The story of DECIPHERMENT

Basalt sphinx of Achôris,
XXIX Dynasty

MAURICE POPE

THE STORY OF
Decipherment

From Egyptian hieroglyphs
to Maya script

Revised Edition

*with 126 illustrations
and a map*

THAMES AND HUDSON

To Johanna

© 1975 and 1999 Thames and Hudson Ltd,
London

This revised edition first published
in 1999 in paperback by
Thames and Hudson Inc., 500 Fifth Avenue,
New York, New York 10110

Library of Congress Catalog Card Number 98-61441
ISBN 0-500-28105-X

Printed and bound in Hong Kong

Contents

Preface 7

Introduction 9

Part One The Egyptian Hieroglyphs

One Through Renaissance eyes 11

ANCIENT EGYPT: OBLIVION AND RECALL 11   THE
ROMAN IMAGE OF EGYPT 14   HIEROGLYPHIC
WISDOM 21   REACTION 33   THE REDISCOVERY
OF COPTIC 36   UNIVERSAL WRITING 39

Two The Eighteenth Century 43

NEW FACTS AND NEW THEORY 43
ZOËGA 55

Three From the Rosetta Stone to Champollion's
Decipherment 60

HOPE AND FRUSTRATION 60   CHAMPOLLION'S
FIRST SOLUTION 68   THE KEY TO THE HIEROGLYPHS 74

Part Two Cuneiform

Four Persian Cuneiform 85

PERSEPOLIS 85   PALMYRA MERCHANTS AND
PERSIAN KINGS 94   THE DECIPHERMENT OF
PERSIAN CUNEIFORM 100

Five Other Cuneiform Scripts 111

THE BABYLONIAN SYLLABARY AND ITS
COGNATES 111   THE UGARITIC ALPHABET 117

Part Three Aegean and Anatolian writing

Six The Cypriot Syllabary   123
THE DISCOVERY OF CYPRIOT WRITING 123
ITS DECIPHERMENT 127

Seven Luvian Hieroglyphic   136
THE SLOW PROCESS OF ITS DECIPHERMENT 136
DECIPHERMENT TECHNIQUES 143

Eight Evans and the Aegean Scripts   146
EARLY INTIMATIONS OF CRETAN WRITING 146
EXCAVATION AND SPECULATION 151   EVANS'
FINAL VIEWS 155

Nine Kober, Ventris, and Linear B   159
ALICE KOBER 159   MICHAEL VENTRIS 162
SUCCESS 172

Conclusion   181
THE HISTORY OF WRITING 181   MORALS 186

Postscript

The Decipherment of Carian   192
THE NATURE OF THE PROBLEM 192   A WAY
FORWARD 192   CONFIRMATION 194

The Maya Glyphs   195
FIRST INTIMATIONS 195   REDISCOVERY 195
THE MAYA CALENDAR 198   READING THE TEXTS 199
ORIGINS AND CONCLUSIONS 202

Notes on the text   204

Glossary of Technical Terms   215

Bibliography   218

Photographic acknowledgments   225

Index   226

Preface

THE scope of this book will be evident from the title-page and the table of contents, and I need not say very much about it here. It is a cross-section through the history of ideas from the Renaissance to the present day taken at a place where literary scholarship and archaeology overlap. If it had not been for the successful decipherments of the last two centuries the earliest voices speaking to us from the past would still have been those of the Greeks and the Hebrews, and our view of the progress of human civilization would have been very different from what it now is. But the interaction has been both ways. Renaissance ideas of history in general and the history of writing in particular would not have allowed the successful decipherments to happen. My aim has been to tell the story of how they did happen, bearing in mind these wider aspects of their importance and not concentrating just on the final steps. These are exciting in the same way as victories of engineering skill, but the excitement is deeper and more memorable if we can discover something about the techniques involved and how they came to be thought of at a particular time and not before.

There are two general limitations which I have had to impose on myself, and which I should perhaps explain briefly. The problem of decipherment is always theoretically capable of solution provided that enough evidence is available, but it has in common with the pseudo-problems of perpetual motion and squaring the circle a strange power of attracting nonsense answers. The earliest example I know of in the modern world is an attempt in 1580 by an Amsterdam medical man, Goropius Becanus, to prove that the sacred language of the Egyptian priests must have been Dutch. Ever since then insubstantial decipherments of one script or another have been appearing with increasing frequency: they now run at the rate, I suppose, of two or three a year. It would be both impracticable and tedious to devote space to considering them. My other limitation concerns the difference between decipherment and interpretation, recognized at least since the time of the author of the *Book of Daniel* (v 8). Decipherment opens the gate, interpretation passes into the field beyond. I have kept strictly to the former. To have done otherwise would have necessitated a far longer book, and would moreover have been trespass. The languages and literatures revealed by the various decipherments now have their own specialists, and these are the only proper guides in them.

Any author must incur a heavy debt of gratitude. My own account begins with my publishers, Thames and Hudson, and Dr Glyn Daniel, the General Editor, who between them encouraged me to write the book in the first place. It continues through many friends in Oxford and elsewhere who have helped me in general conversation on various points, problems, and ideas; of these I must mention in particular Professor George Kilpatrick. Professor Morpurgo-Davies most kindly read and most usefully commented on the draft of my chapter on Hittite Hieroglyphic, and Mr Ray Dawson did the same for my remarks on the history of Chinese scholarship in Europe. Mr Peter Hulin improved my chapters on cuneiform. Professor Bennett of the University of Wisconsin coined for me the words 'biscript' and 'triscript', and Professor Crossland of the University of Sheffield the words 'xenogram' and 'xenographic'. I hope that I have used them worthily. The librarians and their staffs of the Ashmolean and Bodleian Libraries have invariably been helpful whenever I have been in difficulty. Finally, my wife has supported with constant cheerfulness the strain of a husband writing a book. To dedicate the book to her is an inadequate return, but the only one that I can publicly make.

MAURICE W. M. POPE
Oxford, 1973

Preface to the revised edition

Since the publication of the first edition of this book two scripts have been successfully deciphered, and the understanding of another has been significantly improved.

I have described the new decipherments in an extended postscript. The more dramatic of them, and the more wide-ranging in its consequences, has been that of the Maya script: the other is that of Carian. This, though equally meritorious as an achievement, does not have the same celebrity status, and I have dealt with it more briefly. The third script is that which used to be called Hieroglyphic Hittite and is now known as Luvian. I have largely rewritten the relevant chapter.

Otherwise the scripts that were undeciphered in 1975 continue to be so. I have not dealt with the various unsuccessful attempts to solve them, but I have made a brief mention of one curious 'decipherment' I did not then know about – that of Dutch by Japanese medical students in the eighteenth century.

Beyond this I have added one or two minor points of substance, clarified a few passages and updated the notes and bibliography. I should like to thank my publishers warmly for letting me do so and for much else. I must also acknowledge with no less warmth a great deal of scholarly help – from Anna Morpurgo Davies (once again); from Stepanie Dalley; and from Michael Coe and Simon Martin. But what gives me the greatest private happiness is that despite its being twenty-five years since the first edition I can keep the same dedication.

Maurice W.M. Pope
Oxford 1998

Introduction

DECIPHERMENTS are by far the most glamorous achievements of scholarship. There is a touch of magic about unknown writing, especially when it comes from the remote past, and a corresponding glory is bound to attach itself to the person who first solves its mystery. Moreover a decipherment is not just a mystery solved. It is also a key to further knowledge, opening a treasure-vault of history through which for countless centuries no human mind has wandered. Finally, it may be a dramatic personal triumph. Though many decipherments have been carried through by professional scholars as it were in the normal course of duty, this is not so for the three most famous: the decipherment of the Egyptian hiero-glyphs by Champollion, of cuneiform by Rawlinson, and of Mycenaean Linear B by Ventris. These were exceptional feats of exceptional men. The rest of us are tempted to ask of each of them

> Where do you find his star?...
> Have we aught in our sober night shall point
> Such ends as his were, and direct the means
> Of working out our purpose straight as his...?

But there is another aspect of decipherment which makes it worthy of attention and which has nothing whatever to do with any of these romantic considerations; namely, that as a sociological phenomenon it is specific to the modern world. Those who remember 1953, the year when Ventris and Chadwick published the decipherment of Linear B, will recall that it was marked by two other great accomplishments. Hillary and Tensing made the first successful ascent of the highest mountain in the world. Crick and Watson established the structure of the DNA molecule, and so took the first step in explaining the mechanism of life. Whichever is regarded as the greatest personal feat or the most important in its consequences, there can be no question which of them belongs to the rarest category of achievement. People in other societies have climbed mountains. People in other societies have made scientific discoveries about what is not obvious to the senses. But the recovery of the key to an extinct writing system is a thing which has never been attempted, let alone accomplished, by anybody except in the last two or three centuries of our own civilization.[1]

The study of decipherment should therefore be capable of making a valuable contribution to the history of ideas. Two further considerations increase this potential value. The first is that in the architecture of scholarship a decipherment is in the nature of a keystone. It depends on prior results in many different departments of learning, and once in position locks them together. In the hands of a medieval clerk, however well-informed in the learning of his time, the Rosetta Stone would have been as useless as the photograph of a motor-car in the hands of a Roman engineer, however skilful. Neither of them would have had the necessary theories or the necessary techniques at their disposal to turn the gift to account, or even to recognize what it was. It is on the gradual development and elaboration of such theories and techniques that a history of decipherment must concentrate at least as much as on the final anagram-solving steps. This is not only essential for a proper understanding of the ultimate success, but also enormously extends the interest of the enquiry. Neoplatonist philosophers, Church of England bishops, leading mathematicians, grammarians of Chinese are among those who played a significant part in shaping the ideas about Egypt and Egyptian writing which culminated in Champollion's final reading of the hieroglyphs.

The second consideration which makes a study of decipherment valuable in the history of ideas is the certainty of the milestones. No such reliable measures of achievement exist in other fields of literary study except the most severely technical. The theories of literary criticism fashionable in different centuries cannot be graded according to their degree of approximation to the truth. But with decipherments not only can we tell when success has been achieved, but we can to some extent measure the progress that has been made towards it at any one time. Thus the historian of decipherment can combine the precision of a history of science with the richness of a history of the humanities.

PART ONE THE EGYPTIAN HIEROGLYPHS

Chapter One

Through Renaissance Eyes

Ancient Egypt: oblivion and recall

IT IS the normal fate of writing systems, once they are no longer actively employed, to be forgotten. During the Bronze Age in the Near East there existed many different families of scripts. The only one of them to survive is our own. Some passed into disuse and oblivion in the second, or even third, millennium BC. Others continued into classical Greek times. Egyptian, the most durable of them, lingered well into the present era, the latest hieroglyphic inscription we possess having been carved shortly before AD 400. It might have been expected that some knowledge of at least this script, so striking in appearance and so often inscribed on granite monuments, might have lived on; but this did not happen. The great obelisks with which the Roman emperors had adorned Rome and other cities of the West, the small obelisks with which the priests of Isis had adorned their once so fashionable temples, fell, or were felled, one by one. The last inscribed obelisk left standing (which was also one of the first to arrive, having been brought to Rome and erected by Augustus in the Campus Martius in 10 BC) was brought down as the result of fire in the sack of Rome by Robert Guiscard in AD 1084. After this there remained only the Vatican obelisk, originally set up by Caligula – but it was uninscribed. Its Egyptian origin, its very name of obelisk, were alike forgotten.

Memory returned only in the first half of the fifteenth century. It came back partly through the rediscovery of classical authors who mentioned Egypt, partly from travel in the eastern Mediterranean, partly from antiquarianism in Europe and especially in Rome where extensive building development had begun to stimulate interest in the things that were being destroyed. Horapollo's book *Hieroglyphics* – still the only ancient work we possess that is devoted to this subject – was discovered on the Aegean island of Andros in 1419 by Buondelmonte.[1] In 1435 Cyriac of Ancona visited Egypt, taking with him a copy of Horapollo's book, and sending home a drawing of a hieroglyphic inscription to Niccolò Nicoli in Florence.[2] At the same time Poggio was writing on the history of Rome in his *de varietate fortunae*. In it he mentioned Pliny's account of the obelisks imported from Egypt by the early Roman emperors, correctly identified the Vatican obelisk as being the one erected by Caligula, and stated that he had seen a number of fragments of obelisks inscribed with 'the various shapes of animals and birds which the

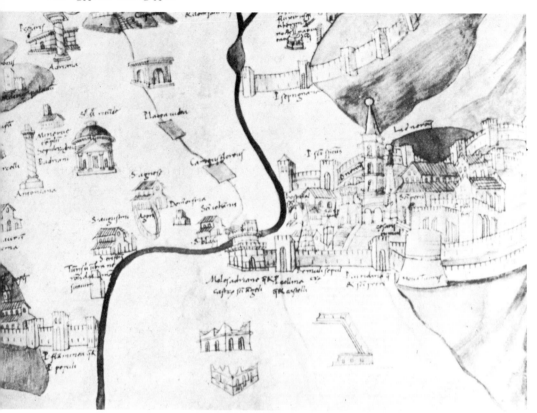

1 Two fifteenth-century maps of the Vatican. *Left*, Traditionalist. By Pietro del Massaio, AD 1471. *Right*, Humanist. By Alessandro Strozzi, AD 1474

ancient Egyptians used for letters'. Yet the obelisks were not of great interest to him; while lamenting their disappearance, he regarded this as a minor matter compared with the vast number of Greek and Roman marble and bronze statues which had been lost. But Poggio's friend, Biondo, devoted rather more space to them – at least to the extent of transcribing much of what Pliny, Ammianus, and Tacitus had had to say. For instance, from Tacitus he quoted that the Egyptians were the first to express mental concepts by animal drawings and that their inscriptions carved on stone were the earliest records of human experience. From Ammianus Marcellinus (the first manuscript by whom had been rediscovered by Poggio in the monastery of Fulda in 1417) he quoted a great deal, most significantly the statement that the ancient Egyptians did not write by letters as we do, but by signs expressing whole words or concepts. The two instances of this given by Ammianus are that a vulture stands for nature because according to naturalists there are no vultures of the male sex, and that a honey-bee represents a king, because kings must exercise their rule with sweetness but also possess a sting.

By the middle of the fifteenth century therefore the existence of ancient Egypt had been rediscovered. Naturally the small humanist circles of the time did not at once alter public opinion. What they did was to introduce and to publicize an alternative manner of understanding history. The situation, as far as concerns ancient Egypt, at the close of the Middle Ages is conveniently

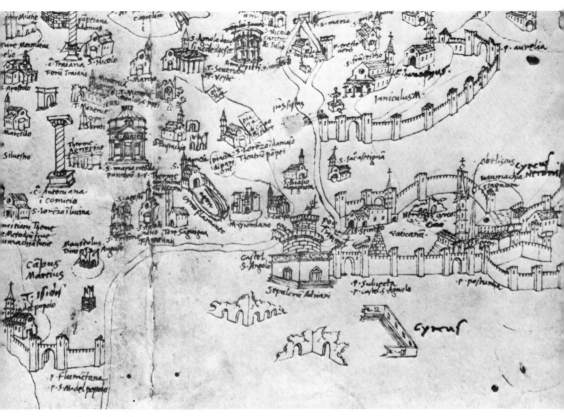

summed up by the contrast between the two maps of Rome, details of which are here reproduced. Both are evidently drawn after the same prototype, thought to have been of the early fifteenth century, but the captions are worlds apart. Massaio's map, in a codex of Ptolemy's *Cosmographia*, gave the medieval view of ancient Rome, the Rome of the Christian pilgrim guides; Strozzi's accompanied a collection of inscriptions from Italian cities and breathed the new spirit of humanism. To take one instance, in a section of the map illustrated, against a building by the Tiber near the Flaminian Gate, Massaio wrote, 'This is the Tower where Nero's Ghost once lingered.' Strozzi, though he included the building, omitted the caption. The omission is significant and does not owe its presence to a desire for fewer words since Strozzi named just over half as many places again as Massaio. It must have been the flavour of credulity and obscurantism to which he objected. But what is relevant to us is the treatment of the Vatican obelisk in the two maps. 'The Needle – Caesar's Tomb' (*Agulia Cesaris tumulus*) is how Massaio described it. This was the medieval explanation, derived from an erroneous identification of the obelisk with the memorial to Julius Caesar described by Suetonius at the end of his life of the dictator. The golden ball at the top was supposed to contain his ashes, still as high above the world as Rome was above all other cities. Strozzi, however, gave the monument its correct ancient title of 'obelisk', thus inevitably implying that he knew it to have come from Egypt.[3]

The Roman image of Egypt

The Egypt that was now beginning to be rediscovered was not the Egypt of the Pharaohs. This had lost its independence to the Persian king Cambyses in 525 BC. Two hundred years later the Persian empire in its turn fell to the Macedonian king Alexander, with the result that Egypt came first under his control and, after his death, under that of the dynasty founded by his general Ptolemy. Eventually in 30 BC it was annexed to the Roman empire, in the eastern half of which it remained until the Arab conquest of the seventh century.

The Egypt that the humanist scholars of the Renaissance could read about was the Egypt of the Greeks and Romans. And what a strange country it had appeared to them! It was quite unlike anywhere else in their experience. It was unique geographically, 'the gift of the Nile' as Herodotus called it, a thin strip of fertility between barren sands. It was unique for the life it bore, the

2 The Roman image of Egypt. Detail of mosaic from Palestrina (Praeneste). First century BC

crocodile and hippopotamus, the papyrus and the lotus. It was unique for its monuments, the vast temples of ancient Thebes, the pyramids like mountains, and the scarcely less incredible single-stone obelisks. It was unique for the number of its priests and for the ancient and mysterious writing in which its piety and wisdom were preserved. The potency of the fascination it exercised need cause us no surprise.

Some of this fascination can be sensed from a mosaic in the Temple to Fortune at Praeneste built by the Roman general Sulla in the early part of the first century B C.[4] Contemporary literature confirms that this mosaic was no isolated fantasy. Cicero, for example, tells us that rich men created artificial streams in their parks and called them 'Niles', a practice which he claims to find ridiculous. But he himself, we are told, once wrote a poem on the Nile.[5] Roman poets and satirists are full of references to this Egyptomania, which was by no means confined to any one rank in society. The chief form it took was, as one would expect in the ancient world, religious. Temples to the Egyptian gods Serapis and Isis became increasingly numerous. There were at least three in Rome itself, and more than twice as many are known from the rest of Italy. The main one in Rome, on the Campus Martius, was founded in the second century B C and continued in use until at least A D 400, but the fashion was perhaps at its height in the second and third centuries. A very good idea of the beauty of the services and of the relief from sin and suffering felt by a convert is given by Apuleius in the eleventh book of his novel, the *Metamorphoses*. What it could all look like to an outsider is well hinted at by Juvenal, a satirist with a healthy scorn for the occult and a nostalgia for the old days of political responsibility. He says of a typical rich lady devotee of Isis (vi 526 ff.):

> . . . if the goddess-cow command,
> She'll go to Egypt's borders and bring back
> Nile-water fresh from sun-baked Meroë
> To sprinkle in the Temple near the Pen
> Where Roman citizens once voted . . .[6]

– that is to say, the Iseum in the Campus Martius. But Juvenal is exaggerating when he talks about Meroë. The homeland of the cult in the Graeco-Roman world was not so far away. It was the Serapeum at Alexandria.

Serapis was originally created as the patron deity of the new Greek colony of Alexandria under Ptolemy I, though his temple was re-founded by Ptolemy III in the next century.[7] To begin with, Serapis was envisaged as predominantly Greek, as his cult-statue shows. His worship spread because when the Greek colonists of Alexandria either returned to their birthplaces or moved to other parts of the Greek world, they were likely to continue his cult in their new homes. Later, as the spell of Egypt began to increase its hold on the Greeks of Alexandria and elsewhere, Isis, who had always been associated with Serapis, began to play an increasingly central part in the cult. The highest point in the life of the Serapeum came in A D 131/2 with the visit of the Roman emperor Hadrian and his wife, but it survived for a further quarter of a millennium.

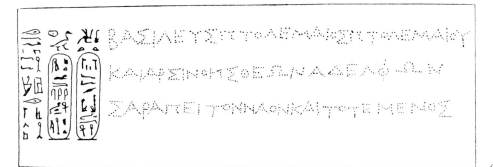

a

3 The Serapeum at
Alexandria. *a*, the foundation
plaque placed by Ptolemy III
(246–221 BC); *b*, bust of
Zeus Serapis found near
the Serapeum; *c*, Roman
coin of AD 132/3 showing
Serapis and Hadrian jointly
dedicating a shrine to the
Emperor; *d*, the final
destruction of the Serapeum
by Christians in AD 391. The
patriarch Theophilus is
shown standing on the ruins
of the Serapeum. From a
fifth-century AD papyrus
chronicle

When it was finally destroyed by the Christians in AD 391, it was
still a live institution, and only succumbed after a struggle.[8]

The destruction of the Serapeum signalled the end of pagan
Egypt, and the end also of the hieroglyphic script. Until then it
had survived, though latterly it was less and less understood even
by the priests, who were its only custodians. By the Greeks and
Romans it had never been properly understood at all. For though
there existed, as we shall see, books which dealt specifically with
the hieroglyphs, none of them came anywhere near explaining
the basic principles of the writing system. Above all, there is
scarcely a mention that any hieroglyphic sign could ever bear a
phonetic value. The explanation of this is not immediately obvious.
To blame lack of curiosity on the part of the Greeks or deliberate
concealment on the part of the Egyptian priests is too moralist and
too facile to be convincing. There was plenty of curiosity – we
know the names of over seventy ancient authors who wrote on
Egypt. And whether or not the priests as a class were jealous of their
secrets, they cannot all have been so as individuals: where the
information about individual hieroglyphs given us by classical
authors can be checked, it usually turns out to be, if not true, at
least descended from the truth and to have come from genuine
inside knowledge. It also seems unlikely that attitudes of this kind
would have persisted unflinchingly through three quite different
periods of relationship – before, during, and after the Greek
political domination of Egypt.

There is a simpler and more universal explanation as to why
the Graeco-Roman literary public never had the hieroglyphic
script, or for that matter cuneiform, Cypriot, or Aramaic,
explained to them. It lies in the nature of ancient literacy and of
ancient books. In the first place, though it would have been
theoretically possible to write a treatise on such a subject, the
result would have been both unpublishable and unusable. Where
would there have been the scribes to copy it, and where would the
potential reader have found the hieroglyphic or cuneiform books
to use his knowledge on? In the second place, writing, in the sense
of forming the actual letters, is a craft. You need someone to show
you how. Ancient books, though they could be on technical
subjects such as architecture or land-surveying, did not deal with
crafts of this nature. Nor could they have usefully encroached on a
sphere where the best teacher is example, the second-best illus-

tration, and the verbal formulation of general principles a poor third.

What then did ancient writers have to say on the subject? Our first authority is Herodotus, who visited Egypt in the fifth century BC, when it was under Persian domination. All that he specifically states about Egyptian writing is in two sentences (ii 36): that it proceeds from right to left, and that there are two types, sacred (*hiera*) and public (*demotica*). This is also stated by Diodorus (i 81) and implied by others. Clement of Alexandria, however, at the end of the second century AD says very firmly that there were three types, hieroglyphic, hieratic, and epistolographic. Which of these contradictory statements was correct, and whether or not they could be reconciled, naturally gave rise to considerable debate among early investigators.

b

As for the hieroglyphic script itself the only other fact that can be inferred from Herodotus is that it was used for the engraving of historical records, particularly royal achievements (ii 102, 106, 125, 135). Other authors lead us to the same conclusion, while others again imply funerary, religious, astrological, or philosophical uses.[9]

The earliest extant writer to suggest the ideographic nature of the hieroglyphs is Diodorus Siculus, who travelled in Egypt in the middle of the first century BC. 'I must include a word on the Ethiopian writing, called "hieroglyphic" by the Egyptians', he says (iii 4). 'The signs are like various animals, or the extremities of the human body, or tools – particularly carpenters' tools. For their script does not work by putting syllables together to render an underlying sense, but by drawing objects whose metaphorical meaning is impressed on the memory. . . .' Among the examples he gives are a falcon for 'anything that happens suddenly', a crocodile for 'evil', an eye as 'the body's watchman' and 'the guardian of justice'. He adds that after a long study of the inherent meanings in things, and with much practice at memorizing them, the recognition of the signs becomes automatic.

c

Diodorus also tells us that among the Ethiopians (whoever he means by them – one would assume the inhabitants of Meroë) the hieroglyphic script is the only one known and is taught to everybody, whereas the Egyptians have a different script for general use.

It is not certain where Diodorus got his information from. The most natural source to suspect is Manetho, an Egyptian priest who served the first two Ptolemies. Manetho wrote on Egyptian history and on Egyptian religion, but none of the fragments that we possess of his work refers to writing. Nevertheless, even if we cannot name it, it is likely that Diodorus had some literary source for his theory and did not pick it up from conversation in Egypt; for very much the same account of Egyptian writing was given in the next century by an Alexandrian, Chairemon, who is alleged to have been a priest (*hierogrammateus*) and who wrote a book on Egyptian writing which contained some genuine information. It would be strange if he had borrowed from a Greek historian on his own Egyptian subject. Yet the account we have from him is extremely like that of Diodorus. It is preserved for us by a late Byzantine writer, Tzetzes, and runs:

d

The Ethiopians do not use letters, only various animals, their limbs, and organs. Earlier priests, in their desire to keep secret their knowledge of natural theology, taught these signs to their own children as an allegorical or symbolic way of writing – a woman beating a drum for 'joy', a man holding his chin and looking down at the ground for 'grief', a tear-filled eye for 'misfortune'. . . .

Chairemon is said to have become one of the tutors of the emperor Nero, and this may be why his theory makes two appearances in the Roman literature of the time. The poet Lucan, who was a member of Nero's entourage and presumably knew Chairemon, devotes some lines to it in connection with the rather unpoetic problem of who invented the alphabet. The Phoenicians, he says, were the first to record language in baldly sketched signs (*rudibus figuris*), and they did so before Egypt had learned to make papyrus scrolls, when stone was its only medium, and when the animals carved on it still gave magic tongue (*sculptaque servabant magicas animalia linguas*). This is very similar to the account, already mentioned, given by Tacitus (and attributed by him to the emperor Claudius) that mental concepts were initially expressed by the Egyptians in the form of animal drawings. He differs, however, from Lucan in regard to alphabetic writing, saying that it too was invented by Egypt and only later adopted by the Phoenicians, who stole the credit for it.

The Greek writer Plutarch, contemporary with Tacitus, gives some half-dozen actual instances of meanings of hieroglyphs in his treatise *de Iside et Osiride*. Two of them are correct (Osiris written with an eye and a sceptre; 'king' or 'southern regions' by means of a rush), and two or three others partially so. There are also some references to the Egyptian language which are correct. In so far as these items of Plutarch's knowledge can be dated they seem to refer to Ptolemaic times. A strange reference to $5^2 = 25 =$ the number of Egyptian letters, and the mention of the ibis as being the first letter of the Egyptian alphabet in another of Plutarch's writings (*quaest. conv.* 9, 3. 2) have been taken as indicating an awareness of Egyptian phoneticism. But it is not a very live awareness, and in any case the inference is not a necessary one.

The only extant ancient work devoted exclusively to Hieroglyphic that we possess goes under the name of Horapollo (or Horus Apollo). It was 'produced in the Egyptian language and translated into Greek by Philip', according to the heading of the first book. The second book (there are only two, both short) has a separate heading explaining that it is in the nature of a supplement. And indeed the greater part of it (paragraphs 31–117) is clearly different, being concerned with animal lore and having no particular connection with Egypt. The rest, however, does. In about a dozen instances Horapollo's information overlaps that given by Plutarch, but for the most part what he tells us is new, including almost a dozen words which he claims to be Egyptian, and which in fact are. The paragraphs, though arranged by subject matter in a moderately coherent way, are in themselves independent entities. Most of them are short: for instance

I 23 'To indicate a man who has never travelled they paint a man with a donkey's head. For he never knows or listens to accounts of what happens abroad.'

II 119 'They paint a hand to show a man who is fond of building. For the hand is what carries out work.'

But some are longer, for instance I 14 on the baboon, whose representation is said to mean any of the following – the moon, the inhabited world, writing, a priest, anger, swimming. The symbolisms by which these various meanings are reached are then briefly explained.

The range of subjects dealt with – the baboon, the vulture, the ibis, sceptres, kings, priests, the Nile flood, etc. – has a decidedly Egyptian colouring. But the explanations are often absurdly Greek. For example I 17, 'The sun is called Horus because it rules the hours', the Greek word for hours being *horai*. Even when he is on Egyptian ground and referring to a recognizable hieroglyph, Horapollo gives us the feeling that we are talking to a very much hellenized Egyptian who knows scarcely more about the hieroglyphs than he can guess by looking at them. For instance he says in I 28, 'To denote hieroglyphs, or a scribe, they draw a reed, ink, and a sieve . . . because the first instrument used in making bread is a sieve . . . and the Egyptian for education is *sbô*, which means adequate nourishment.' True enough, *sbō* means 'instruction' in Coptic, and there are Egyptian words *śb3* – 'instruct' and *šbw* – 'food' which Horapollo may have confused, but where does the sieve come in? The probable explanation (Sbordone's) is that he thought this was what was represented by the Egyptian hieroglyph 𓏞 – which really denotes a reed-pen and a palette with two bowls for red and black ink. Moreover, as Sbordone points out, the bridge between the concepts of 'food' and 'education' looks as if it was the Greek word *trophê*, which, like nurture in English, can imply both. Another aspect of the interpretation which suggests Greek thinking is the order in which it is put: 'If you have enough food you will learn your letters.' In contrast, what we know of Egyptian scribes suggests that they would have been more likely to have said that a good education leads to a good living.

Translations from Egyptian hieroglyphics into Greek were made in antiquity – for instance Manetho undoubtedly used genuine Egyptian sources for his history of Egypt – but the only cases where we have from ancient literature both the original and the translation are an alleged five-sign temple inscription (see page 25), and a translation of two sides of an obelisk in Rome by Hermapion (a person otherwise unknown) reproduced in Ammianus Marcellinus. Which obelisk he was referring to is still a matter of dispute; it may have been the Flaminian, now in the Piazza del Popolo. If so the translation, though excellent in regard to general tone and indeed in its rendering of particular phrases, is too much of a free summary. Champollion, as we shall see, was able to make good use of it in corroboration of his decipherment, but it could never have been of direct help in the initial stages.

I have tried to sketch in outline how Egypt appeared to the Graeco-Roman world, and in slightly more detail what the Graeco-Roman world knew, or thought it knew, about Egyptian writing. Their general picture of two distinct systems, one entirely ideo-

AUTHOR'S NAME	DATE (CENTURY)	DESCRIPTION	EDITIO PRINCEPS	LATIN TRANSLATION (WHERE APPLICABLE)	RELEVANCE TO EGYPT
LACTANTIUS	3/4 AD	Christian philosopher	1467	—	Account of Egyptian myth and religion in *de falsa religione*.
PLINY	I AD	historian of science and technology	1469	—	History of obelisks in xxxvi.
STRABO	I BC/AD	geographer	1516	1469	Description of Egypt in xvii.
APULEIUS	2 AD	lecturer, novelist, mystic	1469	—	The initiation into the rites of Isis of the hero of his novel, the *Metamorphoses*. The Hermetic tract, now known as *Asclepius*, which was printed as his.
TACITUS	I/2 AD	historian	1470 (except *Annals* i–vi) 1515 (including *Annals* i–vi)	— —	Rameses inscriptions *Ann.* ii 60. Egyptian writing *Ann.* xi 14. Serapis *Hist.* iv 81–4.
EUSEBIUS	3/4 AD	Christian historian	1544	1470	Extracts from Philo of Byblos, Apion, Chaeremon, and others, preserved in the *praeparatio evangelica*.
JOSEPHUS	I AD	Jewish historian	1544	c. 1470 (Cassiodorus) 1480 (*contra Apionem*)	Extracts from Manetho in the *c. Apionem*.
corpus Hermeticum	2/3 AD	philosophical and religious tracts	1554	1471	The tracts claim as their author the Egyptian god Thoth, hellenized as Hermes. For the Latin *Asclepius* see under Apuleius.
DIODORUS SICULUS	I BC	historian	1559	1472 (Poggio's translation, which was made in the middle of the century)	Discussion of Egyptian myth, legend, history, geography, and general influence in i. Description of hieroglyphic writing in iii.
HERODOTUS	5 BC	traveller and historian	1474	1502	A first-hand and very full account of Egypt in ii.
AMMIANUS MARCELLINUS	4 AD	historian	1474 (without Hermapion) 1533 (includes Hermapion)	— —	Digression on obelisks in xvii, including the translation of an obelisk inscription by Hermapion.
PLATO	4 BC	philosopher	1513	1483	Many occasional references to Egypt.
PLOTINUS	3 AD	philosopher	1580	1492	Praise of hieroglyphic in V 8, 5.
IAMBLICHUS	4 AD	philosopher and mystic	1678	1497	The *de mysteriis* is intended as an exposition of the religious views and practices of the priests of Egypt and Assyria.
HORAPOLLO	5 AD (?)		1505	1515	On Egyptian hieroglyphics.
PLUTARCH	I/2 AD	historian and moralist	1509	1570	An extended essay on the Isis cult in the *de Iside et Osiride*.
HERMAPION	I BC/AD (?)				See Ammianus Marcellinus.
CLEMENT	2/3 AD	Christian philosopher	1550	1551	Description of Egyptian writing in *Strom.* V 4.
PHILO	I AD	Jewish philosopher and theologian	1552	1554	Allegorical exegesis of Old Testament. (Fifernas' Latin translation, done between 1479 and 1484 was from then on available in MS. in the Vatican Library.)

graphic, the other entirely phonetic, was quite wrong: the details were few, and though they were sometimes correct there was no easy way of knowing when that was. It is no wonder, therefore, that such a long time was to elapse between the rediscovery of Egypt in the Renaissance and the proper understanding of its writing systems by Champollion.

I conclude this section with a list of the main extant Greek and Roman writers who touch on Egypt to any significant extent and the order in which they became available in the Renaissance. It is not exhaustive, nor can rigid conclusions about the non-availability of authors before the appearance of their first printed edition be drawn from it. Manuscript copies of newly discovered works were often in fairly free circulation before their first printing, and of course some authors were read throughout the Middle Ages. For instance there are over two hundred surviving manuscripts of Cassiodorus' sixth-century Latin translation of Josephus.

On the other hand the appearance of an author in print does not necessarily mean that his whole *corpus* as now known was included in the edition. There are three important instances of this in the table opposite. The early books of Tacitus' *Annals* with the account of Germanicus' visit to Egypt were still missing when the 1470 edition of Tacitus was printed. The only manuscript of Ammianus Marcellinus known in 1474 did not transcribe Hermapion's obelisk translation since it was quoted by Ammianus in Greek. The translation of the 'Sais inscription' in Plutarch is absent from all the manuscripts, and could only be restored when the text of Clement of Alexandria became available.

Hieroglyphic wisdom

The abstract admiration felt for the Egyptian hieroglyphs in the latter part of classical antiquity is neatly summarized by the third-century philosopher Plotinus. In the course of an argument to show that the gods do not contemplate propositions but realities, and that ideas, far from being just mental pictures, have a genuine existence, he remarks (v 8, 6):

This is what the wise men of Egypt realized, either by science or by instinct. When they wanted to express their meaning philosophically they did not go through the whole business of letters, words, and sentences. They did not employ devices to copy the sounds of a proposition and how it is pronounced. Instead, in their sacred writings, they drew signs, a separate sign for each idea, so as to express its whole meaning at once. Each separate sign is in itself a piece of knowledge, a piece of wisdom, a piece of reality, immediately present. There is no process of reasoning involved, no laborious elucidation.

Ficino, who translated Plotinus into Latin in 1492, comments: 'Our way of thinking about "time" is complex and shifting. For example "time goes quickly", "time revolves and ends up where it began", "time teaches prudence", "time gives and takes away". This whole range of thought was comprehended in a single, firm, figure by the Egyptians when they drew a winged serpent with its tail in its mouth. And there are many other such figures, described by Horus [=Horapollo].'

4 Hermes Trismegistus giving to Egypt the twin sciences of writing and law. Siena Cathedral pavement mosaic. End of fifteenth century

5 The City of the Past. This illustration and the next three show woodcuts from *Hypnerotomachia Poliphili.* AD 1499

It may seem difficult to believe that the men of the Renaissance took so seriously the wisdom of Egypt when they knew so little about it. But it should not surprise us. 'Nowadays', said Sebastian Munster in his preface to Levita's Hebrew grammar (1525), 'we see the ancient everywhere rightly preferred to the modern, and the springs themselves to the subsequent lakes.' In favour of the superiority of ancient Egypt they had, as we have seen in the last section, the almost unanimous testimony of classical antiquity. Their own experience of contemporary life must have encouraged them to agree. They were learning daily in almost all spheres of literature, science, and technology, from ancient Rome. Rome had learned from Greece; why should not Greece in its turn have learned from Egypt? Indeed, there were plenty of ancient authors who said that this is just what it had done. Diodorus, for instance, lists fourteen founders of Greek culture as having been educated in Egypt, among them Orpheus, Daedalus, Homer, Lycurgus, Solon, Plato, Pythagoras, Eudoxus, Democritus. Other authors have similar lists.

This vision of Egypt as the spring of wisdom was admitted even into the Church. As you enter Siena Cathedral you see in the centre of the nave a great mosaic of Hermes Trismegistus (= Thoth) handing over a book on which is written 'Receive, O Egyptians, the gift of literacy and law.' With his other hand he points to a stone on which is carved 'God, the creator of all, created a second [*secum* is for *secundum*], visible God, and this was the first God he made and the one in which he took pleasure: and he loved His own Son, who is called the Holy Word.' The first inscription comes from Cicero, the second from the Hermetic tract *Asclepius*, both through the medium of the Christian writer Lactantius, who quotes them in his *Divine Institutions*.[10]

4

This great confidence in the virtues of Egyptian writing existed despite the fact that scarcely anybody had ever seen any. Cyriac of Ancona had brought back from Egypt one or two drawings. There were a few inscribed fragments of obelisks lying partly visible in back quarters of Rome; that was the sum of what was available. Nevertheless, imagination could supply the deficiency, and it did. The first hieroglyphs to be printed and published were the modern ones of Francesco Colonna, a learned, allegorical novelist, who wrote in the manner of Apuleius and was a sort of James Joyce of the Renaissance.

The hero of Colonna's *Hypnerotomachia Poliphili* (1499), disgusted with the 'hateful and blasphemous barbarity' of his age, seeks to rediscover Nature. But the only way back to Nature is through a defile, blocked by the tremendous remains of the City of the Past. It is obvious from the woodcut representing this that it is a blend of Rome, Greece, and Egypt. Poliphilus enters the City. In it he finds strange statuary like the elephant transfixed by an obelisk, and encounters various inscriptions. Some of these are in hieroglyphics. Others are in Latin, in Greek, and in Hebrew, Chaldean, or Arabic. It is noteworthy that the hieroglyphic inscriptions are not presented with a translation into any of these languages. Poliphilus has to work out their meaning for himself by thinking about them ('pensiculante' – a word Colonna has characteristically scooped from Aulus Gellius and poured straight into his own Italian).[11] The principles on which Poliphilus works will be clear from the accompanying illustration. Readers who would like to put themselves into his position and consider for

6 Elephant transfixed by an obelisk

7 An invented hieroglyphic inscription, and its interpretation. The Latin means 'Sacrifice with your labour ungrudgingly to the God of Nature. Gradually you will bring your mind back to be subject to Him. In His merciful guidance He will keep firm watch over your life and will preserve you in safety.'

EX LABORE		DEO	NATURAE	SACRIFICA	LIBERALITER	PAULATIM	REDUCES	ANIMUM
oxhead with farm implements	*eye*	*vulture*	*altar*	*bowl*	*jug*	*skein of wool*	*vase*	

DEO	SUBIECTUM	FIRMAM	CUSTODIAM	VITAE	TUAE	MISERICORDITER	GUBERNANDO	TENEBIT
eye	*sandal*	*anchor*	*goose*	*lamp*	*hand*	*olive*	*chariot-pole*	*hooks*

INCOLUMEM	–QUE	SERVABIT
dolphin	*the two ribbons*	*chest*

8 Another inscription seen by Poliphilus in the City of the Past. For its interpretation, and how it seems to have been reached, see note 12 (page 193)

themselves 'the most noble Egyptian hieroglyphs' carved on the bridge leading from the City of the Past to the country of Nature, may like to do so before turning to Poliphilus' own interpretation.[12]

It would be strange to find the hieroglyphs treated in this manner if they were thought of as an object for historical research. But they were not: they were thought of as a source of moral wisdom. This is clear from the table of contents of the first edition of Horapollo, printed by Aldus in 1505. It includes the Fables of Aesop and of Babrius, the allegorical interpretations of Cornutus and of 'Heracleides Ponticus' (i.e. the *Homeric Allegories* of Heracleitus), Palaephatus' 'incredible stories', and a collection of Greek proverbs. These works, heterogeneous to us, were then considered more or less closely interrelated in subject matter.

The first scholar who sought the historical truth about the Egyptian hieroglyphs, and who wrote the first book on the subject in the modern world was Pierius Valerianus. He was Apostolic Prothonotary to Clement VII and his epitaph in Venice claims that his industry in administrative matters was such that nobody would have expected him to have had time to read, let alone write; his publications, however, were of such breadth and learning that one would suppose their author's life to have been an uninterrupted vacation. His work *The Hieroglyphs, or a Commentary on the sacred letters of the Egyptians and other peoples* was first printed at Basle in 1556, and went through several later editions. It consists of fifty-eight books (what we would call chapters), the first thirty-one of which are devoted to animals, and the remainder divided between parts of the human body, human artefacts, and plants.

Pierius' aims and methods are perhaps seen at their clearest in Book xxxiii and its preface.[13] The sources for our knowledge of the hieroglyphs are there listed as the Bembine Table (see page 33), the numerous signs on the obelisks, visits to Egypt and other countries where there are inscriptions, ancient writers in general (though these yield only very few and allusively-hinted-at interpretations), and Horapollo in particular (though this is most disappointing, being summary, superficial, and textually corrupt as well). Other points that he makes are:

1. The hieroglyphs were employed for the purposes of philosophy, poetry, history, theology, and moral aphorism, despite their use of pictures for words.
2. The Greeks, Romans, and Hebrews brought out into the open fields of eloquence the ideas that the Egyptians had confined within the limits of what could be embraced by the eye.
3. Greek, Roman, and Hebrew writers may therefore be legitimately drawn on to interpret what the Egyptians meant in their hieroglyphs.
4. Even Hippocratean dream-therapy, ancient dream interpretation in general, and Etruscan augury-lore are likely to be

descended from Egypt, since they all take their starting-point in the realm of visible things.

These principles explain how Pierius managed to write so large a volume on a subject on which so little was known. For example, they make it relevant to quote even such an apparently obvious metaphor as Cicero's 'devouring books' (*vorare litteras*) when considering the passage in which Horapollo tells us that the Egyptian word *shô* meant both food and education (see page 19).

Pierius' basic procedure is to take each object, animal, plant, or body-part, and consider the various symbolic meanings that can be seen in it. Thus the stork, the subject of his Book xvii, can imply, among other things, filial piety, spring, protection from danger, medical expertise, and prescience. In support of this gallery of meanings he cites Greek and Roman authors, the facts of Roman history, Roman coins, and even contemporary experience. For when Bonzio, he says, was found guilty of an attempted assassination and the razing of his house in Padua was part of the sentence, the stork on the roof left it before the demolition men arrived and built a new nest on the house of Bonzio's political opponent, Cuticelli.

The different symbolisms are generously illustrated with woodcuts. One of the possible significances of the bull, 'sharpness of hearing', is here illustrated. The story comes from Horapollo (i 47):

They paint a bull's ear to indicate hearing. When a cow has the urge to conceive she moos strenuously. The urge never lasts more than three hours, and if it is not satisfied the cow closes her genital passage until the next occasion. But she rarely needs to do so. The bull picks up the mooing very quickly, even from a great distance, realizes that the cow is on heat, and runs to the spot. The bull is the only animal to be summoned to intercourse like this.

9 'Sharpness of hearing'. A hieroglyph illustrated by Pierius Valerianus

In telling the story (iii 7) Pierius adds only the information, derived from Aristotle and Pliny, that the next occasion is nineteen days off.

Most of Pierius' work is taken up with the illustration and usage, including the modern usage, of individual symbolisms. But he does sometimes have occasion to discuss hieroglyphic groups, and in one lucky instance (xxxi 6) we are in the position of an examiner able to grade his answer. This is where he deals with an inscription said by Plutarch (*de Iside et Osiride*, 32) to have been 'in front of the Temple of Athena at Sais' and to consist of a child, an old man, a falcon, a fish, and a hippopotamus. The alleged translation 'O young, O old, God hates impiety' had dropped out of our Plutarch manuscripts, and can only be supplemented from Clement of Alexandria, who happens to give the same example. The supplement seems to have been first made in Squire's edition of Plutarch in 1744: it is not in the Frankfurt edition of 1620, and was certainly unknown to Pierius. So Pierius had to translate unseen, helped only by the symbolisms given in Plutarch's surviving explanation – that the falcon stands for 'god', the fish for 'hatred' (because fish live in the sea which eventually swallows up the life-giving Nile), and the hippopotamus for 'violence and immorality' (because it kills its father in order to be able to rape its mother).

11 Cartouche of Osiris from Philae. Ptolemaic

12 Imaginary reconstruction by Pierius of an inscription described by Plutarch

10 The god Horus after overcoming Seth. Scene from the inner girdle wall of the temple at Edfu. Ptolemaic

Pierius also shows us what he imagines the original to have looked like. We cannot control this exactly. No such inscription has been found, and so un-Egyptian would it have been that it is unlikely that there was ever one like it even in Ptolemaic times. But if there was, either it would have borne some resemblance to

11 the Osiris cartouche from Philae with the hieroglyphs of a child and an old man at the beginning and end respectively, or else, if Plutarch is not describing a hieroglyphic inscription but a large-scale bas-relief, it may have been after the type that can be seen at

10 Edfu and of which something was known in the Graeco-Roman world.

We can now examine the reconstruction made by Pierius. The

12 drawing is, except for the obelisk frame, about as unlike anything Egyptian as it could be. His translation too departs from what one would expect an Egyptian to have said, and is certainly not the translation that Plutarch and Clement gave. Pierius captions the five hieroglyphs 'birth', 'age', 'life', 'death', 'dissolution', and comments that 'the message is the precariousness of our human life, moving from childhood to old age and second childhood. . . . When the harmonious discord created by the mixture in our

bodies begins to break up and the elements begin encroaching on each other by violent means, the inevitable consequence is death.'

It looks as if Pierius arrived at this elaborate interpretation by visualizing a symmetry in the inscription – two propositions separated in the centre by the falcon, which, he says, 'signifies God, hence Love, the Divine Element in us, and the essential Life'. Put more simply, the whole will run, 'Youth and Age make up Life, and Life ends through Hatred and Violence.' His explanation of the last part draws heavily on Greek medical theory and Greek theology, but, as we have seen, the principles on which he operates make it relevant for him to bring in Greek ideas, for he assumes that they were derived from Egypt in the first place.

The complex mixture of truth, fallacy, and fantasy that went to the making of a Renaissance hieroglyph can be seen in the accompanying illustration. The sceptre presumably began as a walking-stick with a side-shoot left on it for a handle. It was then animated. Since the Egyptian word for this kind of staff or sceptre *w:s* could also mean 'well-being', and since the word for a simple stake λ *śḏb* could also mean 'mischief', the sign could be punningly taken as 'well-being over mischief'. Then, the verbal nature of the pun coming to be forgotten, the sign could be seen as a hoopoe over the claws of a hippopotamus (Horapollo i 55, 56), whence Pierius, changing the hoopoe into the more familiar stork as an emblem of filial piety, evolved his own hieroglyph.[14]

Before we leave Pierius we should notice one passage where the gathering clouds of contemporary religious conflict are hinted at. Pierius always tried to consider the truths of animal symbolism in connection with the truths of natural history, and he therefore wondered why the hippopotamus should possess a divided hoof and yet not ruminate. The answer, he says (xix 8), is that this hits off very well the nature of the heretic, always rooting up quibbles and distinctions yet never finding wisdom. And it is perhaps the shadow of Luther that makes him, at the beginning of his book on Isis (xxxix), so firmly define the limits of admiration for antiquity in general and Egypt in particular – 'supreme in human accomplishments, though ignorant of true religion' (*veteribus verae pietatis nesciis sed rerum humanarum peritissimis*).

Fifteen editions of Horapollo and an even greater number of original works devoted to hieroglyphs and emblems appeared in the sixteenth century. Most of them were seen by their authors as a contribution, not to Egyptology but to what we should nowadays call the science of communications. They were for the use of 'public speakers, preachers, designers of seals and devices, sculptors, painters, draughtsmen, architects, and inventors', to show them how to represent symbolically 'everything that can occur in human thought', to quote the title-page of Ripa's *Iconologia* (1593 and many subsequent editions). They are therefore irrelevant to our own enquiry except in so far as they helped stimulate the re-erection of obelisks in Rome. Between 1582 and 1589 no less than six obelisks were either re-sited or put up again for the first time since antiquity.[15] One important consequence was that in future engravings of obelisks and of hieroglyphic inscriptions had to be very much more accurate.

a

b

c

d

13 The evolution of a Renaissance hieroglyph. *a*, normal form of the sceptre ideogram in Egyptian writing; *b*, animated representation of the sceptre, from the inside of the coffin of Sebk-o. Middle Kingdom; *c*, stork accompanying the figure of *Pietas* on a coin struck by the Roman emperor Hadrian to celebrate his adoption of an heir, AD 137; *d*, *Impietati praelata Pietas* ('Devotion over Selfishness'), a hieroglyphic by Pierius

27

14

2

This is certainly true of the handsomely proportioned obelisks shown opposite. Even the fact that they are represented as a pair is itself a significant increase in accuracy; for it was now realized from travellers' reports (such as Belon's book of 1553), confirmed by the discovery in about 1600 of the Praeneste mosaic, that obelisks had originally been sited in pairs to flank the entrance to temples. It was therefore appropriate to make them flank the title-page of a book on Egypt's symbolic wisdom. Its author, Nicolas Caussin, tells us that he conceived of it as a supplement to his previous work on Eloquence, but since he also wished it to be authentic he has confined himself to the ancient authorities more rigorously than Pierius. Accordingly, the main substance of Caussin's book consists of a Latin translation of Horapollo and relevant extracts from Clement, together with a commentary on them. But what is particularly interesting in it is the introduction. This is not only because he gives a clear definition of the distinctions between Symbol, Enigma, Emblem, Parable, Apologue or Fable, and Hieroglyph,[16] but also because he makes a firm and conscious defence of the study of Egyptian hieroglyphic. Luther had been suspicious of allegory: the Lutherans too. Hieroglyphic and allegory were closely related. Caussin's defence of them therefore – he was a Jesuit priest – is intimately bound up with the Counter-Reformation.

Caussin admits that the Hebrews may have had wisdom of the Egyptian type before Egypt herself did. For all ancient wisdom was 'concealed in the cloak of symbol or enigma', and Abraham, who had lived with the priests of Heliopolis and taught them about the stars according to one ancient account, may well have taught them this too. It would not be surprising. The rich variety of the created world was a sort of gallery of images or symbols for early men to puzzle out. All the things that Adam and Enoch saw were like letters illuminated by God. But it was the Egyptians who carried this science of symbolism furthest and who are therefore rightly looked on as its real founders. Egypt has generally been considered, as by Plato, to have been the birthplace of writing; Greek learning began in Egypt, Moses (*Acts* vii 22) was learned in all the wisdom of Egypt. Philo in his Life of Moses tells us that this consisted not merely of arithmetic, geometry, and music, but also of philosophy written by means of symbols and with drawings of animals, which is to say the hieroglyphs.

This last point of Caussin's was of great importance. The Reformers might attack the classical and humanist view of Egyptian wisdom, but they could not escape the biblical references to it. What exactly it was about the wisdom of Egypt that had caused Moses to regard it as so important was to remain one of the central questions in discussions of Egyptology for the remainder of the century and beyond.

Like the agave, which blossoms monstrously before it dies, the doctrine of hieroglyphic wisdom was to experience a final climactic flowering in the large and numerous folios of another Jesuit priest, Athanasius Kircher. Kircher's main positive contribution to Egyptology was his work on Coptic. Coptic manuscripts had only recently become available in Europe (see pages 36–9), and

▷
14 Title-page of the *de symbolica Aegyptiorum sapientia* ('The Symbolic Wisdom of Egypt') by N. Caussin (Cologne 1631)

De symbolica
AEGYPTIORVM
Sapientia, in qua
SYMBOLA, PARABOLÆ,
HISTORIÆ SELECTÆ,
quæ ad omnem
EMBLEMATV, ÆNIGMATV,
Hieroglyphicorum
Cognitionē viā præstat.
Autore Nicolao Caußino
Trecensi è Soc.
IESV

COLONIÆ AGRIPPINÆ
Apud IOANNEM KINCKIVM sub Monocerote
ANNO M.DC.XXXI.

Kircher was attracted to their study partly by their usefulness as a weapon against the heretics of his 'most calamitous century'. Many of the rites, liturgies, and doctrines attacked as being Roman inventions could, he thought, be decisively shown to be nothing of the sort but to date back to very early Christian times by the fact of their existence in the Coptic Church (Kircher, 1636, chapter 2). Nevertheless, he thought Coptic equally important for the assistance it might be expected to give to the understanding of ancient Egypt. He argued from the Coptic vocabulary (the words for father, son, and holy spirit) that the language differed from all known neighbouring languages (Hebrew, Chaldean, Syriac, Arabic, Ethiopian, Armenian, Samaritan), and tried to show from the Egyptian words quoted in *Genesis* and in Horapollo that it must have been the language of ancient Egypt. This was all level-headed enough. Kircher was, however, disingenuous about his claim to originality (see page 37). He was also unsound in his argument that Greek was derived from Coptic, and immodest in that he had his book prefaced with outspoken testimonials to his ability by quite such an exotic range of characters as a Maronite Archbishop, a Professor of Arabic, two Professors of Hebrew, an Armenian, and a small committee of Abyssinian priests.

Modesty was not, however, a part of his character. He was grandiose in all things, and wrote voluminously on a voluminous range of subjects, including Chinese, Universal Writing, and the Art of How to Think. Almost none of his work is reliable. Nevertheless, among his inaccuracies and his fantasies there is some brilliance and enough learning to make it unjust to label him a charlatan. He belongs rather to the category of the fashionable academic. He became, in Rome at least, the accepted pundit on matters Egyptian. When the Pamphilian obelisk was re-erected in the Piazza Navona in 1651 by Innocent X it was he who was entrusted with its publication. Later he was given the publication of the Minervan obelisk, put up by Alexander VII in the Piazza della Minerva in 1666/7.

The latter may stand as the crowning achievement not only of Kircher himself but of the whole school of Hieroglyphic Wisdom. The setting was designed by Bernini, and though he evidently had Colonna's woodcut in mind, everything is fresh and relevant. The tone is set by one of the inscriptions on the pedestal:

15 Wisdom supported by strength. Sixth-century BC Egyptian obelisk brought to Rome in the first or second century AD and re-erected in the Piazza della Minerva to the design of Bernini in AD 1667

SAPIENTIS AEGYPTI
INSCULPTAS OBELISCO FIGURAS
AB ELEPHANTO
BELLUARUM FORTISSIMA
GESTARI QUISQUIS HIC VIDES
DOCUMENTUM INTELLIGE
ROBUSTAE MENTIS ESSE
SOLIDAM SAPIENTIAM SUSTINERE

The learning of Egypt
carved in figures on this obelisk
and carried by an elephant
the mightiest of beasts
may afford to those who look on it
an example

of how strength of mind
should support weight of wisdom

The words *robustae mentis* allude to Alexander VII's own robustness of mind in overcoming the handicap of his weak health, and also, as Iversen (1968, p. 99) has brilliantly observed, identify him with the elephant through Mercier's Latin translation of Horapollo (ii 84), where it is said that the robust man (*robustus homo*) who is simultaneously prudent and sensitive is depicted by an elephant with its sensitive and practical trunk. The elephant's attitude shows, in Iversen's words, 'that it is approaching the monument cautiously and reverently in order to probe its way toward the Divine Wisdom which it represents, and to scent and grasp the Divine Truth'.

Kircher's book on the Minervan obelisk opens with a fine array of Latin epigrams on the monument composed by contemporaries. One exclaims that the elephant is now a Master of Arts. Instead of a howdah it carries Egyptian learning on its back, no longer just the most prudent of beasts, as Cicero had called it, but the most literate too. Another begins:

> *Monstra refert obelus: latitat sapientia monstris:*
> *Bellua, quae molem gestat, et ipsa sapit. . . .*

Here on the obelisk are shown
　Strange beasts wherein strange wisdom lies:
Another beast bears up the stone,
　And this beast too is just as wise.

while the shortest and neatest brings in a reference to the site in the Piazza della Minerva:

> *Es prudens, elephas, Minerva prudens,*
> *Foro quam bene praesidetis ambo!*

Wise beast, wise Goddess, a fit pair
　To be joint guardians of the Square!

The purpose of Kircher's book is to interpret this obelisk wisdom. He has no doubts of his own ability to do so, saying in the introduction '. . . the Sphinx has been killed, her riddles answered, and all the secrets of the Hieroglyphic Art, its rules and methods and principles are by the Influence and Grace of the Divine Spirit fully comprehended by me.' To go through all his interpretations (even though he gets tired of giving them half-way through, saying that the meaning of the other two faces is much the same as that of the first two) would be a long and painful procedure. It will be enough to give what he says of a single cartouche. Cartouches, which are generally found in pairs, are groups of hieroglyphs enclosed in an oval outline. They give the name and titles of the Pharaoh concerned, though this was not known at the time, and the matter was therefore open to speculation. Kircher affirms that they were *sacrae tabulae* of great value and mystery in summoning or placating different Genii. His interpretation of one on the Minerva obelisk (now known to be the name of the Pharaoh Psammetichus) runs:

The protection of Osiris against the violence of Typho must be elicited according to the proper rites and ceremonies by sacrifices

16 Drawing by Kircher of the east face of the Minervan obelisk

17 Scarab on the 'Bembine Table'. *a*, photograph; *b*, as drawn by Kircher

and by appeal to the tutelary Genii of the triple world in order to ensure the enjoyment of the prosperity customarily given by the Nile against the violence of the enemy Typho.

All this the priests, according to Kircher, understood at a glance. Indeed more than this. For Kircher says that each inscription has 'a quadruple sense, literal, tropical, allegorical, and analogical, to express one and the same thing.'

He nowhere gives all four levels of meaning, but he does attempt two in a passing interpretation of the man-faced scarab on the Bembine Table.[17] They will make clear, as nothing else can, the total lack of value, despite its high contemporary reputation, of Kircher's interpretative work. The only element of his publications on Egypt, other than those concerned with the Coptic language, which had any positive value, was his drawings of the inscriptions. They were not all that accurate, but in some cases they remained the only ones available even to the time of Champollion. An example is shown on the previous page.

17, 18

16

Reaction

Kircher's extravagances were such that in due course they stimulated opposition and produced their own antidote. They can thus in a negative way be said to have assisted the birth of the Age of Reason.[18] But before this happened there had been two notable moments of sanity in Egyptian studies.

The first of these came in 1605 with the publication of the Bembine Table by Lorenzo Pignorio. Pignorio was a classical scholar of sufficient reputation to have the offer of a post at Pisa transmitted to him in person by Galileo; but he declined it, preferring to remain in his native city of Padua. The Bembine, or Isiac Table, was, apart from the obelisks, the most famous Egyptian artefact of the time. Found in Rome in the ruins of the Iseum in or shortly before 1527, when it passed into the hands of Cardinal Bembo, it was actually a bronze table-top made in Rome not earlier than the middle of the first century AD as is evident from the fact that it carries a cartouche of the emperor Claudius. It was presumably made for use in the Iseum. The very accurate plate used by Pignorio in his edition was engraved by Enea Vico in 1559.

19

Pignorio's book was an iconographical commentary on the large figures on the table, and he declines to comment on the small hieroglyphs that accompany them ('though with the exercise of much imagination', he says, 'I could have invented for them

18 Kircher's decipherment of the scarab on the 'Bembine Table'

Iuxta fensum proprium ita lege .		*Iuxta fensum mysticum ita lege .*
Anima Mundi vita rerum ·		Hemphta fupramundanum Numen, Sol Archetypus .
Totius orbis moderatrix.		Ofiris .
Cœlorum orbitas .		Genij cœleftes .
Solem .		Horus .
Lunam ,		Ifis .
Elementa .		Læmones fublunares velati per potentem .
Amore connectit & in fuo effe conferuat .		Amoris catenam trahuntur alliciunturque .

19 Detail of the 'tabula Bembina' from Vico's copperplate as reproduced by Pignorio

explanations of little utility'). Strictly speaking, therefore, it falls outside the scope of this book except as an instance of the small importance attached at the time to the difference between the hieroglyphic script proper and the representations of Egyptian art. Nevertheless, Pignorio's scepticism is relevant to us since it was to introduce a new note into the discussion of Egypt. 'I shall do my best', he writes, 'to explain the pictures on the table by quoting evidence from ancient authors and not by means of allegory. I am as firmly opposed as anybody can be to the extravagant and generally irrelevant interpretations which Platonists, forgetting what their master Plato said on the matter, introduce to buttress their own insecure myths.' Pignorio is full of quotations from ancient authors, Christian and pagan, particularly Juvenal, on the absurdity of Egyptian superstitions, and approves the remark of the Spanish archbishop Agustìn that Horapollo and Clement are about as useless for our understanding of the hieroglyphs as the few mutilated lines of Punic surviving in Plautus' *Poenulus* are for learning that language.[19]

Pignorio had merely stated his position against the Neoplatonists. A more positive blow against them was struck by Isaac Casaubon in 1614. Taking exception to the doctrine that the coming of Christ had been foretold by the Sibyls and by Hermes Trismegistus (see page 22), and in particular to a recent expression of it by Cardinal Baron, Casaubon sets out (i 10) to demolish the credentials of the *corpus Hermeticum*. He wields in turn the weapons of philosophic, stylistic, and historical analysis to show that these tracts, far from being the most ancient heir-looms of Egypt were composed in Greek and in the Christian era. They contain Platonic concepts (Mind, Archetypal Form, the Infinite, Demiurge) and Christian concepts (Son of God, Word, Consubstantial); vocabulary items that are elsewhere of late appearance only (*authentia*, 'authority'; *hylotês*, 'materialness'; *ousiotês*, 'essentiality'); word-plays that are inevitably Greek (*thanatos/athanatos*, 'death' and 'immortal'; *kosmos/kosmei* 'world' and 'arranges'); and references to specifically Greek institutions (such as prytanies and athletic festivals), to say nothing of the mention of a statue by Phidias. Moreover Galen and Plutarch, who both show knowledge of Hermetic books, dismiss them as of no validity. It is therefore clear, concludes Casaubon, that the Hermetic treatises are Christian, or rather semi-Christian, compositions fathered on the Egyptian god Thoth to lend them importance. He adds that the practice of false attribution existed in antiquity, and even in the early Church before the Council of Rome; but that, however laudable its motives, it is a bad practice since it is an injury to Truth to suppose that she is strengthened by the support of Falsehood.

There could be no appeal against arguments as strong as these. As a result, the doctrine of Egyptian Wisdom lost the only actual exponent of that wisdom to which it had ever been able to point.

The next significant advance in the attempt to present an intel-ligible picture of ancient Egypt was made in a work against atheism by Edward Stillingfleete in 1662. Stillingfleete was then Rector of Sutton, but he was to become Bishop of Worcester, a power in the Church of England, and the first employer and patron of the greatest of English classical scholars, Richard Bentley.

According to Stillingfleete one of 'the most popular pretences of the Atheists of our Age has been the irreconcileableness of the account of Times in Scriptures, with that of the most learned and ancient Heathen Nations'. He therefore devoted the first volume of his book to the discrediting of all secular history, including Egyptian.

He began by arguing the general case. New colonies, he pointed out, have difficulty in getting subsistence, they tend to become dictatorships, and they frequently have wars of rivalry with their neighbouring states before they settle down. Learning is unlikely to flourish in them. In particular they will probably not retain much knowledge of their own origins – 'all certain histories of their former state must vanish and dwindle into some fabulous stories'. At this stage the reader can be excused if he thinks that Stillingfleete's mind has been wandering. But not at all. For all gentile societies started as colonies, colonies established by Noah's children. It follows that no true historical knowledge can be expected of them.

A further factor made it even more unlikely that these very early colonies should preserve knowledge of their history. This was the lack of means of communication. Stillingfleete does not pretend to know when writing was invented, but points out that it came comparatively late to Greece, and may have been late elsewhere. Speech is obviously impermanent, and oral tradition depends on memory, which is frail. This only leaves the use of signs and symbols, and in ancient times the use of signs and symbols, such as the Egyptian hieroglyphs, was indeed the chief medium of written communication. But they are inevitably obscure and ambiguous. Knowledge transmitted by their means cannot be reliable.

As for Egypt herself, there is no evidence for her possession of ancient learning now that the Hermetic books have had 'their vanity and falsehood . . . sufficiently detected by learned men'.[20] Nevertheless, there must have existed some sort of Egyptian wisdom for it to have been mentioned in *Acts* vii 22, and *I Kings* iv 29–31. So what could it have been? Medicine, geography, astronomy, and geometry are mentioned by different ancient authors. The last of these would naturally have been in demand for re-surveying land boundaries after the annual floods. Even so the standard of geometry could not have been very high. For it is clear from Euclid (i 47) that Pythagoras did not learn his proposition from the Egyptians, despite the twenty-two years he spent in Egypt.

Nor can their 'Hieroglyphical and Mystical Learning' have been very advanced, to judge from the inscription at Diospolis recorded by Clement and 'so much spoken of by the Ancients'. Its meaning, 'God hates Impudence', is no more than 'an ordinary and trivial observation'. If this sort of thing is what the celebrated wisdom of Egypt amounted to, then 'all these hieroglyphics put together will make but one good one, and that will stand for *labour lost*'.

A splendidly scornful remark to dismiss nearly two centuries of neoplatonist fancy. But Stillingfleete concluded on a more positive note. Egypt's wisdom must have been Political and Civil. Her laws were highly spoken of by Diodorus and Strabo, and borrowed by Solon and Lycurgus. Pharaoh's counsellors are referred to as 'wise' in the Scriptures. And the facts would seem to bear out this opinion for, as a state, Egypt enjoyed a particularly long and peaceful history.

Stillingfleete's views – a gust of fresh air and commonsense – were to be taken up and extended by Warburton. But Warburton deployed a wider range of evidence than was available to Stillingfleete, and before we can come to him we must first see how it was discovered.

The rediscovery of Coptic

Egypt, O Egypt, all that will remain of your religion will be words carved on stone to record your piety and stories that not even your posterity will believe. Scyths or Indians or such barbarians will inhabit the land of Egypt. Deity returns to heaven, leaving Man to die, and Egypt will become a wilderness empty of men and gods alike. And you, too, O most sacred river Nile, I tell you of what is to come. Inundated with blood you will burst your banks. Blood will pollute, nay desecrate, your divine water. There will be more tombs than living men. The few who survive will be recognized as Egyptian by their speech alone. In all their acts they will be as foreigners.

So the author of a Hermetic tract (*Asclepius* 24). He was treading
the beaten path of apocalyptic cliché, as Festugière shows (ed.
Budé ii 374), not being wise after the event. Indeed his last threat
is an understatement. For though the ancient Egyptian language
survived into Christian times and became the official language of
the Egyptian Church, after the Arab conquest it began to lose
ground to Arabic, and by the time of the European Renaissance it
was dying fast. In 1677 Vansleb claimed to have met the last surviving speaker of the language in a village in Upper Egypt. The
claim was premature, but only slightly. As a spoken language
Coptic was soon to die out.

The memory of it was, however, rescued in Europe just in time.
There were occasional people in Rome who were aware of its
existence. For instance (according to Quatremère, 1808, 45 ff.),
Leonard Abela, a Maltese who became Bishop of Sidon and died in
Rome in 1605, could speak it. In 1610 a ten-language Polyglot
Bible, to include Coptic, was planned in Rome, but never
executed.

The two earliest European collectors of Coptic manuscripts
were the Italian traveller Pietro della Valle, who went himself to
the Middle East and who brought back as well as Coptic manuscripts the first copy of a cuneiform inscription (see page 86), and
a Frenchman, Peiresc, who sent an agent, Theophilus Minuti, to
the Middle East in 1629 to hunt for manuscripts and other antiquities and purchase them on his behalf. Minuti returned in 1630
with a hoard of one Samaritan, two Syriac, several Arabic manuscripts, as well as Coptic ones, coins, and two mummies. To work
on the Coptic material Peiresc first engaged Samuel Petit. He was
not a great success (for his 'decipherment' of the Palmyra script in
1632 see page 95). Peiresc then turned to Salmasius, a sound
scholar of considerable repute, and to assist him tried to borrow
the manuscript of a Coptic–Arabic lexicon from Pietro della Valle.
But Pietro would not part with it, either because he did not want
to run the risk of sending it to France or because he was reluctant
to have it published by a scholar who was a Protestant, which
Salmasius was. However, he was in need of somebody to work on
the manuscript, and Peiresc suggested to him the name of Kircher,
whom Peiresc had met and who was then in Rome. To the great
disappointment of Salmasius (*Epist.* i 83) della Valle took up this
suggestion and so gave Kircher the opportunity that was to lead
him to his fantastic career in Egyptology.

Kircher published his *Prodromus Coptus sive Aegyptiacus* ('Introduction to Coptic, or Egyptian') in 1636 and *Lingua Aegyptiaca
Restituta* ('The Egyptian Language Restored') in 1643. These works
were enthusiastically received at the time, and, though it was not
long before numerous faults were found in them, he has generally
been given credit for having played the major part in founding
Coptic scholarship. But it now seems somewhat doubtful if he
deserves this. Not only had the potential importance of Coptic
been previously recognized by Pietro della Valle, Peiresc, and
Salmasius, but Thomas Obicini, the scholar to whom Pietro had
originally entrusted the study of his Coptic material, is now known
to have made much greater progress than had previously been

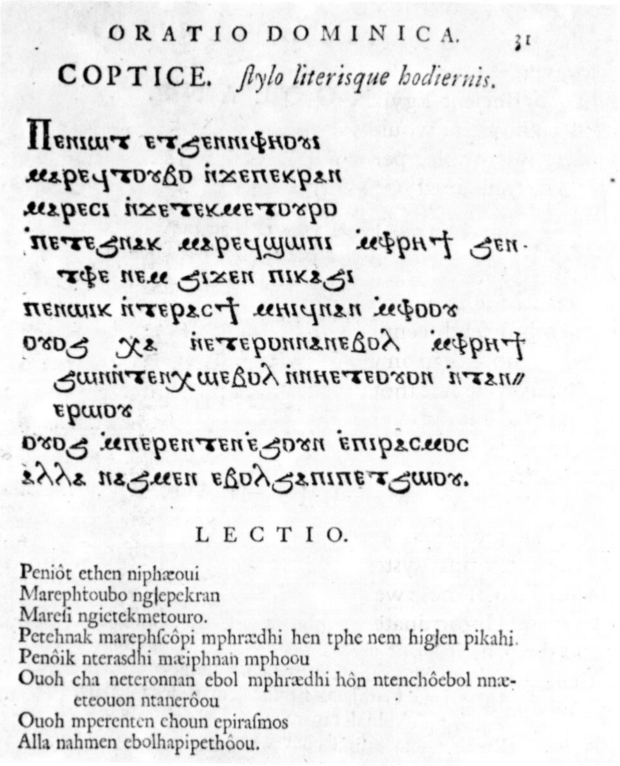

ORATIO DOMINICA. 31

COPTICE. *ſtylo literisque hodiernis.*

Ⲡⲉⲛⲓⲱⲧ ⲉⲧϭⲉⲛⲛⲓⲫⲏⲟⲩⲓ
ⲙⲁⲣⲉϥⲧⲟⲩⲃⲟ ⲛϫⲉⲡⲉⲕⲣⲁⲛ
ⲙⲁⲣⲉⲥⲓ ⲛϫⲉⲧⲉⲕⲙⲉⲧⲟⲩⲣⲟ
ⲡⲉⲧⲉϩⲛⲁⲕ ⲙⲁⲣⲉϥϣⲱⲡⲓ ⲙⲫⲣⲏϯ ϧⲉⲛ·
ⲧⲫⲉ ⲛⲉⲙ ϩⲓϫⲉⲛ ⲡⲓⲕⲁϩⲓ
ⲡⲉⲛⲱⲓⲕ ⲛⲧⲉⲣⲁⲥϯ ⲙⲏⲓϧⲛⲁⲛ ⲙⲫⲟⲟⲩ
ⲟⲩⲟϩ ϫⲁ ⲛⲉⲧⲉⲣⲟⲛⲛⲁⲛⲉⲃⲟⲗ ⲙⲫⲣⲏϯ
ϩⲱⲛⲓⲧⲉⲛⲭ ⲱⲉⲃⲟⲗ ⲛⲛⲏⲉⲧⲉⲇⲩⲟⲛ ⲛⲧⲁⲛ/
ⲉⲣⲱⲟⲩ
ⲟⲩⲟϩ ⲙⲡⲉⲣⲉⲛⲧⲉⲛⲉϩⲟⲩⲛ ⲉⲡⲓⲣⲁⲥⲙⲟⲥ
ⲁⲗⲗⲁ ⲛⲁϩⲙⲉⲛ ⲉⲃⲟⲗϧⲁⲛⲓⲡⲉⲧϩⲱⲟⲩ.

L E C T I O.

Peniôt ethen niphæoui
Marephtoubo ngǀepekran
Mareſi ngietekmetouro.
Petehnak marephſcópi mphrædhi hen tphe nem higǀen pikahi.
Penôik nterasdhi mæiphnan mphoou
Ouoh cha neteronnan ebol mphrædhi hôn ntenchôebol nnæ-
        eteouon ntanerôou
Ouoh mperenten choun epiraſmos
Alla nahmen ebolhapipethôou.

20 The Lord's Prayer in
Coptic as published by David
Wilkins in Chamberlayne's
Oratio Dominica

20

thought, owing to the discovery, made in 1938, of Obicini's
manuscript notes in the Vatican Library (van Lantschoot, 1948).

The credit for the rescue of Coptic is therefore to be shared, but
the important thing is that it was rescued. Its inclusion in books of
more general appeal, such as Chamberlayne's edition of the Lord's
Prayer in 152 different languages in 1715 brought the existence of
Coptic to the notice of a much wider public, and Coptic studies
made steady progress during the eighteenth century, one of the
landmarks being the printing of Lacroze's *Dictionary* in Oxford
in 1775.

Almost all the Coptic manuscripts recovered from Egypt were
ecclesiastical – liturgies, biblical translations, lives of martyrs. The
content was therefore of little direct value for illuminating ancient
Egypt. Even so, there are occasional glimpses, such as the following
from a sermon in a MS. in the Borgia collection noticed by
Zoëga (1810, p. 455),

Woe to him who puts his hand to his mouth and worships saying
'Hail PRE, Victory to thee, POOH!.' What are the crocodiles, and
all the water-creatures you adore? Where is Kronos, also called
PETBE, who chained his parents and castrated his father? Where
is Hephaistos, also called PTAH?

Zoëga missed the point of the last phrase, translating it 'Hephaistos
the butler', and it was only Champollion who realized that here
was the name of the ancient Egyptian god, Ptah. Champollion
managed too, as we shall see, to extract a large amount of infor-

mation about ancient Egyptian place-names and personal names from the Coptic manuscripts.

However, the primary importance of Coptic for the understanding of ancient Egypt was linguistic. Without it Champollion's decipherment would certainly not have taken place as it did. Indeed it is possible, perhaps probable, that ancient Egyptian would have remained permanently obscure.

Universal writing

Coptic scholarship was to prove indispensable for the ultimate decipherment of the hieroglyphs, but this was not foreseen in the seventeenth or eighteenth centuries. Nobody then believed that it could be more than an aid towards their interpretation; for the hieroglyphs were not thought to be a record of language, or even to operate on linguistic principles at all, but to go straight to the heart of reality.

The question was how. We have seen the attempts to provide an answer by following up clues given by Greek and Roman writers. But there was another resource: comparative evidence from other writing systems might be brought to bear on the problem. Two of these were thought relevant, namely, Mexican[21] and Chinese. Unfortunately the principles of the former had been lost and the principles of the latter had not as yet been described. But there were at least reports from the Jesuit missionaries in China of the general nature of Chinese writing. Joseph d'Acosta (1590) had stressed its complexity and the difficulty of writing foreign proper names in it because of its non-phonetic nature. Fuller information came from Trigault (1615). The language itself was monosyllabic, briefer and less ambiguous than ours, and therefore nearer to being truly philosophic. The writing system was, however, independent of it and intelligible to those who spoke other languages. The characters, though different in appearance, were similar in function to the Egyptian hieroglyphics, and represented things or ideas, not letters of words. There were some seventy or eighty thousand of them.

What caught the imagination of the seventeenth century was the hint of universal intelligibility. Could not Europe too have a writing system that would be understood by everybody, whatever language they spoke? The want was stated by Bacon, and a number of attempts were made to supply it.[22] The most important was that of John Wilkins (Dean of Ripon, later to become Bishop of Chester), *An Essay towards a Real Character and a Philosophical Language* (1668). The book had been commissioned by the Royal Society and, to judge from its Dedication, Wilkins had high hopes of its utility. It was to serve as a remedy against the Confusion of Tongues and to assist Commerce, Science, the spread of true Religion, and the cure of religious quarrels, 'by unmasking many wild errors that shelter themselves under the disguise of affected phrases'.

After two chapters on the history of languages and their tendency to multiply, Wilkins turned to the history of writing. He attributed a Hebrew origin to the alphabet, rightly using the order of letters in derived alphabets as an argument for diffusion. But the alphabet, he said, was not the only possible method of writing. 'Besides this common way of writing by the ordinary *Letters*, the Ancients have sometimes used to communicate by other *Notes*, which were either for *Secrecy* or *Brevity*.' Into the latter category came shorthand, ancient and modern: into the former the Egyptian hieroglyphics 'as they are commonly esteemed'. But he expressed some hesitation as to whether they really were intended to conceal mysteries from the vulgar people, and a strong scepticism in any case as to their profundity. 'There is reason to doubt whether there be anything in them worth the enquiry, the discoveries that have hitherto been made out of them being very few and insignificant. They seem to be but a slight, imperfect invention, sutable [*sic*] to those first and ruder Ages: much the same nature with that of the *Mexican* way of writing by *Picture*. . . .' Precisely Stillingfleete's views.

Wilkins had higher hopes of the Chinese script – at least if it was, as commonly supposed, a single form of writing read by all the inhabitants of the country despite language differences. Nevertheless, Chinese was reported to be difficult to learn, which was also the trouble with Latin (pp. 450, 453). In fact no existing language or writing system approached the ideal; it was therefore necessary to invent one.

The first and basic requirement was 'a regular enumeration and description of all those things and notions to which names are to be assigned', arranged in a descending order from the general to the particular. (Users of Roget's *Thesaurus* – a descendant of Wilkins' book, though composed on somewhat different criteria – will be able to form an approximate idea of what the resulting scheme looked like.) Each major concept (e.g. MEASURE) was differentiated into a limited number of aspects (e.g. *NUMBER, SIZE, WEIGHT, STRENGTH, DURATION*), and each of these taken separately was further speciated (e.g. *DURATION* into *year, summer, winter, month, 24-hour day, daytime, morning, hour*). Three ciphers will therefore be all that is needed to reach any of these specific concepts. It remains to find a convenient notation for them. Thus:

INTEGRALS Forty in all. A bold line with a distinctive variation in the middle. e.g.:
⊤— STONE   —○— DISEASE

DIFFERENCES limited to nine for each integral. Marked by a semaphore-like system operated at the left hand of each integral line. The third differentiation of stone is precious stone; of disease, tumour. So
⌐⊤— *PRECIOUS STONE*   ⌐○— *TUMOUR*

SPECIES the same, but on the right hand of each integral line. The fifth speciation of precious stone is turquoise; of tumour, wart. So
⌐⊤⌐ *turquoise*   ⌐○⌐ *wart*

Naturally the user of the system must refer to the book for the representations of the integrals and the manner in which they are differentiated and speciated until he has it by memory. But the process of looking up is straightforward and quick.

A further modification of the signs gives them verbal or adjectival force. The system therefore sets out to be able to express all the major notions of human thought in any of the three major grammatical guises – noun, verb, or adjective.

But there still remain grammatical particles. These follow a separate system, which I shall not attempt to set out in detail. In a running text they are used concurrently with the signs for the major notions, and are placed in between them wherever needed; for what they express is the interrelationship of the major notions. The illustration at the top of the page shows what the result looks like. The key is as follows, the major notions being in italics:

21 Ideographic and phonetic scripts invented by John Wilkins. *a*, (top of page) the Lord's Prayer in 'real character'; *b*, (foot of page) the English version of the Lord's Prayer in characters representing the sounds as pronounced

21a

1. our *parent* who art in *heaven*, thy *name* be *hallowed*, thy *kingdom come*, thy *will* be *done*, so in *earth*
2. as in *heaven*, *give* us on this *day* our *bread expedient* and *forgive* us our *trespasses* as we *forgive*
3. them who *trespass* against us, and *lead* us not into *temptation*, but *deliver* us from *evil*, for the *kingdom* and the *power*
4. and the *glory* is thine *for-ever-and-ever*, a m e n so be it.

Notice how he cannot cope with 'amen'. This is a foreign word, and cannot be expressed except with the help of a phonetic notation. So Wilkins needs yet another system. Interestingly, he does not choose an alphabet, but a rationalized syllabary after the model of the Amharic (Ethiopian) syllabary published by Kircher. He employs thirty-one consonant-signs and six vowels. The consonants are systematized as far as possible – for example voiced and unvoiced are made upside down to each other:

c	⊥	g	T
f	⊦	v	⅂
t	⌊	d	⅂ etc.

and the vowel-signs are attached to the part of the consonant-sign appropriate to the vowel sound it is desired to express. How the system works can be seen in the illustration below.

21b

Wilkins was optimistic enough to hope that one day his Real Characters might develop from script to language, there being in his view no necessary reason why writing should come later than speech. Historically it may have always done so, but the opposite way, he thinks, would in this case be easier. 'To proceed from the Language to the Character would require the learning of both', whereas by proceeding in the other direction it would be possible to take the stages one at a time. For the Real Character could be used while retaining one's own language.

Needless to say Wilkins' writing systems have not conquered the world. Whether this is because they were too complicated, as Horne Tooke thought, or too systematic and therefore more suited for computers than for people is not here our concern. What does concern us is how far the attempt to construct them contributed to progress in understanding ancient scripts. Surprisingly, it would appear that the answer is a great deal. It clarified many things that might otherwise not have become clear. The most striking of these was the difficulty, if not the impossibility, of writing proper names, foreign proper names in particular, in an ideographic script. It was this point that was to become central in the early decipherments, and in Champollion's initial decipherment of the hieroglyphs. Another possible contribution was Wilkins' adoption of a syllabary and the use of a grid system for displaying it on the printed page. This must have had a useful effect in making it easier to think about the nature of syllabic scripts. He also provided the original hints for some ingenious but false theories. For instance, the theory of language development entertained by Champollion's tutor, Sacy (see page 65) has for its main point of departure the probable inability of ideographic scripts to express the smaller parts of speech – for which Wilkins had found he needed a wholly separate system. Champollion himself entertained the hypothesis that the way the hieroglyphs might work was by classifying concepts into genus and species – in the same sort of way therefore as Wilkins' Real Character. Even Wilkins' mistakes may have contributed something. He was not able (as a glance at Ill. 21a will show) to escape from the order of ideas of his own language, even though this was one of the points on which he had criticized his predecessors. This was to highlight one of the main theoretical problems of an ideographic script. It was from consideration of this problem that Zoëga was to argue that the order of hieroglyphs in a hieroglyphic text must be linguistically determined, a conclusion which was to have a conscious effect on Champollion.

In short, Wilkins' scheme, except in so far as it had a share in the ancestry of modern symbolic logic and of Roget's *Thesaurus*, was a failure as a practical project. But viewed in the light of what is nowadays called a 'model' or a 'game', it made a useful, perhaps even a necessary, contribution to progress.

Chapter Two

The Eighteenth Century

New facts and new theory

During the eighteenth century new evidence from Egypt came to be discovered, acquired by European collectors, and published on an increasing scale; in particular specimens of non-hieroglyphic Egyptian writing were found and recognized for the first time. By the same token, the mysteries and fantasies of the Kircher-type interpretation of ancient Egypt became progressively out of tune with the intellectual atmosphere of the age. A new synthesis was needed and the person who did more than anyone else to provide it was William Warburton.

These are, respectively, the new facts and the new theory of the section heading.

The story begins just before the century opened. In 1692 a long band of material from a mummy burial was unwrapped in the presence of M. de Maillet, the French Consul in Cairo.[1] It carried figures drawn in the ancient Egyptian style which were accompanied by an ink-written text in a hitherto unknown sort of writing. It was cut up, presumably at the time of unwrapping, into seven or eight pieces, and sent to France. One of the pieces came to the notice of Jean-Pierre Rigord, a collector of antiquities, who discussed the find in the *Mémoires de Trévoux* of June 1704.

Rigord's article was illustrated with plates of an ordinary hieroglyphic inscription, a specimen of the mummy text, and another stone inscription from Egypt from his collection. With the aid of the passage about Egyptian writing in Clement, he identified the first as 'symbolical hieroglyphic', the second as either 'hieratic' or as 'cyriological hieroglyphic', and the third as 'epistolographic'. He thought that this last one, written from right to left, was probably Phoenician.[1a] The script was said to have been in public use, and Phoenician might have come in as a mercantile language with the Shepherd Kings. The divergence of the language from Hebrew (the original tongue of mankind) had obviously reached the point of unintelligibility in Joseph's day for an interpreter to have been considered necessary between him and his brothers, and Jerome had said that Phoenician was half-way between Hebrew and Egyptian. Finally, Rigord suggested that the language might have been the same as Punic. In any case he dismissed the last form of Egyptian writing, Coptic, as irrelevant: it was purely Greek and must post-date Alexander, or at least Psammetichus (*c.* 700 BC). It was perhaps Psammetichus, he thought, who introduced the Coptic language into Egypt.

23a
22a

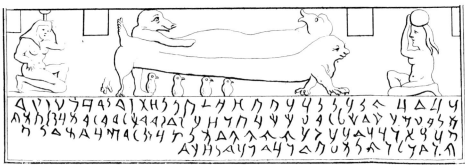

22 Early publications of a
funerary stele bearing non-
hieroglyphic writing from
Egypt. *a*, by Rigord (1704),
who thought the script to be
Punic, which he identified
with epistolographic; *b*, by
Montfaucon (1724), who
thought it to be in the same
Egyptian cursive script as the
others, which he identified
with Herodotus' 'public'
script *c*, by Caylus (1752),
with a commentary by the
Abbé Barthélemy, who
thought it to be in the
'vulgar' script, similar to
inscriptions found on Sinai.
It is in fact Aramaic (v. note 1)

The article[2] is unpretentious and even muddled. Witness the
apparent confusion between the Coptic script and the Coptic
language. Nevertheless, it contained two new ideas of great
importance.[3] The first was that hieroglyphic was not a secret script
at all but the opposite, a public one for use on public monuments,
devised for the benefit of those who were illiterate and unable to
read the (Hebrew-derived) alphabetic script. The temple-
entrance inscription in Clement, which Rigord realized to be the
same as that presented without a translation in our manuscripts of
Plutarch, was given by him a totally non-mystical interpretation:
in the context, 'God hates Impudence', could only mean 'one must
approach a Temple with the reverence due to the presence of God'.
Rigord's second novel suggestion, which was to remain dormant
until Champollion, was that the meaning of 'first elements' (*prôta
stoicheia*), referred to by Clement as being used to express words
in 'cyriological hieroglyphic', must be alphabetic letters.

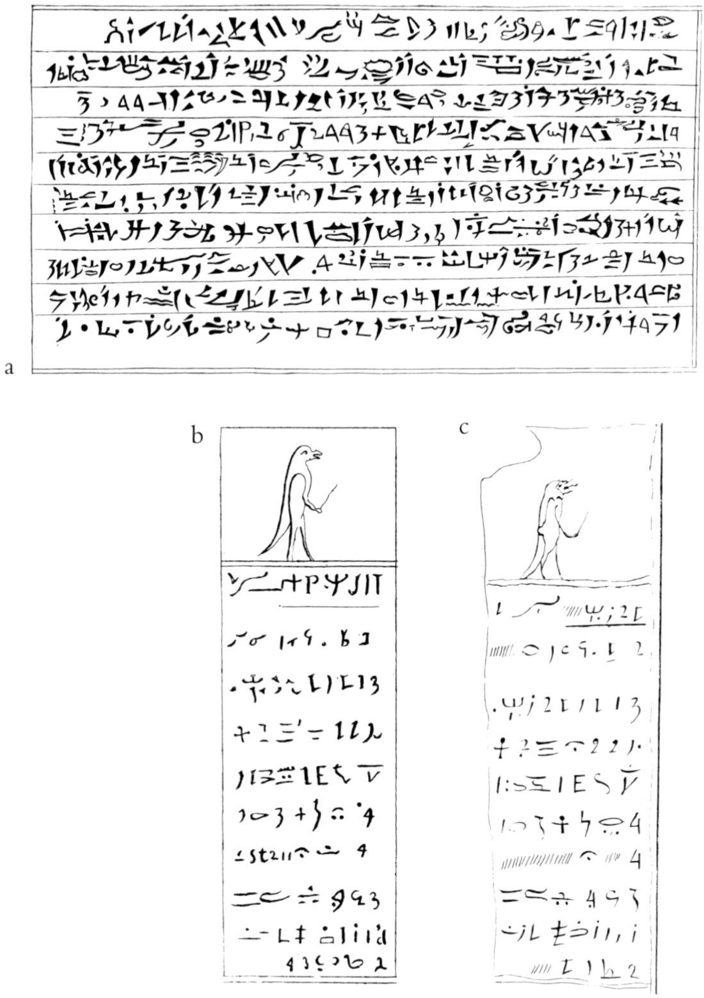

a

b   c

23 Early publications of sections of texts in non-hieroglyphic Egyptian writing from Egyptian graves. *a*, by Rigord (1704), who thought it to be part of a book of theological consolations written in the priestly, or sacred, script; *b*, by Montfaucon (1724), who thought it to be in the same script as that on the stele; *c*, by Caylus and Barthélemy, who thought this same text to be a specimen of the 'sacred' script as opposed to the 'public' or 'vulgar'

The totality of non-hieroglyphic inscriptions known were collected and published by Bernard de Montfaucon, a classical scholar who had travelled extensively in Italy in his younger days but who since 1701 had been living and working at the monastery of St Germain-des-Prés. They occupy two large plates (II ii 140; supp. vol. II 54) in his *L'Antiquité expliquée*, an encyclopedia of ancient life and religion in ten folio volumes containing over 1,100 full-page illustrations – scarcely a large proportion. Nor was the quality good; the engraving of the 'tabula Rigordana' in the second of the two plates is a particularly clear example of how badly an eighteenth-century author could be served by his illustrator. Montfaucon himself is fully aware that this is a scene of Anubis laying out the dead, but who would guess it from the plate?

22b

Montfaucon does not discuss the texts at great length. He points out that the writing is proved to be Egyptian by the totally Egyptian character of the accompanying drawings, and takes them as

23b

examples of Herodotus' 'public' script. He then goes on to consider the question of Coptic. Coptic as a language, he says, is now almost extinct except in some corners of Upper Egypt, but it is what the ancient Egyptians spoke. The Coptic script is the Egyptian language written in Greek characters supplemented with some eight extra characters taken from Egyptian to meet the specific needs of the language. The reason for its creation, Montfaucon thought, was the spread of Greek influence and literacy after Alexander's conquest. Finally he expresses the hope that the publication of the new texts will allow these extra characters of the Coptic script to be identified in cursive Egyptian, and that thereby, or with the aid of a Greek-Egyptian bilingual whose discovery one day is not to be despaired of, the script may be deciphered. Such a decipherment would be made easier by the fact that because of Coptic the language was already partly known. It should also prove rewarding. For since Egypt was the schoolmaster of Greece, as Greece was of Rome, and since Egyptian buildings, and the Egyptians' ability to move vast weights attest an able technology, there should be considerable interest and profit in reading their literature, once more of it becomes available.

Montfaucon's calm and level-headed appraisal of the possibilities and purposes of Egyptian research could not have been more distant from the erratic imaginings of Kircher. Yet from the philosophical standpoint, to answer the question where Egypt stood in human history, there was still nothing to replace Kircher and the Neoplatonists. True, the ideas so confidently alleged by them to be Egyptian must have aroused scepticism or embarrassment in any participating member of the Age of Reason. Witness for instance the half-hearted way in which Alexander Pope accepted but for all serious purposes ignored the belief that Homer and Hesiod received their wisdom 'through Egyptian strainers'. But there was no alternative; no intellectually respectable way of denying the major propositions of Egyptomania had yet been put forward.

24   This was to be the contribution of William Warburton, the future Bishop of Gloucester, whom Champollion (*Précis* 371) described as the first sensible man to have tackled the subject.

Champollion's evaluation is not the one which would occur to anyone who, picking up Warburton's book, let his eye stay at the title-page. Its title is *The Divine Legation of Moses demonstrated on the principles of a Religious Deist, from the Omission of a Future State of Reward and Punishment in the Jewish Dispensation*. This might well appear the strangest and most difficult of all possible ways of proving the divine nature of Moses' mission. But not at all; according to Warburton it is entirely straightforward. For 'it is clear that to inculcate the doctrine of a future state of rewards and punishments is necessary to the well-being of society'. It follows from this that 'whatever Religion or Society have no future state for their support, must be supported by an extraordinary Providence'. Jewish religion and society having no such state for its support, it must therefore be supported by an extraordinary Providence, and the Law of Moses must accordingly be of divine origin. *Q.E.D.*

Warburton suggests that this would indeed be self-evident if it were not for men's passion for paradox. As it is, he will have to go more deeply into the demonstration.

He does so. *The Divine Legation* is divided into nine books, and even so was unfinished. Egypt is dealt with in the fourth, where the ostensible purpose was to defend the antiquity of Egypt against Sir Isaac Newton. In a book on the chronology of the world, published in 1728, Newton, employing a mixture of sophisticated mathematical arguments and naïve mythological assumptions, had reached dates such as Daedalus' invention of carpentry in 989 B C, the Pyramids of Gizeh built respectively in 838, 824 and 808 B C.[4] Newton's chronology, though absurd, continued to have adherents down to Champollion's time, so doubtless Warburton was justified in taking it seriously. But his main purpose clearly extended beyond this negative one. He wished to establish a coherent account of human history as a whole, and this could hardly be done without full consideration being given to Egypt's place in it.

24 William Warburton, 1698–1779

The importance of Egypt lay of course in her contribution to learning. According to Warburton, Egypt's learning must have consisted largely of a traditional body of detached tenets, moral and scientific, without regard to system (for instance Pythagoras, despite his twenty-two years in Egypt, had to evolve his theory on the square of the hypotenuse after his return to Samos – a point made by Stillingfleete, see page 36), or the cult of controversy; it was not eristic according to Clement (viii *ad init.*), but could be advanced (for instance the doctrine that the earth went round the sun, thought by Newton to be Egyptian). But the chief thing it consisted in was 'legislation and civil polity'. In particular what was invented in Egypt was the 'double doctrine'.

The existence of this 'double doctrine' is a major theme of Warburton's book. What he means by it is that all ancient philosophers and philosophical sects that concerned themselves with morals, politics, legislation, and such matters (therefore not the Ionians or the Epicureans) promulgated publicly the belief in future rewards and punishments since they thought that such a belief was politically useful or even necessary, but that they themselves rejected it as being untrue.

To prove this strange proposition Warburton assembles a massive and impressive array of quotations, not only from what he calls the 'grand quaternion' of theistic philosophy – Pythagorean, Platonic, Peripatetic, Stoic – but also from individuals like Cicero, whose letters and occasional remarks in speeches show that he personally thought of death as the end of feeling despite what he says in his public works devoted to the subject.

In Warburton's opinion, two tenets of ancient theistic philosophy explained why it was impossible for serious thinkers to believe in a future state of reward or punishment. The first was that God cannot be angry. Warburton shows how universal was the agreement on this point among ancient philosophers, and how it was singled out for attack by early Christian Fathers, especially Lactantius, who devoted a treatise, highly praised by Jerome, to this one point (*de ira Dei*) establishing that if you take away either anger or its opposite (*gratia*) from your concept of God there can be no religion. The other tenet was that soul is a substance. It was therefore not created nor could it be destroyed. On death one's portion of soul rejoined the universal stock, just as one's portion of body returned to its material elements. There could therefore be no individual reward or punishment for it.

The 'double doctrine' clearly came to Greece from Egypt. For who brought the 'scattered tribes' of Greece into the condition of 'civil society'? Orpheus, and others of his time. Where does tradition say they were educated? Egypt. And what particular institutions did they found? The Mysteries. And we know that the Mysteries came from Egypt, and that they taught about future life. Yet the flow of the tradition was not wholly unruffled. There came an age, the age of the tyrants, when speculation on political and moral matters became unsafe. The philosophers of the time, Thales and others, consequently took from Egypt only its physical and mathematical knowledge. They had no need for the 'double doctrine'. This was, however, to return later with men like Plato when liberty had been regained and legislation and morality had become once again a concern of philosophy.

In short, legislation and political skill was the particular *forte* of ancient Egypt. This is confirmed by the practical success of the Egyptian state in maintaining its power and stability for so long (Stillingfleete again, see page 36). It is also confirmed by Horapollo. The reader may gasp to hear such a witness called on behalf of such a cause. But Warburton finds no difficulty in leading his man where he wants. For is it not evident that all Horapollo's hieroglyphic interpretations 'relate to civil life, and are altogether unfit for the abstruse speculations of philosophy and theology'?

This brings us to Warburton's theory of the hieroglyphics and of writing in general.

Men communicated first by sounds, then, to 'perpetuate their conceptions' or 'to communicate them at a distance', by figures. The first and most obvious way to try to do this is by pictures. Attempts in this line are universal, but were developed to the furthest extent by the Mexicans.

But 'the inconvenience attending the too great bulk of the volume in writings of this kind would soon set the more ingenious and better civilized people upon contriving methods to abridge their characters'. Hence what was in the Mexican stage 'a simple painting' became in Egypt 'a pictured character'. The abridgement was of three kinds:

1. *Curiological Hieroglyphic* by putting an important part for the whole, as a scaling-ladder to mean a siege.

2. *Tropical Hieroglyphic* by putting the instrument of the thing for the thing itself, as an eye to mean divine omniscience.

3. *Symbolic Hieroglyphic* by using 'any quaint resemblance or analogy' collected from the observation of nature or traditional superstition, as the two eyes of a crocodile to mean the sunrise, or a black pigeon to mean a widow who does not re-marry.

Egyptian hieroglyphic therefore came about in the normal course of human progress. It was 'the second mode of invention for recording men's actions and conceptions; not, as has been hitherto thought, a devise of choice for secrecy, but an expedient of necessity, for popular use.' This was Rigord's view (see page 44).

Even so 'the scantiness of hieroglyphic characters' led to obscurity, and the number of straightforward pictures still retained made the script cumbersome. So there was a third change in the history of hieroglyphic writing, of which Chinese is the most famous example. We know from 'the concurrent testimony of the best writers on the arts and manners of this famous people' that their present method of writing by arbitrary signs 'was deduced, through an earlier hieroglyphic, from the first simple way of painting the human conceptions'.

These three stages of Warburton's history of the hieroglyphic class of writing can be presented schematically thus:

METHOD	EXAMPLE	DESCRIPTION
by representation	Mexican	pictures
by analogy or symbol	Egyptian	pictures and 'contrasted and arbitrarily instituted marks'[5]
by arbitrary institution	Chinese	marks only, but 'increased to a prodigious number'

Summing up this section of his exposition, Warburton writes, 'Thus we have brought down the general history of writing, by a gradual and easy descent, from a FIGURE to a LETTER; for Chinese marks, which participate of Egyptian hieroglyphs on the one hand, and of alphabetic letters on the other . . . are on the very border of letters; an alphabet invented to express *sounds* instead of *things*, being only a compendium of that large volume of arbitrary marks.'

On this point, cardinal to his theory, Warburton was to receive a confirmation of his views that must have been as gratifying as it was apparently decisive. In preparing the publication of the non-hieroglyphic Egyptian texts in the collection of the Comte de Caylus, the Abbé Barthélemy, who had read Warburton, made the experiment of looking for letters that might have been taken over from the hieroglyphs. And he found them – just as he should have done on Warburton's hypothesis. In the next (1765) edition of his book Warburton included Barthélemy's table of the signs so found.

But Warburton is not yet finished. There are many things left to explain. One is how the hieroglyphs, 'the simplest and plainest means of instruction', were converted into 'one of the most artificial and abstruse'.

That originally the hieroglyphics were employed 'to record openly and plainly laws, policies, public morals, and history, and, in a word, all kinds of civil matters' is the most natural conclusion to be drawn from several lines of evidence. The most reliable ancient authors, Diodorus, Strabo, Tacitus, say of the obelisk inscriptions that they recorded the achievements of ancient kings. Hermapion's surviving translation of an obelisk inscription is a panegyric on Rameses and a history of his conquests. Horapollo's interpretations all refer to civil life. The Sais temple-entrance inscription 'God hates Impudence' was rightly ridiculed by Stillingfleete if it was intended as a piece of recondite wisdom: but taken simply 'as a very plain and important truth to be read and understood by the people', as a sort of public notice in fact, it was perfectly appropriate to its position.

As time passed, however, the script became more recondite. The 'method of contriving tropical hieroglyphs, by similar properties, would of itself produce refinement and nice enquiry into the hidden and more abstruse qualities of things.' This process of research, assisted perhaps by a more theologically inclined temper, introduced 'a new species of zoographic writing, called by the ancients SYMBOLIC, and employed for SECRECY; which the high speculations conveyed in it required; and for which it was well fitted by the aenigmatic quaintness of its representations.' Tropical symbols operated by means of the less well-known properties of things. For instance a cat could indicate the moon because, as Plutarch tells us, its pupil dilates and contracts with the waxings and wanings of the moon. Enigmatic symbols operated by associations that were not obvious, such as a scarab beetle with a round ball in its claws for the sun.

The script thus became 'at length and by insensible degrees' very different from its plain beginnings. The Greeks realized this difference to the extent that they distinguished the terms 'hieroglyphic' and 'symbolic'. But they assumed that both were secret writing. This was an error, and it has 'involved the whole history of hieroglyphic writing in infinite confusion'.

The same process eventually led to alphabetic writing. This was invented by the secretary of an Egyptian king (for that is what the ancient traditions about Thoth must imply). The reason was the need for clarity in administration: hieroglyphic instructions must have tended towards the obscure or the ambiguous. It is not the case, says Warburton, predictably rowing against the stream of all ancient and modern opinion, that the invention of the alphabet would have been difficult. All it needed was the realization that selected arbitrary marks could be combined on paper just as the basic elements of human speech are combined in sound. A repertory of arbitrary marks was already to hand in existing hieroglyphic writing.[6]

The administration having invented alphabetic writing, it is reasonable to suppose that they kept it to themselves for as long as they could as a secret cipher. But the secret must have leaked out, and this before the time of Herodotus, because Herodotus calls the non-hieroglyphic form of writing 'public'. But possibly it did not happen long before, as Herodotus does not mention the sacerdotal script; nor does Diodorus. The inference is that it was not invented or not known. But it is mentioned by Clement, who makes it clear that it was alphabetic 'by the first elements of words'.[7] The only conclusion which fits all this evidence is that the sacerdotal script was the last form of Egyptian writing, and that it was invented for the use of the priests to replace the original alphabetic writing when it had ceased to be a secret and become public.

Having completed his history of writing, Warburton turns to the history of language. For writing and language run parallel courses and can shed light on one another. The main difference is that we know the origin of language from Scripture – the direct instruction of Adam by God. Otherwise the account normally found in Greek and Roman writers, says Warburton, of a gradual growth from animal noises would have been plausible enough. Even so the language as taught to Adam could only have been a start. 'We cannot reasonably suppose it to be any other than what served his present use: after this he was able to improve and enlarge it, as his future occasions should require: consequently the first language must needs be very poor and narrow.'

Divine intervention thus obscured the parallelism in the initial stages, but thereafter the growth of language, writing, and even literary style, was concurrent. Warburton's description of their growth can be most conveniently plotted by means of a table, provided we bear in mind that a table is bound to make his distinctions look more hard-and-fast than he intended.

	WRITING		LANGUAGE	STYLE
1	pictures		signs and gestures	pleonasm
2	proper hieroglyphic	curiological	fable	metaphor
		tropical		
3	symbolic hieroglyphic	tropical	parable	wit
		enigmatical	riddle	

When language was 'rude, narrow, and equivocal' it had to be helped out by signs. For instance we are told that North American Indians speak by gesture as much as by voice. But what arose from necessity passed, as often happens, into ornament, and lasted long after the necessity was over. Thus the Delphic Apollo, according to Heracleitus, 'neither speaks nor keeps silent, but reveals himself by signs'. In the Old Testament we read of Isaiah being ordered to go naked for three years, of Jeremiah hiding the linen girdle, and of God giving instructions by sign to Abraham in regard to the sacrifice of Isaac. It is similar in the sphere of style. Pleonasm is frequent in early language, and particularly in Hebrew, 'the scantiest of all the learned languages of the East'. For 'when the speaker's phrase comes not up to his ideas, he naturally endeavours to explain himself by a repetition of the thought in other words.'

Fables, for instance the speech of Jotham (*Judges* ix, 7) and the thistle that presumed an equality with the cedar (II *Kings* xiv 9), were necessary when 'language was yet too narrow, and the minds of men too undisciplined, to support . . . abstract reasoning'. Fables that became popular were distilled into proverbs. In the

25 Comte de Caylus,
1692–1765

field of style 'rusticity of conceptions' and the inability to express abstract ideas except in a material image leads to frequency of metaphor.

Parables are intentionally arcane and mysterious (see *Ezekiel* xx 49; *Luke* viii 10), and riddles still more so (*Ezekiel* xvii 2; *Proverbs* i 5–6; *Psalms* xlix 4). Stylistically, wit 'consists in using strong metaphoric images in uncommon yet apt allusions: just as ancient Egyptian wisdom did in hieroglyphic symbols fancifully analogized.' The basis, however, was serious observation. 'The Egyptians studied all the singular properties of beings, and their relations, in order to fit them for representatives of other things.'

Such is Warburton's account of the development of human techniques of communication. It is among other things an account admirably adapted to the position of an eighteenth-century churchman. He reminds us that 'the illiterate cavils of modern libertines' are fond of attacking the prophetic language of the Scriptures as 'absurd', 'fanatic', and 'the peculiar workmanship of heated imagination'. This can now be recognized as misplaced criticism. Absurd means extravagant, fanatic means affecting unusual or foreign modes. But the prophetic style is 'a speaking hieroglyphic' and the 'sober and established language of the time'. On the other hand the attempts, not uncommon among Dissenters, to revive the style of Old Testament speech and imitate the 'significative actions' which it describes are unnecessary in the present stage of human communications and can properly be labelled both absurd and fanatic.

However, the main purpose of Warburton's review of Egyptian writing was not to prove the centrality and correctness of the position of the religious deist but to give the internal evidence for the high antiquity of Egyptian civilization. The key lies in the dating of the symbolic hieroglyphs. They occupy a middle point in the course of the history of Egyptian writing. Yet that middle point must have been a long time ago. It was before the invention of alphabetic writing; it was also before the fashion for animal worship. (This last is a new point. Warburton's reasons for it, briefly, are that animal worship was unique to Egypt, not confined to useful animals, or even to real ones, and that it extended even to plants: it has all these points in common with the symbolic hieroglyphs, and so must have been derived from them.) But both alphabetic writing and animal worship existed at the time of the Exodus; for Moses brought with him the letters of the Egyptian alphabet, and he also found it necessary to forbid the cult of animals. The symbolic hieroglyphs must therefore be earlier than the time of Moses. Since the system of symbolic hieroglyphs was inevitably of slow growth, however, the origins of Egyptian civilization must have been considerably earlier still.

We have spent a long time with Warburton. This will not be grudged by those who enjoy ingenious argument. Warburton, however, was not only ingenious but also important. To ask whether or not the decipherment of the hieroglyphs would have taken place without him is very much like asking whether or not the discoveries of modern science and technology would have taken place without the theoretical shelter for them erected by

Francis Bacon. That is to say, it is a question with two sides and no visible answer. But what is evident is that Warburton created the framework for Egyptological speculation, particularly in France, in the latter half of the eighteenth century and beyond. The section of *The Divine Legation* that deals with Egypt was translated into French under the title *Essai sur les hiéroglyphes des Égyptiens* by Léonard des Malpeines in 1744, and its ideas were enthusiastically received by Condillac (*Essai sur les origines des connaissances humaines* 1746), by the *Encyclopédie* (articles on *écriture égyptienne* and *hiéroglyphe*), and indeed found general favour. It was therefore Warburton who shaped the climate of opinion in which Champollion was brought up.[8]

We must now turn to the Abbé Barthélemy, who was one of Warburton's admirers. He approved the outlines of Warburton's theory of Egyptian writing, and in helping to publish the Egyptian inscriptions in the collection of the Comte de Caylus (Caylus 1752, 69–70) he set out to test Warburton's theory of the inter-relationship of the hieroglyphic and alphabetic systems. As we have seen, Warburton's theory predicted that some of the signs of the hieroglyphic would have been borrowed by the alphabetic script, and this prediction was apparently confirmed by Barthélemy's findings.

The large number of separate characters in Egyptian hieratic might have been expected to have warned Barthélemy against a too ready acceptance of the hypothesis that it was an alphabetic script; indeed Barthélemy did notice the problem ten years later when he was publishing another text in Caylus' collection. However, he managed to save the alphabetic hypothesis by the assumption that Egyptian could be like 'Ethiopian' (i.e. Amharic) writing, which is composed of only twenty-six letters, but in which, because the vowel-signs are attached to each letter and the system includes syllabic signs, the total number of different-looking characters mounts to 202.

It was on this occasion (Caylus 1762, 79) that Barthélemy made his most fruitful and important suggestion. This was that the obelisk cartouches might contain the names of kings or gods. Oddly enough, he was led to it by two false observations. The first was that he thought he could detect in the alphabetic script of the mummy-bandage he was publishing 'a combination of characters forming a sort of square', which might be the cursive equivalent of a hieroglyphic cartouche. The second was that he thought that the particular hieroglyphs contained in the cartouches were different from those found elsewhere.

The Comte de Caylus, for whom Barthélemy was working, deserves a few words at this point. He was a French nobleman who had had, in the normal way of things, a commission in the army. After the peace of Rastadt, finding that army life no longer gave him a sufficiently purposeful outlet for his energies, he resigned his commission, and travelled to Turkey. There he saw Colophon and Ephesus and other of the *claras Asiae urbes* under the protection of Karakaiuli, a brigand who then enjoyed virtual control of the Smyrna area. The nobility of the ancient Greek cities and the striking contrast they offered to the shoddiness which had taken

26 The difficulties
confronting an
eighteenth-century
decipherer who relied on
published transcriptions can
be seen by comparing the
last lines of the copies of the
funerary stele (ill. 22) made
by (*a*) Rigord, (*b*)
Montfaucon, (*c*) Caylus

their place, resolved Caylus to devote his life to the promotion of classical standards in architecture and art. He became a collector, and a patron of classicizing designers; he interested himself in the improvement of engraving techniques; he even re-invented the process of encaustic painting from the pages of the elder Pliny – in his own eyes his greatest achievement.

His most direct contribution to the study of Egyptian writing was his collection of Egyptian texts, both hieroglyphic and non-hieroglyphic. This provided a body of material for French scholars – including, later, Champollion himself – to work on. But almost as important as his collections was Caylus' interest in promoting accurate reproduction. In this his example may have been less potent than his influence. The supreme importance of accurate reproduction for any decipherment, obvious from a close comparison of the copies here illustrated, was pointed out by Caylus himself, and came progressively to be realized. The next generation of travellers set out with the equipment and the resolve to make them.

One of these, and the most successful, was Carsten Niebuhr, a Danish scholar and the father of the distinguished ancient historian. Although, as we shall see later, it was his copies of the Persepolis inscriptions that made the decipherment of cuneiform possible, he also travelled in Egypt. The accompanying illustration, which represents no more than a small part of what Niebuhr succeeded in copying *in situ* in a Cairo street, will give an idea of the quality of his work. In this connection he makes the sound, though unexpected, point that one of the main conditions for accurate copying is the ability to have good relations with the Arabs. He also tells us, and this is clear from the confident style of his copying, that he had so familiarized himself with the hieroglyphic script by dint of the amount of it he took down, that he could write it with almost as much ease as Greek or Arabic. This enabled him to point out firmly and for the first time that the term 'hieroglyphs' should not be used for the large-scale figures on Egyptian reliefs and paintings, but be reserved exclusively for the small characters which are written in a uniform and script-like manner. This was a point on which even Warburton had been confused (see note 5).

Niebuhr was also able to provide for the first time a proper table, not, as he knew, a complete one, of hieroglyphs arranged in an order determined by objective criteria and therefore giving a base for judging the total number of signs and the limits of variety for each one.

27 A section from Niebuhr's copy (1774) of a granite coffin in the streets of Cairo

With Niebuhr we have at last emerged from the forests and the foot-hills on to the open mountainside. But before we follow the

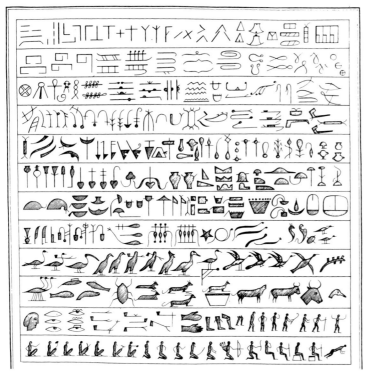

28 Niebuhr's table of selected hieroglyphs

explorers up it, we must survey the possible routes as they appeared from that point in time. Our guide will be another Danish scholar, Georg Zoëga. Zoëga lived most of his life in Rome, where at the request of Pope Pius VI he wrote and published the most comprehensive and dispassionate survey of Egyptology that had yet appeared. It must have the next section to itself.

29

Zoega

Zoëga's great book on Egyptology *De origine et usu obeliscorum* ('On the origin and purpose of the obelisks') was published in Rome, where Zoëga lived for the last half of his life, and carries the date 1797. Its purpose was to collect and examine all the evidence, from ancient author or modern explorer, that had a bearing on the obelisks of ancient Egypt. Since Zoëga interprets this brief widely, the book is in effect one on Egyptology as a whole. Nevertheless, he declares a specific interest in Egyptian writing, and devotes a sizable part of his book to it. It is this part which concerns us.

Zoëga's main quality is his reliability; from it flow his other characteristics. He is enormously industrious, giving on each topic a fair summary of all that his predecessors have said on it, and not shirking the duty of giving his own verdict, which is invariably a sane and balanced one. He is cautious: the twin pillars of his subject – or, as he puts it, the twin obelisks that flank the entrance to it – are ancient testimony and surviving monuments, and no conjectures about things Egyptian derived from the customs or practices of other peoples can be considered secure without their support. This principle would rule out among other things the use of the analogy of Chinese writing to answer questions about Egyptian, and Zoëga, unlike Champollion, abides by it. He is thoroughly objective. For instance, he gives a long and patient exposition of the various arcane theological and astrological significances which had been attributed to the shape, proportions, and material of the obelisks but, absurd though most of them are, he does not just dismiss them with *a priori* scorn. He shows by detailed measurements that most of the classifications proposed are not even consistent within themselves. His own sane, though perhaps over-rational, opinion is that the granite material and the slender pyramidal shape arose from considerations of aptness, beauty, and durability, so that there was no mystery about it. There is no good evidence, he says drily (*desunt testes idonei*), that the Egyptians were different in nature from other people.

It is in this objective attitude that Zoëga's modernity lies. Stillingfleete, and even Warburton, were still men of the Hebrew Renaissance. The most important thing in human history to them was the position held in it by the Jews. But if there was a special historical position for the Jews, it followed that there were probably special positions for other peoples too, particularly ancient peoples. To elucidate their specific historical roles was the task of the historian, and by fulfilling it he would be illuminating the divine purpose. Zoëga does not have this preoccupation. What he has instead is a conviction of the gradual and anonymous progress of human society and human institutions. The words that we would now use to describe this, 'evolution' and 'evolutionary' were not then available. Zoëga's words were of the type 'slow', 'gradual', 'transition', 'advance', and his analogies were either from plant life ('birth . . . growth . . . maturity . . . spread . . . decay') or from the diffusion of crafts or inventions ('small beginnings . . . a long period of private use . . . slow diffusion . . . unconscious transition to public use').[9] This vocabulary and these images are significantly frequent in Zoëga's work. They reveal an important difference in kind between Zoëga's idea of human progress and Warburton's. Warburton saw progress as having taken place in comparatively large steps that had been made possible either by the special characteristics of a particular race, or by the special inventiveness of a particular individual. Zoëga on the other hand saw it as occurring by means of continual but almost imperceptible improvements, piecemeal by nature, and independent of race or personality.

What Zoëga regarded as Warburton's main achievement was the explanation of how hieroglyphs had developed out of representational into symbolic pictures, and this was one advance which Warburton had gone out of his way to stress as having taken place 'by insensible degrees' (1788 ed. ii 423). Contrast the two men's treatment of the origin of alphabetic writing. While both believed it to be Egyptian, Warburton assumed an inventor, the secretary of an Egyptian king, later mythologized as Thoth; Zoëga on the contrary stressed the difficulty of the invention – it needed not only the analysis of the vast range of human speech sounds, but also of the different stages of utterance from sentences to words, from words to syllables, from syllables to single sounds. It would have been impossible for a single man to accomplish it. But for the same reason, namely that its creation must have depended on slow growth and acceptance, it must have originated within a single nation. This is confirmed by the observed fact that all the alphabetic writings we know hark back to a small group of contiguous countries in the Near East. Zoëga, however, agreed with Warburton on the question of dates, regarding the demotic or 'public' script as pre-Mosaic and the hieratic as a later elaboration by the priests 'for the sake of refinement or secrecy'.

On the question of the likely content of the hieroglyphic inscriptions, Zoëga agreed with Warburton that the record of historical achievements was the use vouched for by the most reliable ancient authors. On the other hand it was possible that they had been misled by false evidence. The real meaning of the obelisk inscriptions at Thebes may have been forgotten by the Egyptians themselves. The interpretations of them that we find in Diodorus, Strabo, and Tacitus – that they record the empire of Rameses – may have been based on wishful thinking and the desire to give Egypt a past glory equal to that of Persia. If so, we had no solid evidence at all for what the obelisk inscriptions may have really contained.

29 Zoëga, 1755–1809

This was a depressingly negative conclusion. But elsewhere Zoëga was able to establish firm starting-points for further research, either through the thorough sifting of what his predecessors had said, or by the contribution of new arguments of his own.

He stressed the important distinction between the hieroglyphic script and the large-scale drawings which it often accompanied (438 *n.* 1).

He established (436–7) the late appearance of the Coptic script, though in attributing its introduction to Christianity and dating it to the third century A D he was only partly correct. There have since been discovered magical papyri written in Coptic script (i.e. Greek with extra demotic letters) dating from as early as the first century. But there was no way in which Zoëga could have foreseen this discovery of magical papyri, and his conclusion was undoubtedly the best available on the evidence at his disposal.[10]

He showed that the direction of hieroglyphic writing was indicated by the figures facing the start of the line (464). (A deduction from repeated formulae: if a sign-group, known to be such from other occurrences, is split over two lines, it is at once clear which are the beginnings and ends of the lines concerned.)

On the question of cartouches his position was that they were likely to contain either religious formulae or personal names (465–6).

He attempted (466–97) to count and classify the number of separate signs, reaching the total of 270 for the obelisks which he considered on stylistic evidence (not always correctly) to belong to the days of Egypt's independence, and of 958 if one included all the inscriptions in European museums. He realized that these totals were nothing like as high as would be expected in an ideographic script. Any language must inevitably have had far more words than this, and therefore there could not have been a one-word/one-sign equivalence. The difficulty was a serious one, and Zoëga suggested two possible ways out of it. First, the signs might stand, as indeed some were said to do in Horapollo, for more than one concept. Second, two signs might receive an altogether new meaning by being juxtaposed. This was, he adds, reported to be the case in Chinese, whose vast signary had grown from a mere 214 basic signs. The possibility could only be investigated by preparing an index to show what signs were found next to one another. It was neglect of such necessary preliminaries in counting, classifying, and indexing that had hitherto produced so many solutions and so much scepticism (463–4).

The most important suggestion made by Zoëga (454, 552–3), and the one that he himself considered his most important, was that some hieroglyphs might be, in some measure at least, phonetic signs. In making it, Zoëga also made his major contribution to linguistic terminology, this being the first appearance in modern European usage of the word phonetic or the phrase phonetic signs (*notae phoneticae*). Zoëga's argument stemmed from Horapollo i 7. Here it is said that a hawk could stand for the 'soul in the heart', and the Egyptian words are given as *baiêth* (hawk), *bai* (soul), and *êth* (heart). The Coptic words are in fact close enough to Horapollo's transliterations to make his information look reliable. Zoëga picks on it for its significance in showing us how the bridge between word-sign and syllable-sign may have been crossed. For it would be easy to imagine that once a word like *baiêth* was thought of in terms of its constituent syllables, the same principle could be extended to the drawing. The front of the hawk (its head) could then perhaps be used for the front syllable (*bai*), and its afterpart (the legs) be used for its rear syllable (*êth*). There would result a class of characters which were in appearance parts of animals or other bodies, but in function phonetic signs. Such a class would belong to the broad category of 'enigmatic hieroglyphs'.

The emergence of the two different Egyptian writing systems might, Zoëga thought, have come about as a result of this. For, assuming multiplication in the class of phonetic hieroglyphs, it might have so complicated the script as to necessitate a reform. Such a reform might have separated the phonetic and ideographic signs, thus simultaneously restoring the ancient script and creating a new one in the form of a syllabary. This may then have been in its turn refined down to the alphabet, which Plutarch tells us consisted of twenty-five signs, probably, like other ancient alphabets and in view of the unstable treatment of vowels in Coptic, exclusively consonantal. But we cannot check this, says Zoëga, as no demotic survives. The lack was to be made good almost within the year by the discovery of the Rosetta Stone, but the demotic script which it brought to light was not to be confined to the predicted twenty-five letters.

In addition to suggesting the presence of actual phoneticism in the hieroglyphic signs, Zoëga argued that the hieroglyphic texts must proceed in the order of thought as it would be expressed in language. He had two reasons for thinking this. One was that Egyptian hieroglyphs, unlike Mexican, seemed to stand in a text as independent entities and not as pictures in mutual relationship with each other; the other was that in the very few translated inscriptions offered in ancient literature the order of signs and the order of thought seemed to run parallel. So hieroglyphic, unlike Mexican, was a genuine script – pictorial only in outward appearance, writing in respect of arrangement (*quoad figuram, pictura*; *quoad ordinem, litterae* p. 438).

Finally, the reader may like to see how Zoëga's reconstruction of Egyptian writing fits into his vision of the history of human writing as a whole. Here is what he says (422):

Early men made rough sketches, using colouring matter or a knife to make lines. Slowly and insensibly they progressed to the stage of making proper representations. The arts of painting, carving, and sculpture were discovered. The origin of writing, the noblest human invention, was similar. The transition was from the delineation of the forms of things to their abbreviation, from simple pictures to tropical ones, until finally, in the various combinations of metaphor, symbol, and enigma, there grew up hieroglyphic writing. In the broader sense of the term this was common to many peoples: in the restricted sense it was specific to Egypt. From it developed two types of writing, which can be called arbitrary and conventional. The one is suitable for the representation of things in a manner divorced from their outward appearances. Chinese writing, and what are commonly called ciphers, are examples of this. The other aims at representation of sound. The alphabets now used by the greater part of the civilized world are an example of this type. It is probable enough that the Chinese characters originated in a form of hieroglyphic once used by the Chinese: and as for alphabetic writing, it can be argued, I believe correctly, that it derived from Egypt.

Here we must leave Zoëga. Even though his one attempt to give a specimen interpretation of a hieroglyphic inscription may not be impressive, his book is. It is comprehensive and judicious, a fine monument of eighteenth-century learning, and in its determination to treat Egyptian history for its own sake a herald of modern scholarship. It was completed as the French expedition to Egypt was about to be planned, just before the discovery of the Rosetta Stone, and in the early boyhood of Champollion, who was finally to fulfil the hope expressed by Zoëga in his preface.

30

My limited aims have been those which at the present day an interpreter of Egyptian antiquity can hope to pursue with some success. Further goals I have thought best left to posterity. When Egypt is better known to scholars, and when the numerous ancient remains still to be seen there have been accurately explored and published, it will perhaps be possible to learn to read the hieroglyphs and more intimately to understand the meaning of the Egyptian monuments.

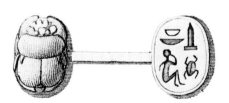

30 Scarab conjecturally interpreted by Zoëga to mean 'Contemplation of the World can teach Man to reverence the Eternal Power of God'

Chapter Three

From the Rosetta Stone to Champollion's Decipherment

Hope and frustration

In the month of May 1798 some sixty or more French scholars and scientists who had been independently requested by their revolutionary government to muster at the naval port of Toulon were secretly conducted aboard men-of-war of the Republican fleet. The tone of their initial instructions, the military preparations around them, the presence of Bonaparte as Commander-in-Chief made it clear to them that they were to form part of an expeditionary enterprise of major importance, but it was not until they were already at sea, indeed not until they had captured Malta and set sail again towards the East, that its destination was to be known. They were bound for Egypt. Egypt held the keys to the dominion of the modern, and the wisdom of the ancient world. The army was to seize the former, they the latter. But it was a joint enterprise. They were to help the army establish a modern government based on scientific knowledge of the resources of the country: the army was to help and protect them in their exploration of whatever was of scientific or antiquarian interest. The expedition contained among its members archaeologists, architects, sculptors, painters, draughtsmen, and printers equipped to measure and to copy, to draw and to publish the monuments that were so widely but still so inaccurately known.

For a crash programme organized in so short a time (a mere two months) and accompanied throughout by such risks (on the way out the accidents of first a broken mast and then a fog prevented Nelson intercepting and almost certainly destroying the overladen French fleet; the two years in Egypt were constantly harassed by the alarms and excursions of war and rebellion; and when the adventure was over the *Oiseau* in which the mission was trying to make its escape back to France came within an ace of being sunk by the English fleet) the final result must be counted a success, and Champollion's claim (*Précis* 374) that the study of Egyptian writing could only become scientific after the accurate and plentiful reproductions of hieroglyphic texts in the *Description d'Égypte* was justified.[1] Nevertheless, the most famous archaeological prize of the expedition was not in the first instance due to its academic arm at all but to its military. It was in the course of fortification works that the Rosetta Stone, or Rosetta Pillar as it used to be called, was noticed. It had been built into some comparatively modern walling. The presence of the inscription on the stone was spotted and its potential importance realized by the

31

31 The Rosetta Stone

32 Silvestre de Sacy,
1758–1838

32

engineer officer in charge, by name Bouchard. The general was informed, and the stone removed to Alexandria. But it was never to reach France. After the surrender of the French expedition in 1801 it passed into the possession of the British Army, and is now in the British Museum.

The Rosetta Stone is a triscript, containing a decree in honour of Ptolemy V of 196 BC in hieroglyphic, demotic (which it refers to as the *enchorial* or local writing), and Greek. The Greek text assures us that the other two parts carry the same message. The whole inscription is of substantial length. In short it was just what everybody had been hoping for. In the case of the Palmyra inscriptions (see page 95 and Ill. 62), much briefer and scrappier though they were, the first accurate publication (by Dawkins and Wood in 1753) had been followed within weeks, days almost, by two independent, correct decipherments. The same speed and success might have been looked for in the case of the Rosetta Stone; yet its decipherment was to take over twenty years.

One of the earliest and best articles on the new discovery was the *Lettre à Citoyen Chaptal* (1802) by the Professor of Arabic at the School of Living Oriental Languages in Paris, Silvestre de Sacy. This is the first time we have had occasion to mention him, but as he will be a central figure in the sections that follow, a brief description of his life and career will be in place. Externally his life was not an exciting one. He was born in Paris in 1758, left the French capital for the only time in his life for a brief visit to the library in Geneva in 1805, and died peacefully in Paris in 1838, having done a full day's work, including the delivery of a speech in the House of Peers, two days before his death. But few men can have had such a tranquil career in so turbulent a time. He established his reputation in 1787 with his decipherment of the Sassanid Persian inscriptions of Naqš-i-Rustam in a paper read to the Académie des Inscriptions (see chapter 4), and began to rise in the world of the *ancien régime* with an important preferment by the king in 1791 and election to the Académie in 1792. During the Republic Sacy rose higher still, being appointed in 1795 to the Chair of Arabic that he still occupied forty-three years later. Under Napoleon he was made Professor of Persian at the Collège de France in 1806 and a Baron in 1813. One of the first acts of the Bourbon government on its restoration was to appoint him Rector of the University of Paris. But he was not an opportunist, and though through all these political changes he retained his rank he also retained his honour.

When the course of the revolution became violent in 1792 Sacy resigned all his public appointments and memberships of public bodies in protest, and retired with his family to a small house in the country near Paris. In October 1795, when an oath of hatred towards the monarchy was imposed on all holders of public office, he refused to take it and resigned his newly acquired Professorship of Arabic, offering only to continue teaching until a replacement was found. None was, and Sacy was allowed to remain without taking the oath. To fill academic posts with honour at such a time was praiseworthy enough: but Sacy succeeded in filling them with distinction too. He published steadily throughout his life. As an administrator he played a general part in the formulation of educational policy and specifically fostered the foundation of the *Société asiatique* and of Chairs in Chinese, Sanskrit, and Hindustani. As a teacher he had many outstanding pupils, two particularly so: Bopp, the founder of the science of comparative philology, and Champollion, the decipherer of the hieroglyphs.

At the time of his *Lettre à Citoyen Chaptal* Sacy was already eminent for his Sassanid decipherment and for his competence as an Arabist, in which capacity he was particularly interested in Egypt. He also knew Coptic. If there was any man of the time qualified to discuss the new inscription of the Rosetta Stone, it was he.

The plan of attack decided on by Sacy was, first, frankly to abandon the hieroglyphic part for the time being. It was the most damaged of the three texts, only fourteen lines surviving, and not even those intact. Moreover 'the hieroglyphic character, being representative of ideas, not sounds, does not belong to the domain of any particular language' (p. 5). One had therefore to concentrate on the 'Egyptian text', which consisted of thirty-two lines and except for the beginnings of the first few was virtually complete. The first step was to locate the proper names. Their approximate whereabouts was likely to be given away by the Greek text, especially in the case of names which occurred two or three times. If the same letter occurred more than once in the Greek spelling of a name, it would probably do the same in the Egyptian, and so serve to identify it. Thereafter it should prove possible to proceed from the known to the unknown, starting with words frequent in the Greek text ('god', 'king', 'son') the Egyptian for which was likely to be similar to their known Coptic equivalents.

The programme was a sound one, and to help him carry it out Sacy used three copies of the inscription – a print taken (under the direction of M. Marcel, the Director of the Imprimerie Nationale that had been established in Cairo) from the stone itself as if it were a lithograph, a corrected copy of this lent to him by Marcel, and an engraving. Nevertheless, he did not get very far. He located some of the names correctly, but read them wrong. For example, the group of signs that stood for the name of Ptolemy he trans- 36(2) literated as 'Aftuulma' (instead of 'Ptolmês'), being thrown off course at the very beginning by taking the first three letters together as the same as that which he had identified as the first letter of Alexander, and thereafter further entrenching himself in error 36(1) by fancied resemblances of the shape of the letters he called 'f', 't', and 'm' to the shapes of the corresponding Coptic, Hebrew, and Samaritan letters respectively. From here he proceeded to the transliteration of other names, such as Arsinoe, by the same unsuccessful method of cross-script letter-recognition.

Nevertheless, Sacy sanely stopped short of attributing any certainty to his preliminary results, and his essay contained many remarks of independent value. For instance he drew attention to the large number of different characters in the Egyptian text, many more than the twenty-five letters mentioned by Plutarch. This was an important point to have made. Eventually it led to the overthrow of the hitherto universally held hypothesis that the non-hieroglyphic writing of Egypt was 'alphabetical'. But this was not the conclusion drawn by Sacy at the time. Instead he offered the rather weak suggestion that the letters might alter their shape according to their word position (as in Hebrew, Syriac, and Arabic), and – even less likely – that they might have miniscule and majuscule forms.

The attempt to transliterate the proper names of the demotic text on the Rosetta Stone was prosecuted with greater success by Åkerblad later in the same year. Johan David Åkerblad was a Swedish diplomat and orientalist to whom Sacy had lent a pre-publication copy of the inscription. Acknowledging that the correct method was to begin with proper names as Barthélemy had done in 1754 and Sacy himself in 1787 (see chapter 4), Åkerblad used as his starting-point the same three sign-groups as Sacy (though he claimed to have identified them independently), and managed to transliterate them in such a way as to yield a dozen further names. But his attempts to use his alphabet beyond the proper names did not succeed, and the decipherment of demotic was to remain for a long time at this unsatisfactory half-way stage. Åkerblad published his proposed solution in the form of a letter to Sacy, together with a courteous, though not fully convinced reply of Sacy's.

After this Sacy does not seem to have renewed his own attempts at decipherment. But he did not give up his interest in Egypt. Since he was to become Champollion's tutor it is important for us to follow his ideas on the subject. They would in any case be interesting enough in themselves to make it worth while.

In 1808 he reviewed in the *Magasin Encyclopédique* a series of articles on the language and literature of Egypt by a former pupil of his, Étienne Quatremère. Quatremère's main concern was with the Coptic dialects, but his book contained a restatement of the arguments that Coptic was descended from the language of ancient Egypt. In reviewing the book, Sacy accepted Quatremère's conclusions on this, and added one very interesting, and to us curious, argument of his own. What shows the independence of a language, he pointed out, is not so much its vocabulary as its grammatical structure. This was a significant departure from the vocabulary-oriented concepts of seventeenth- and eighteenth-century linguistic theory and the seed from which the science of comparative philology was to grow.[15a] But Sacy's immediate moral was a different one. Coptic grammar, he said, preserves specific traces of its hieroglyphic origin. Thus, the plural is usually the same as the singular except for a monosyllabic prefix. Distinction of gender is shown by a separate word (either a preceding article or a subsequent word for 'male' or 'female'). Cases are shown, not by inflectional changes but by the prefixing of particles. Verbal in-flections signifying tense and person also have the look of indepen-dent words, being able to come before or after their verbs, and even allowing infixed words to come in between. The same goes for the principle of building words by juxtaposition, for instance *met-ref-er-pet-ôou* = quality – of a person – who does – what is – bad = 'malice', with which, says Sacy, one may compare the Chinese *ti-ten-tie-gin* = shave – head – of man = 'barber'.[2]

From these observations Sacy concluded that Coptic originally had no inflections but consisted of independent, invariable, units. Now this was just what one would expect a language written in a hieroglyphic script to have been like, for in a hieroglyphic script each sign stands for a whole word and cannot vary.

This concept of a 'hieroglyphic language' strikes us today as odd, if not bizarre. But it is a logical consequence of the then fashionable belief that writing was the sole fixative agent of language,[3] and was to be further elaborated by Sacy in the next few years. Languages could be divided into three classes, scriptless, hieroglyphic, and phonetically written. Scriptless, or Barbarous, languages are in a state of continual change – which is why there are so many of them. Hieroglyphic languages (Egyptian and Chinese) have a stable vocabulary because their hieroglyphic script can fix words, but lack a permanent grammar and therefore the means to express nuance. Phonetically written languages, like Greek and Latin, combine the stability of a written, with the flexibility of a spoken language. This is why they could be cultivated to such a high pitch of refinement. Coptic, however, is not a full grammatical language in this sense, having been first stabilized in the hieroglyphic stage of writing. It therefore inevitably retains some of the stiffness and monumentality of that stage.

This generalized version of his theory is given by Sacy in a letter to Thomas Young of 20 January 1816. The ideas must have been in Sacy's mind during the intervening period when he was teaching Champollion. Indeed it is clear that Champollion's initial reflections on the Coptic language (see page 70) owe a great deal to it. We may even see its influence in the intimate relationship between phoneticism and the writing of grammatical inflection which is assumed in Champollion's final decipherment (see pages 82–3). A final echo of it is still to be heard sixty years later in Sayce's speculations about the Hittites (see page 138).

Let us now turn from this to another and more practical suggestion of Sacy's.

Some general notions about Chinese language and Chinese writing had been current in Europe since Acosta (1590) and Trigault (1613); such as that the language was 'monosyllabic' and that the script was entirely ideographic with up to eighty thousand characters. But it was not until the eighteenth century that any grammars became available. The most widely known were those by Bayer (1730) and by Fourmont (1737 and 1743). Neither did much to dispel the philosophical haze through which the whole subject of China was fashionably regarded, and of which we have seen some of the consequences in our section on Universal Writing. But they did contribute some new information on the question of phoneticism in Chinese writing. 'To show how characters are read,' says Bayer somewhat briefly in discussing the practice of Chinese lexicons, 'two characters are generally written, of which the first indicates the vowel, the second the consonant.' The same practice is more fully described by Fourmont (1737, pp. 31 and 126). Neither of them makes any mention of its use for writing foreign words. The idea that the Chinese contrived to write these in a phonetic manner was introduced to Europe by another pupil of Sacy's, Abel-Rémusat, in 1811, in his description (p. 36) of the '*Tsiĕ*, or method employed by Chinese lexico-graphers to express the sounds of characters and sometimes also to render the sounds of certain foreign words.' As an example he gives the character for *kò* followed by the character for *hán* followed by the character for *tsiĕ* (= 'divide') to make the Mongolian word '*khan*' = 'emperor'.

It seems to me clear that this is what Sacy had in mind when he wrote, reviewing a second book on Egypt by Quatremère, in the latter half of 1811:[4]

We know that the Chinese experience this difficulty [namely, in writing foreign names] and that they are sometimes obliged to employ a special sign to show that the characters used in expressing a proper name are reduced to a simple [phonetic] value. *I con-jecture that in the hieroglyphic text of the Rosetta inscription the line that encircles a series of hieroglyphs is employed for this same function.* (The italics are mine.)

Though Barthélemy had made the passing suggestion that cartouches might contain the names of a king or a god, and Zoëga had thought them to be either religious formulae or royal names, this footnote of Sacy's is the first time, as far as I can discover, that the proposal was put forward that they might signify a name written phonetically. Strictly speaking, the suggestion was in-correct. The cartouches signify royalty, not phoneticism. How-ever, the suggestion, which became a commonplace among all who worked on the hieroglyphs during the next ten years, was to lead to Champollion's first solution, and through that to the decipherment proper.

We must now turn our attention to the Englishman Thomas Young, whom we have just glimpsed as the recipient of a letter on language from Sacy. Young's name is often bracketed with that of Champollion as a decipherer of the hieroglyphs. The practice stems from Young himself, but it is a particularly odd one; for though Young claimed for himself the credit of Champollion's decipherment, he never accepted its validity. Indeed he died still denying it.[5] What he did accept was Champollion's first solution, and his claim, reduced to its minimum and most realistic terms, amounts to his having been the first to propose some of the elements in it. Even so it is scarcely justified, and would have doubtless been forgotten long ago if it had not been fanned to life again by an irrelevant patriotism every time it was on the point of expiry. The reader who is interested in the question can see Young's claim mercilessly and definitively refuted in Renouf's article of 1897.[6]

Young was a man with a grievance. After a brilliant youth, finishing up at Emmanuel College, Cambridge, where he was nicknamed 'Phenomenon Young', he made original contribu-tions to such diverse subjects as the theory of insurance, natural history, medicine, physics, and above all the history of technology, but never reached the first rank in any of them, except perhaps in optics in his work on the interference of light. Instead he rose to a position of considerable power in public life, becoming what would now be called a scientific and cultural administrator or adviser. Yet the rewards of this world did not satisfy him, and he clearly hankered for something with a promise of immortality in it. This shows itself in the way he signed his numerous articles in the *Encyclopaedia Britannica Supplement* (1816–25) with two consecutive letters from the phrase *fortunam ex aliis*, an allusion to Vergil's *Aeneid* xii 435–6:

> Learn, Boy, true toil and manliness from me:
> Success from others!
>
> (tr. C.J. Billson)

His interest in the problem of the Rosetta Stone dated only from the beginning of 1814, and it was during this year alone that he carried out any serious and original work on it (mainly during a summer holiday in Worthing where he took a copy with him). He began with the generally accepted assumption that the demotic text (or 'enchorial' as he always called it) was an alphabet, and that the large number of different characters was to be explained by the same letters having different forms. He hoped that Åkerblad's values would prove good not only for the proper names but also for the ordinary words, of which some ought to be recognizable as Coptic. His plan was to limit the range of possibilities by demarcating as rigidly as he could all the places where the demotic text must correspond to the Greek, using for section-boundaries groups of characters which were repeated in the demotic and which therefore looked as if they might correspond to repeated words in the Greek. This process of demarcation he called his 'translation' of the demotic text.

He entered into correspondence with Sacy. In his first letter (August 1814) he had already begun to fear that this line of attack might prove abortive and that the demotic characters were perhaps like the Chinese, which he thought had a phonetic significance only in expressing the sounds of a foreign language. As he continued he found his fears confirmed. Writing to Sacy at the end of the year (though he could not send the letter till August 1815) he explained his 'unexpected' and 'discouraging' conclusion. Greek writers had misled us about the demotic script. It was not alphabetic (apart from its use in writing foreign words), and therefore could be no help in deciphering the language of the inscription. The reason for his thinking this was his discovery that many of the demotic characters 'had a striking resemblance to the corresponding hieroglyphs'. So the directions of enquiry would have to be reversed. 'Instead of being led to a knowledge of the hieroglyphic characters by the assistance of the Coptic language and of alphabetic characters', one must in future start with the hieroglyphs and proceed from them to the derived demotic, which, Young feared, might even subsume a different language. On the hieroglyphic script itself he observed that it could not be quite like the Chinese since there were only a thousand or so characters in all. There could not therefore be a simple one-to-one correspondence between words and signs. Rather it seemed that 'a combination of two or three of them was often employed to form a single word'. We have seen this idea already in Zoëga (see pages 57–8).

This letter was published together with several preceding ones in *Museum Criticum* vi of 1815. It was the first time that any query had been raised against the accepted simple equation Hieroglyphic = Ideographic, Demotic = Alphabetic. Even though Young did not draw the correct conclusion from his doubts, their expression was in itself an important step forward – more important than the few positively correct suggestions of detail that he was later to propose; for these were accompanied by a much larger mass of incorrect suggestions, and there was no way to tell which was which.

After this letter Young does not seem ever to have changed his mind, or to have done any more original research on the subject. He transferred himself, as it were, from the playing field to the selectors' box. It is true that he noticed (1823, p. 15) the existence of parallel texts from the reproductions in the *Description d'Égypte* lent to him in 1816 by Sir William Hamilton, and used them to work out in greater detail the correspondences between the hieroglyphic and non-hieroglyphic characters (he never grasped the distinction between hieratic and demotic). It is true that he continued to publish, but his work amounted to no more than the extension of his previous interpretations by identifying further characters (generally wrongly) in the light of the principles he had laid down and by their application to new finds that his friends brought him. He believed that he had settled the correct lines for further research, and that he need do no more than foster it, especially by midwifing publications.

This was useful enough work. It is a pity that Young spoilt it by laying claim to a glory that was not his.

Champollion's first solution

33 Jean-François Champollion, 1790–1832

Jean-François Champollion – 'this new Achilles' as Young called him, characteristically adding *'fortemque in fortia misi'* (''twas I who sent the warrior to war') – was born at Figeac in the valley of the Lot in southern France in the last week of the year 1790. It was the time of the Revolution, and the accompanying social disorganization meant that there was no early school for him to attend. Instead, he was privately taught Latin and Greek by a displaced Abbé. This seems to have been greatly to his profit. It is said that he could already read Homer and Vergil when, at the age of nine, he was moved to Grenoble to join his elder brother, Champollion-Figeac, and to attend the Lycée there. At Grenoble he came into contact with Fourier, the mathematician, who had been secretary of the Mission in Egypt, and who was now Prefect of the Isère. Fittingly it was Fourier, Napoleon's man, not Young at all, who sent Champollion into the battlefield of Egyptology. The young Jean-François turned to the study of eastern languages, and announced – rather precociously it must have seemed – the plan of his proposed life's work to the Grenoble Society of Arts and Sciences on 1 September 1807 in a paper on the Coptic etymology of Egyptian place-names preserved in Greek and Latin authors. He was then turning seventeen and on the point of leaving the Lycée for Paris.

In Paris he studied oriental languages, chiefly under Langlès for Persian and Sacy for Arabic. In addition to attending their courses he worked on the Coptic manuscripts in the Bibliothèque Nationale (which at that time included the manuscripts of the Vatican collection brought to Paris as the result of the revolutionary wars). What mainly interested Champollion was not the subject matter of the manuscripts (mainly ecclesiastical) but the grammatical structure of the language and the incidental memories of ancient Egypt that were preserved in them, particularly personal and place-names.

After three years in Paris, Champollion, still only nineteen, returned to Grenoble to become assistant Professor of History to the titular holder of the Chair, who was an octogenarian. Fourier saw to his being exempted from military service, and he was able to proceed with his project.

The general subject was to be Pharaonic Egypt, 'so different from the Egypt of the Persians, from the Egypt of the Greeks, and above all from modern Egypt, which so richly deserves a happier destiny'. The treatment was to be in three parts, the first devoted to geography, the second to social institutions, the third to language and letters, both alphabetic and hieroglyphic.

The first part was published in two volumes in 1814 under the title *L'Égypte sous les Pharaons*. In the Preface Champollion states that his aim has been 'to establish the Egyptian names of the country of Egypt, its river, provinces, and towns'. The bulk of the two volumes is given over to the well-disciplined pursuit of this rather remote quarry. By the end of them he has amassed the Coptic names of some 200 towns and 36 nomes in Upper and Lower Egypt together with the names of oases and regions outside the Nile valley, and in doing so has drawn on more than 40 ancient authors and over 60 Arabic and modern ones, to say nothing of the numerous Coptic manuscripts on which the whole is founded. The exploration, survey, and charting of so much virgin ground was a formidable accomplishment for a man in his early twenties. It is also an eloquent testimony to the quality and range of the European scholarship of the previous two centuries that an enquiry of so specialized a nature should have been possible to undertake at all, let alone complete within a reasonable time.

The interest of the modern reader in Champollion's first book is not likely to centre on the details of Egyptian geography so much as on what he may have to say about Egyptian literature, language, and writing. Is there anything of striking brilliance or originality to mark Champollion off as the future decipherer of the hieroglyphs? The answer must be no. His opinions are all perfectly orthodox. What is remarkable about the book is not the flash of ideas, but the extent and up-to-dateness of its author's knowledge. His position is very much in the mainstream of contemporary thought.

He claims, for instance, in his introduction that it was the antiquity, glory, wisdom, and science of Egypt, qualities confessed by the Greeks and more than confirmed by the discoveries of recent times, that had inspired and maintained his resolution in carrying out the work. This was partly, of course, the ritual obeisance to rhetoric demanded of an exordium; but only partly. It is evident that Champollion believed it himself from the enthusiasm he shows when he comes to Dendera, the site of one of the most complete surviving Egyptian temples (i 232): 'It is here that we must look for the ancient form of the orders and the principal beauties of Greek architecture. Egyptian architecture has proved to be the source of all that has been subsequently thought admirable.'

A strict judge would have to give this a low mark. The Dendera temple is Ptolemaic, and therefore later than the Greek architecture whose glories it is said to have inspired. This was, however, not known at the time. Ironically the late date of the temple was to be one of the most important first-fruits of Champollion's decipherment.

Champollion shows the same theoretical enthusiasm for the Coptic language. It is monosyllabic; its structural rules are constant; it possesses the unalterability that characterizes all the institutions of ancient Egypt. In its way of expressing grammatical relationships it has substantial analogies with the principles of Chinese writing, though one should not assume, as is sometimes done, a common origin for Egypt and China. All these views of Champollion's fit easily into the pattern of current linguistic doctrine.[7]

In an equally orthodox manner he divided Egyptian writing into three stages, hieroglyphic, alphabetic, and Coptic. On the first of these, the hieroglyphic, the only hope that he professed was to be able to present some relevant observations on a huge topic. About the second class he was more optimistic. He thought that he had already been successful in making out much of the Egyptian text of the Rosetta Stone, and he hoped that his knowledge of Coptic and his nearly complete collection of copies of Egyptian non-hieroglyphic texts would between them enable him to master the alphabetic script. As for Coptic, he accepted without hesitation that it was the Egyptian language written in Greek characters with an additional seven letters of the old Egyptian alphabet for representing sounds not catered for by Greek letters.

These, then, were the aspirations and ideas with which Champollion began his academic career. It is clear that he had as yet no new theory. But his concentration of knowledge, of Coptic, of the Egyptian monuments, and of the relevant ancient and modern literature, was probably already unique.

The next year, 1815, saw Napoleon's return from Elba, his welcome in Grenoble and the Hundred Days (during which Champollion played an active political part), the second Restoration, and the closure of the Faculty of Letters at Grenoble, allegedly for reasons of economy. Champollion, now without a post, divided his time between championing the cause of primary education and compiling a Coptic dictionary. He regarded this as a necessary tool to have before he could usefully turn to the problem of the ancient scripts. For these the available evidence was becoming rapidly more plentiful. In addition to the publication of the great volumes of the *Description de l'Egypte* which were still appearing, there was a constant succession of new texts being brought back from Egypt by travellers and published or circulated in private copies. It became possible to recognize (from the fact that the accompanying illustrations were the same) different copies of the same text written in hieroglyphic and non-hieroglyphic script. This was of tremedous importance, and Champollion devoted much energy to the comparison of such texts. He was able for the first time to establish firmly the distinction between the three, or rather, four, systems – hieroglyphic, 'linear' or 'cursive' hieroglyphic, hieratic, and demotic – and to draw up tables of their equivalent signs. It was this work which was the foundation of his subsequent decipherment. Both in the number of texts he examined and in the exactness of his examination of them he carried these researches far beyond the scope of Young (who never even became clear on the difference between hieratic and demotic or so much as suspected the existence of linear hieroglyphic), but reached the same conclusion – that the pattern of the other scripts was the same as that of the hieroglyphic and that therefore they must be equally ideographic. In 1821 and 1822 he read papers to the Académie des Inscriptions on the hieratic and demotic scripts. He summarized their conclusion as follows:

I hope it is not too rash for me to say that I have succeeded in demonstrating that these two forms of writing are neither of them alphabetic, as has been so generally thought, but *ideographic*, like the hieroglyphs themselves, that is to say, depicting the *ideas* and not the *sounds* of the language.

These words come from the first paragraph of Champollion's famous *Lettre à M. Dacier*, read on 27 September 1822 before the Académie (Dacier was its secretary), and published the same year. It was Champollion's first major publication, though only some fifty pages long, since his two volumes on Pharaonic Egypt.

Its subject was the 'phonetic hieroglyphs', not the 'pure hieroglyphs'. Champollion considered the latter a separate subject, and had earmarked it for future treatment (*Lettre*, p. 41). There was nothing novel in the concept of a class of phonetic hieroglyphs. The theoretical necessity for such a device in an ideographic script for the writing of foreign names was by now generally accepted. It was thought to be confirmed by the existence of a similar practice in Chinese, and that the place where the names were to be found was in the cartouches (see page 66). It was also in accordance with Champollion's previous conclusion on the basic identity of the hieroglyphic, hieratic, and demotic systems: for in the demotic text of the Rosetta Stone proper names and foreign words were written phonetically, as Åkerblad's decipherment of them had shown.

Once granted the existence of an acknowledged class of phonetic hieroglyphs it might have been thought that those on the Rosetta Stone could have been readily deciphered. But it was not so easy. The only cartouche on the surviving part of the hieroglyphic text of the Rosetta Stone was that of Ptolemy. As Champollion pointed out, this was not enough. To enable any decipherment to be cross-checked one needs to find at least a pair of names in which the same letters recur, for instance Ptolemy and Cleopatra, or Alexander and Berenice (*Lettre* 6).

So far nothing new: this was the pitch that had foiled previous climbers. But Champollion had found a new foot-hold. Around

January of that year he had been able to see for the first time a copy of the inscription on an obelisk from Philae which had been brought to England for William Bankes by Giovanni Belzoni. From a Greek inscription found on the base pedestal near by, the obelisk seemed to have been dedicated in the names of Ptolemy and Cleopatra. One of the cartouches on the obelisk contained the same signs as the one found on the Rosetta Stone. The other terminated in the two signs which were already suspected of indicating a female name. It was highly probable then that these were the names of Ptolemy and Cleopatra, and indeed Bankes had already assumed them to be so. Given confidence that the signs were phonetic, a knowledge that the script proceeded against the way the signs faced, and the expectation that the representation of vowels would be irregular or absent – and these three items of data were commonly accepted at the time[8] – it was an easy step to make a preliminary decipherment.

There was, however, one stumbling-block. The second sign of Ptolemy and the seventh of Cleopatra ought to have been the same; but they were not. One was a semicircle, the other a hand.

Nevertheless, the phonetic value of these twelve signs was, as Champollion says (p. 9), 'already probable and will become indisputable if, on being applied to further cartouches, it proves possible to read them in a regular manner without straining the evidence, and to produce the proper names of kings which are foreign to the Egyptian language'.

Champollion now proceeded to do this. He began with two cartouches from Karnak published in the third volume of the *Description de l'Égypte*. Applying to the first of these the values he had already guessed, he found A L – S E – T R – . Since the name

34 The obelisk from Philae which Giovanni Belzoni brought to England for William Bankes, now at Kingston Lacy in Dorset

a PTOLMÊS
(Ptolemy)
ever-living,
loved by Ptah

b PTOLMÊS
(Ptolemy)

35 Champollion's decipherment of Greek royal names in hieroglyphic writing. Cartouches from the Rosetta Stone (*a, b*); from the Philae obelisk (*c, d*); from Karnak (*e, f*)

f ALKSNRES
(Alexander)

e ALKSANTRS
(Alexander)

▷

36 Champollion's decipherment of Greek proper names in demotic writing. The first of the twelve names are from the Rosetta Stone, the last eight (continuation overleaf) from a papyrus

c PTOLMÊS
(Ptolemy)
ever-living,
loved by Ptah

d KLEOPATRA
(Cleopatra)
followed by two
signs signifying
the feminine

of Alexander as deciphered by Åkerblad in the demotic text of the Rosetta Stone ran A L K S E N T R S, it was not difficult to supply to the Karnak cartouche the missing letters K, N, and S. But here we come to two new stumbling-blocks. The K of Cleopatra took the form of a quarter-circle, whereas in the name of Alexander it is a basin with a handle. And in the name of Alexander the final S is different from the middle one.

It is the way in which he removed these stumbling-blocks that marks Champollion as more than just a successful solver of anagrams. He first argued that the Egyptians would not be likely to abjure completely the ideographic nature of their sacred writing on the few occasions where they were compelled to use it phonetically. If different word-signs suggested the same sound it could be expected that different word-signs would be used to represent it. For instance the semicircle, basically a female determinative, might have suggested the feminine article *te*, and therefore have been used for the sound *t*: but this did not mean that the same sound could not have been represented by the sign for a hand (Coptic *tot*). This was the germ of the acrophonic principle which Champollion was later to develop extensively. But he did not leave the matter at this level of an appeal to general probability. He was able to produce facts. The first letter of the demotic form of Cleopatra's name was the regular equivalent for a particular hieratic sign, and this hieratic sign was itself a regular equivalent for the hieroglyphic basin-with-a-handle. The only possible conclusion to draw from this was that the Egyptians themselves regarded the quarter-circle and the basin-with-a-handle as homophones.

It was this ability, derived from his methodical and thorough work of the previous years, to call in demotic and hieratic evidence to supplement the hieroglyphic that made it possible for Champollion to carry his suggestions through to the domain of proof. But he did not always need this resource. For instance, in another cartouche of Alexander at Karnak the twin-sceptre sign is used for S in the middle as well as at the end of the name, thus showing directly that it is an alternative for the hooked line in the middle of the other cartouche.

There is no need for us to pursue Champollion's further identifications in detail. Suffice it to say that he followed the same method, gradually extending his alphabet, until he had read the names of Berenice, Tiberius, Domitian, Vespasian, Nerva, Hadrian and his wife Sabina, and Antoninus, together with the additional names used by some of these emperors, Germanicus, Claudius, Dacicus, and Augustus (in its Greek guise of Sebastos). Some of the names come out strangely in the transliteration, for instance TOMTÊNS for Domitian, but for all that they are unmistakable. At the end of it he had identified some forty hieroglyphic signs which can represent the sounds of some seventeen Greek letters.

Besides names, the Egyptian cartouches also contained titles. Champollion found that he could transliterate two of those employed by the Roman emperors – Caesar (KESR, KSRS, etc.), and the Greek word for emperor, Autokratôr (AOTOKRTR, AOTKRTR,

1. ALKSANTRS (Alexander)
2. PTLOMÊS (Ptolemy)
3. ARSÊNE (Arsinoe)
4. BRNÊKE (Berenice)
5. AÊETOS (Aetes)
6. PRE (Pyrrha)
7. PÊLÊNS (Philinus)
8. ARÊE (Areia)
9. TÊEKNS (Diogenes)
10. IRENE (Irene)
11. SNTKSS (σύνταξις)
12. OUÊNN (*Ionian*=Greek)
13. ALKSNTROS (Alexander)
14. PTOLMÊS (Ptolemy)
15. ARSÊN (Arsinoe)
16. BRNÊK (Berenice)

17. KLOPTR
(Cleopatra)

18. APLONÊS
(Apollonius)

19. ANTÊCHOS
(Antiochus)

20. ANTÊKNS
(Antigonus)

etc.). Other titles, such as 'the immortal' or 'loved by Ptah', whose meanings were known from the Greek text of the Rosetta Stone, were considered by Champollion at this stage to be expressed purely ideographically (p. 18).

At the end of his paper Champollion revealed, without giving details, that he had already been able to extend the use of his alphabet in a quite unexpected way, and to read the names of the Pharaohs of ancient Egypt and not just their successors of Graeco-Roman times. Thus 'Europe, which received from old Egypt the elements of the arts and sciences also owed to her the priceless benefit of alphabetic writing' (p. 43). Nevertheless, it is abundantly clear from everything that Champollion says and does not say, and from the alterations which he made when reprinting the *Lettre à M. Dacier* in 1828 (usefully listed in Sottas 1922), that when he delivered his paper he never suspected that his alphabet would have any application beyond the sphere of proper names and foreign words, or that it was going to prove the long-looked-for key to the hieroglyphs.

The key to the hieroglyphs

At the end of his *Lettre à M. Dacier* Champollion had stated that he was able to identify and read phonetically the names of some pre-Greek Pharaohs. Soon afterwards, and still following up this line of enquiry, he approached a fellow-orientalist, Antoine Jean St Martin, who was interested in the problem of Persian cuneiform, with the suggestion that they should make a joint inspection of an alabaster vase from the collection of the Comte de Caylus and which carried inscriptions in both cuneiform and hieroglyphic. The inscriptions, which they rubbed with vermilion, proved more easily legible than they had expected (St Martin, 1823, 85). The first word of the text written in the first variety of Persepolis cuneiform consisted of seven characters, of which the second was the same as the sixth, the fourth as the seventh. It was a word already known from Persepolis where it had been read by Gotefend (see page 101) as the name of Xerxes. St Martin claimed to have arrived at the same conclusion independently. His transliteration of the cuneiform name was *kh-sch-é-a-r-sch-a*. The hieroglyphic cartouche also consisted of seven signs. As in the Persian, the second and sixth, the fourth and seventh were alike. On the sign-values already reached by Champollion in the *Lettre à M. Dacier*, the cartouche could be read ? – ? – e – a – l/r – ? – a. Supply *kh* and *sch* for the two unidentified signs (values which Champollion seems already to have suspected[9]) and the agreement is complete.

This, as far as it went, was a remarkable confirmation of the two decipherments. St Martin read an account of it from his side to the Académie at its meeting of 20 December 1822. Champollion included the name of Xerxes among the thirty Pharaohs' names (Dynasties XVI–XXIX) which he had collected, and sent the list to the *Journal Asiatique* where it was published in the News Column for January 1823.

Champollion's next commitment, as we have seen, was to consider the 'pure' hieroglyphs, that is to say those outside the cartouches. At the time he, like everybody else, assumed that they were exclusively ideographic. But it is not clear how he thought such an ideographic script would work, or what first caused his change of mind. It must have been quick, as he read the first of his papers to the Académie announcing his general decipherment in April 1823, but he does not describe it. He was naturally more concerned to give a rational and convincing account of his decipherment than to trace the full sequence of ideas that had led him to it. All we can do therefore is to fall back on the somewhat hazardous process of trying to understand from remarks made at other times some of the probable landmarks and turning-points of these three months.

The most certain of these landmarks is to be found in a passage in an article on the Dendera zodiac published in the *Revue Encyclopédique* of August 1822, a month before he read his *Lettre à M. Dacier*. He says (p. 7) that his study of the three Egyptian writing systems has shown him that 'the majority of proper names of *individual members of a species* are always either preceded or followed by a hieroglyphic sign to express that *species*'. Thus the names of gods are followed by a single sign for GOD, the names of months preceded by a single sign for MONTH. This observation, sound though it was in itself and to be proved correct by future knowledge, was also very much in line with seventeenth- and eighteenth-century conceptions of how an ideographic, or even a philosophic, writing system should work.

I have not succeeded in finding in anything else that Champollion published any further hints of how he thought an ideographic script operated. On the other hand there are several indications of his having felt frustrated. He points out that if one looks at the hieroglyphs as pictures one can catalogue them into well over twenty different classes – celestial bodies, animals, plants, human artefacts, geometrical forms, and imaginary combinations such as human bodies with animal heads or vases with human legs, yet in any one inscription all these classes of sign may be impartially mingled in apparently total disorder. 'The look of a hieroglyphic inscription is a veritable chaos. Nothing is in its place. There is no relation to sense. The most contradictory objects are put right next to each other, producing monstrous alliances.' (*Précis* 255.) Yet the regularity of the script and of the combinations of signs showed that writing and sense must be intended. The purpose could not be just ornamental.

Nor could it be straightforwardly representational, for what could the monsters and other imaginary combinations represent? (p. 171). Possibly the majority were symbolic, yet this did not seem plausible either. A predominantly symbolic script would have been 'inevitably very obscure, being compelled to express its ideas by a string of metaphors, comparisons, and barely soluble riddles' (p. 295). The hieroglyphic inscriptions on the other hand were everywhere. The script looked like a monumental and public one, not like an arcane and secret mystery (p. 272).

Another striking point about the script was its difference from Chinese, as recently described by Abel-Rémusat (1822). According to this 'learned and brilliant academician', as Champollion calls

Latus III Occidet.

37, 38 The name of a private
Roman citizen in
hieroglyphic writing.
37, A part of Kircher's
drawing of the Barberini
obelisk.

him (p. 304), 'the first to clear the study of Chinese from the darkness, one might say the mystical darkness, in which his predecessors had enveloped it', the Chinese script contained some 500 simple characters (both representational and symbolic), and many thousands of compound characters (i.e. ligatures) composed from them and symbolically signifying a host of different ideas. The Egyptian hieroglyphic signary was, however, quite different, both in total numbers and in proportion. Champollion counted some 860 different signs, of which at most 20 appeared to be ligatures, and the remainder simple (p. 298). Moreover, even with their ample signary, the Chinese, according to Rémusat, still found it necessary to have a class of phonetic characters, called hîng-chîng ('representing the sound'). What was more, these characters 'constituted a good half of normal written Chinese' (p. 305).[10]

It seems to me very likely that it was this new information, so totally different from anything that had previously been reported about Chinese writing, that encouraged Champollion to try out his phonetic alphabet on a wider front. But there were also two more immediate considerations. One of them (p. 266) concerned the Rosetta Stone. The 14 lines of the hieroglyphic text correspond to 18 lines of the Greek. On Champollion's count the Greek text contained just under 500 words, the hieroglyphic text 1,419 signs. This was a disturbingly large number if the writing system was really ideographic with one sign standing for one word. But what was just as disturbing was that there were only 66 different signs making up the 1,419.

The other consideration was the very great frequency with which the few dozen signs that Champollion had deciphered phonetically in the proper names recurred in the ordinary run of hieroglyphic inscriptions. They were only a handful of signs in comparison to the total signary of over 600, yet Champollion reckoned (p. 50) that their overall frequency of occurrence in running texts was higher than 66 per cent.

Enough has been said to show what the problem of the 'pure hieroglyphs' must have looked like to Champollion after the publication of his *Lettre à M. Dacier* and before he realized that he already held the solution in his hand. It was becoming increasingly difficult to understand how the writing could be totally ideographic. At the same time it was becoming less outrageous to suppose that it might be, to a large extent at least, phonetic. But how far these theoretical considerations preceded, ran parallel with, or followed Champollion's first attempts to make the hieroglyphs spell out Coptic words must always remain an open question. The only person who could perhaps have given an answer to it was Champollion himself; but he does not.[11] Let us, then, turn to what he does give us, and give us in full – the general application of his decipherment and its proof.

Champollion's *Précis du système hiéroglyphique*, published under the imprint of the Imprimerie Royale in 1824, runs to over four hundred (quarto) pages, and includes a total of forty-six plates. The body of the book consists of an introduction and ten chapters. The former begins by referring to the *Lettre à M. Dacier*, and the decipherment made in it of the phonetic hieroglyphs used for the writing of proper names. Champollion goes on to say that in following up his discovery he began to realize that it had a far wider application than he had at first suspected. The phonetic use of the hieroglyphs was not ancillary but central, and in fact the 'soul' of the whole writing system (p. 3). This discovery was very much more important than his previous one, and he would have liked to present it to the world in a full-scale and comprehensive work. But he had been forced into publishing his results in a comparatively summary form. The historical value of the decipherment in enabling the Ptolemaic and Roman cartouches to be read (and thus, for instance, certifying the lateness of such an object as the astrological zodiac from Dendera[12]) had brought both fame and a rival claimant. The rival claimant was Dr Young. Champollion was bound to point out to the public that his alphabet was very different from Young's, both in its detailed values, and in its general application. It was used not only in the royal cartouches of Greek and Roman times, but in those of Pharaonic times as well, and in ordinary inscriptions of all periods to represent *alphabetically* the sounds of the spoken Egyptian language. So the discovery of the phonetic hieroglyphs was the 'true key of the whole hieroglyphic system' (p. 11). All these positions Young denied.

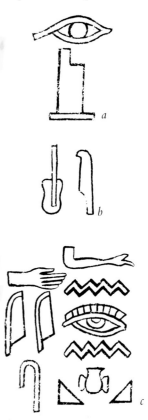

38, Sign-groups from the top of the second column isolated by Champollion; *a*, the name of Osiris; *b*, signifying 'deceased'; *c*, the name of the deceased – to be read ANTEIN.S

Thus the *Précis* begins on a polemic note. Even though everything that Champollion said was both moderate and justified, time has inevitably made the details of the dispute seem trivial. It is a pity that there should be this slight tarnish, on one of the most important and original works of modern scholarship.

However, we do eventually sail clear of Dr Young, and enter on a majestic series of chapters, each of which establishes a new sphere of usage of the phonetic hieroglyphs. Champollion does not conduct us in the order that his own investigations took him. The principle of the tour is from the less to the more surprising, and from the more modern to the more ancient.

First comes the application of the phonetic hieroglyphs to the proper names of Greek and Roman private individuals. Since these were foreign to the Egyptian language it was only to be expected, on the then fashionable Chinese analogy, that they would be written phonetically. Champollion confirms this expectation, beginning with the Barberini obelisk. He had shown in the *Lettre à M. Dacier* that this carried the cartouches of the Roman emperor Hadrian and his wife Sabina. He now points out (p. 42) that the general inscription of the obelisk contains several times a group of eight characters, and that this group is 'in all cases preceded by the most usual name of Osiris, and followed by two characters, which, in all the manuscripts, on all the funerary stelae, on the mummies, etc., regularly follow the name of the deceased – before which with equal regularity occurs the name of Osiris just mentioned'.

The eight characters were obviously a name. Application of the phonetic values to them yielded ANTEIN.S: and since Hadrian had a much-commemorated favourite who was drowned during their visit to Egypt and whose name was Antinous, there could be no doubt at all that this was the name intended and that the obelisk must have been carved in his memory.

37

38a, b

Other obelisks of the Roman period are now made to yield other names, the most certain being Lucilius, Sextus, and Africanus, each of them being followed by the hieroglyph for MAN 🕱.

The deductions drawn by Champollion from these results (p. 48) are that in Roman times at least there existed two separate orders of sign – phonetic and ideographic – and that these could be used together in the same inscription without any special distinguishing mark to show which was which. There was no warning sign to indicate phonetic usage.

Champollion now pauses and invites us to consider these deductions in the light of a further fact. The hieroglyphs of which he has found phonetic values when they are used in proper names are also the most frequently used hieroglyphs when there is no question of names being intended. They constitute at least two-thirds of all inscriptions of all epochs. Are they, when they are not applied to names, ideographic, as has been always thought? Or can they still be phonetic – as the lack of any external differentiating sign for proper names might lead one to suppose?

Champollion now recounts (p. 50) how he settled the question for himself by a totally objective experiment ('une opération toute matérielle').

It will be remembered that the alphabet as worked out from the Greek and Roman royal cartouches contained numerous homophones (⏝ and ▭ for *k*, 𝍖 and — for *s*, etc.), which could be used as alternatives. Champollion decided to take two hieroglyphic texts containing the same material, and to work through them noting down all the alternative spellings of ordinary words which occurred. He collated several texts in this manner (the fact that he was able to do so at all shows what enormous progress in discovery and publication had been made in the previous twenty years), and after extracting from them the signs that seemed to alternate in arbitrary fashion in the spelling of the same words he found that he had 'produced a table which was a veritable copy, almost a replica, of the phonetic alphabet formed from the Greek and Roman proper names' (p. 52).

Readers who find it difficult to visualize Champollion's experiment may be helped by an English example. A search through the different ways of spelling English proper names would reveal some homophones – for instance *s* and *z* in Isaac/Izaac. Susie/Suzie; *g* and *j* in Gill/Jill. Now if we searched with equal diligence through the spellings of ordinary words we would find the same letters alternating – for instance jeopardise/jeopardize; gibe/jibe. This would show that the same rules of usage must apply to the letters whichever category of word they are used in. Of course the analogy is only a rough one. In Egyptian the apparent homophones are more numerous, and the pictorial nature of the characters makes the conclusion more surprising.

Since the only possible non-bizarre explanation for this phenomenon was that the hieroglyphs in question were equally phonetic in value whether being employed in proper names or in ordinary words, the script must be to a large extent a phonetic one. Moreover, continued Champollion, it must be alphabetic, not syllabic, though to the pattern of Hebrew or Arabic where the

vowel-notation is less regular than in our own. For a sign might stand either for the consonant itself or for the consonant followed by a vowel (e.g. the open-hand *t* in 'ΤΡΑΙΑΝΟΣ', 'ΤΙΒΕΡΙΥΣ', 'ΑΥΤΟ-ΚΡΑΤΟΡ'). A vowel-sign might or might not be added (e.g. *tmitans, tmtians, tmitians, tomtins*, etc., for 'Domitianos'). As for the precise sound values represented by his hieroglyphic alphabet, Champollion considered that the Hebrew alphabet offered the most helpful analogies, and the rest of his third chapter is spent considering them.

This discussion of principles completed, the tour is now resumed. The fourth chapter shows us phonetic hieroglyphs being employed for writing ordinary words and grammatical inflections. Sign-groups that can be identified from their contexts on funerary stelae, as indicating degrees of relationship such as son, daughter, father, mother, brother, sister, and two groups identifiable on the Rosetta Stone as indicating king and place, are seen to yield on the hypothesis of the alphabetic values (sometimes helped out by the assumption of still more homophones) recognizable Coptic words. But more persuasive even than these words is their combination with the appropriate Coptic masculine, feminine, and plural forms of the article (*p, t, n*), and most persuasive of all is the coherent system of demonstrative adjectives (*his* father / *her* father: *his* mother / *her* mother, etc.) and pronouns. The evidence, mainly from funerary stelae, was corroborated not only by the Rosetta Stone ('received the kingdom *from his father*'), but also by obelisk inscriptions – such as that of the Pamphili obelisk in the Piazza Navona which carries the cartouche of Domitian and refers to '*his father* Vespasian' and '*his brother* Titus'.

Where the evidence of common words, grammatical forms, context, history, and a bilingual all pointed in the same direction, little corroborative weight could be added by a single small detail. Nevertheless, Champollion tells us (p. 77) that one of the things that contributed most powerfully to convince him personally of the general use of the phonetic hieroglyphs was the coincidence between the hieratic and demotic forms of the horned viper and of the Coptic letter *fei*, and the fact that in both Hieroglyphic and Coptic it was this letter which was employed to denote the sound *f* of the third person pronoun.

39 Champollion's discovery of grammatical forms in hieroglyphic writing. *a*, a section of his table showing hieroglyphic groups compared to the Coptic demonstrative pronouns *ntf* or *ntof* 'he' (1), *nak* or *nek* 'to you' (2), *naf* or *nef* 'to him' (3); *b*, his drawing of the ancient Egyptian forms (hieroglyphic, linear hieroglyphic, hieratic, demotic) of the Coptic letter ' ϥ '; *c*, detail of the Rosetta Stone, showing three occurrences (here shown in a darker tone) of the group ⸘ recognized by him as marking the third person of the future plural (Coptic *sene/sena*)

39a

39c

39b

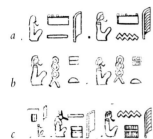

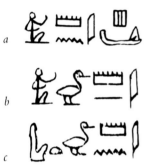

40 Champollion's decipherment of the names of Egyptian gods in hieroglyphic writing. *a, amn* – Ammon; *b, ptḥ* – Ptah; *c, anp* – Anubis

41 Champollion's decipherment of individual Egyptian names in hieroglyphic writing. *a, ptamn MAN* = Petamon; *b, amns MAN* = Amonse; *c, amnst WOMAN* = Amonset

In his fifth chapter Champollion presents us with the phonetically written names of Egyptian deities. Their occurrence on the monuments is not only frequent, as one might expect, but also easily detectable, for the name of a god is always followed by a 'species sign', as Champollion called it. This meant that he could make a full collection of the names of gods as they were written in hieroglyphic, and indeed in hieratic too. Since a large number of names of Egyptian gods had been transmitted to us by Greek and Roman authors, this list offered a good test for the applicability of the phonetic values. In the event Champollion has no difficulty in showing us the spelled-out names of numerous deities, of which three are here illustrated. His full list included Amun, Rê, Ptah, Satis, Anukis, Tefnut, Nut, Osiris, Arouêris, Anubis, Amset, Bes, Apis, Sobek and Apopis. But though the gods' names may be written phonetically, they might also be written, for brevity or display, ideographically, either by representation or by symbol. Examples of the first method were Amun indicated by the conventional picture of a god, but with a ram's head, Anubis with the head of a jackal, and so forth: examples of the second were an obelisk for Amun, a solar disk and uraeus for Rê, a Nilometer for Ptah. Sometimes these methods might be employed simultaneously, as in the second example of Anubis' name.

Having seen a number of divine names we can now be shown the names of individuals, which were largely composed from them. This fact was already known from personal names recorded in Greek and Coptic – Ammonius, Petosiris, etc. Archaeological discovery had now made it possible to compare these with a vast number of names from actual burials. The names in the hieroglyphic script were always followed by the 'species-sign' for MAN or WOMAN, as the case might be. There could therefore be no mistake in their location. Reproduced here are three examples. Champollion illustrates some fifty or sixty.

Foreign names, ordinary words, articles, pronouns, grammatical inflections, divine names, ordinary private names – clearly the phonetic hieroglyphs were used in all these categories. But so far none of the evidence used has been clearly datable to Pharaonic times. It is still just conceivable that the alphabetic use of the hieroglyphs was an innovation introduced into Egypt by the Greeks.

To disprove this Champollion now invites us to inspect the obelisks and other great monuments which were generally considered (e.g. by Zoëga) to be ancient. These contain the same grammatical forms, the same ordinary words, the same divine names as the inscriptions of Graeco-Roman times. If they are phonetic in the latter case, they must be so in the former. But more interesting is the occurrence on the ancient monuments of the same royal titles as are found on the Ptolemaic.

We have seen some Ptolemy cartouches, and may have noticed 35a, c that they contain more signs than are needed to spell his name. To judge from the Greek text of the Rosetta Stone these signs ought to carry the meaning 'ever-living, loved by Ptah'. Transliterated according to Champollion's phonetic values the final signs read *pt.mai*. If the still-undeciphered third sign is given the value *ḥ*, the phrase will be plausible Coptic for 'Ptah-loved'. Confirmation of

42 Alabaster vase with bilingual inscription, *c.* 460 BC. *a*, the vase; *b*, Champollion's drawing of the inscriptions; *c*, his transliteration of the hieroglyphic text into letters of the Coptic alphabet. *khschearscha* is the name of Xerxes. *irina* was taken by Champollion to mean Iranian.

b

c

this is the frequency with which the same three signs occur after the name of Amun in royal titles at Karnak. They ought then to mean 'loved by Amun'. Was this a royal title? There is evidence that it was. ὃν Ἄμμων φιλεῖ, ὃν Ἄμμων ἀγαπᾷ ('whom Ammon loves', 'whom Ammon cherishes') are descriptions or titles of the Pharaoh in Hermapion's obelisk translation preserved in the text of the Roman historian Ammianus Marcellinus. The Pharaoh concerned is said to be Rameses. If this is true, then the title must be an ancient one.

Champollion proceeds to show us parallels to other titles preserved in Hermapion's translation (e.g. ⟨hieroglyphs⟩ *ms* GODS on the Flaminian obelisk for Hermapion's θεογέννητος 'god-engendered'), and afterwards to assemble from the monuments a collection of previously unattested titles formed in the same general manner and phonetically expressed.

It is still, however, not absolutely certain that the monuments on which these titles appear are pre-Greek. To make it so, the cartouches of pre-Greek Pharaohs have to be identified.

This is the purpose of Champollion's eighth chapter. Its first exhibit is the name of the Persian king, Xerxes, written in both cuneiform and hieroglyphic characters on the Caylus alabaster vase we have discussed on page 74. This proves that the phonetic hieroglyphs go back to at least 460 BC, and therefore pre-date Greek rule in Egypt.

42

43 Basalt sphinx of Achôris,
XXIX Dynasty (see also
frontispiece); *below*,
detail of the titles and
cartouches of Achôris

There are also in Paris two basalt sphinxes which date from the comparatively brief period in the fourth century when Egypt recovered her independence from Persia. They bear the names of Nepherites and of Achôris.

43

To establish this result and to clear his way for the rest of the chapter Champollion had to prove, against Young, that each king had two cartouches, one giving his titles, the other his name, with the formula *sche-rê* ('child of the sun') coming in between. The unfortunate Young had taken this intervening formula to mean 'son'. Champollion points out that if this were so one would expect to find the second cartouche of one king recurring as the first cartouche of another, since according to Manetho's king-lists many a Pharaoh was succeeded by his son. *But this never happens.* Moreover the cartouches of the Roman emperors Tiberius, Gaius (Caligula), Nero, and Domitian are preceded by this formula – yet none of them had sons! On the other hand the sign-groups of the first cartouches generally make plausible sense as titles when transliterated according to the phonetic values, e.g. *autokrator*, *amun-mai*, etc.

44

This point clear, Champollion is free to march back into the past, reading the names of fifteen further Pharaohs, the earliest being of Dynasty XVIII. This is the climax of the tour. There can no longer be any doubt that the phoneticism of the hieroglyphs is original. It is also the most immediately useful discovery. For the identification of so many cartouches will enable many temples and other buildings to be securely dated for the first time.

The practical part of the *Précis* is now concluded. There follows a long ninth chapter of over a hundred pages in which Champollion sets out his general conclusions on the Egyptian writing system as a whole. He describes the different scripts, and how they were written; analyses the sign-forms and the three different ways by which, according to him, they could convey meaning (pictorially, symbolically, phonetically); surveys the history of modern opinion on the subject; and gives a new interpretation of the main ancient Greek account. By no means all of what he says in this chapter would be considered correct today. For instance his distinction between directly pictorial and symbolic signs is not a very useful one, whereas he takes no account of the important distinction between logograms which give information and determinatives which classify information otherwise given. In defending the numerous homophones of his alphabet he invokes the rather questionable principle of acrophony (arguing that an Egyptian would readily recognize the object depicted, its name, and the initial sound of that name, so that reading it correctly would present no great problem either of skill or of memory), but does not notice the specifically bi-consonantal or tri-consonantal values of some of the signs. He is wrong too in supposing that Horapollo's interpretations refer only to allegorical bas-reliefs, and the ingenious interpretation of the famous Clement passage put forward by himself in conjunction with Letronne – that the phrase πρῶτα στοιχεῖα ('first elements') refers to the alphabet of the phonetic hieroglyphs – is open to objection.[13]

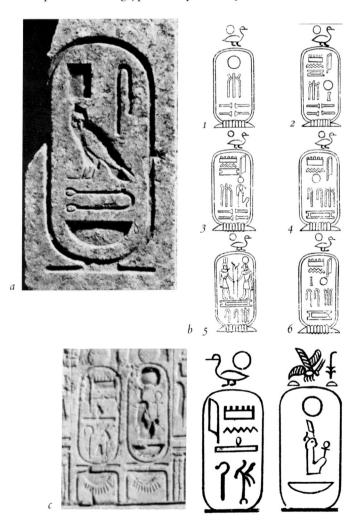

44 Champollion's decipherment of the names of early Egyptian Pharaohs. *a*, cartouche on the Campus Martius obelisk brought to Rome by Augustus, revealed by Champollion's alphabet as being the name of Psammetichos (*psmtk*); *b*, various forms of the cartouche of Rameses II, as drawn by Champollion. According to his alphabet they read: 1 *rmss*, 2 *amnm remss*, 3 *ammm RÊ mss*, 4 *amn rmss m*, 5 *AMON RÊ m mss*, 6 *amn remss m ; c*, the cartouches on the so-called Colossus of Memnon, and Champollion's drawing of them. The statue is known to have been really that of Amenophis, and on Champollion's alphabet the first four signs of the second cartouche read *amnph*

But these are trivial points in comparison to the overwhelming correctness of the decipherment as a whole. Champollion's decipherment was accepted by Sacy, in an admirable review which appeared in the middle of 1825, as being already beyond the need for confirmation. Champollion was enabled to travel to Italy to work on the Egyptian collections there, and afterwards to Egypt and Nubia. On his return a Chair was created for him at the Collège de France, but his health broke down. He died, after a series of strokes, within a very short time of taking up his duties, at the age of forty-one – tragically early for a man who still had so much to contribute to the world. He had, however, completed his Egyptian Grammar. This was seen through the press by his elder brother who had from the beginning been his constant protector and promoter, and who was himself an ancient historian.

But success attracts jealousy. Neither the personal career of Champollion nor the public reputation of his decipherment enjoyed quite the plain sailing that this summary description would suggest. Criticism ranged in tone from the inanities of Young ('Champollion's conjectural Coptic', 'his precipitation and love of system' – letters of 7 July 1827 and 24 November 1827) to the venom of Klaproth ('M. Champollion's versatility of mind' – *Examen* 41, 53), to the obstinacy of Sir George Lewis who forty years on was still stating firmly that the Egyptian language, having died out, was in theory irrecoverable and any decipherment that claimed to be recovering it must in principle be wrong. In substance the criticisms bore a quite remarkable similarity to the criticisms of more recent decipherments, and will be discussed briefly later on (see pages 114, 177). Their main usefulness today is to serve as a reminder that there can be smoke without fire; for Champollion's decipherment has stood the test of one and a half centuries, and its essential correctness has been repeatedly confirmed by new evidence.

Chapter Four

Persian Cuneiform

Persepolis

Your majesty shall shortly have your wish
And ride in triumph through Persepolis.

Marlowe's Tamburlaine, overhearing these words, was fired to
treason and to the usurpation of the crown of Persia, so desirable
did it seem to him to have Persepolis. But Marlowe could have
known neither what Persepolis looked like, nor where it was.   45
Persepolis, the seat of Darius the Great, Xerxes, and the subsequent
kings of the Achaemenid dynasty, was generally located at the site
of the modern town of Shiraz,[1] while the actual ruins of the
Achaemenid palace (locally known as Chehel minar, 'The Forty
Pollars') were identified as the courts of Jamshid.

  The correct identification of Persepolis was first made in 1618
by the Spanish ambassador to Persia, Garcia Silva Figueroa.
Figueroa disliked the country, and was particularly disappointed
in the squalor and modernity of its towns, built as they were of
crude brick, 'a transient material, unlikely to last for days, let
alone years'. But he was correspondingly impressed by the clean-
cut lines, beauty, and permanence of the ruins of Persepolis. He
devoted a thousand words to them in the very short account of the
country which he published on his return to Europe. He identified
them correctly on the grounds of the descriptions of the site given
by the ancient authors Quintus Curtius, Diodorus, and Plutarch,
pointed out the unique value of the bas-reliefs in preserving evidence of Achaemenid life and clothing, and gave the first-ever
description of cuneiform.

There is a remarkable inscription carved on black jasper. Its characters are still clear and sparkling [*integrae et venustae*], astonishingly
free from damage or deterioration despite their very great age. The
letters themselves are neither Chaldean nor Hebrew nor Greek nor
Arabic nor of any people that can be discovered now or to have
ever existed. They are triangular, in the shape of a pyramid or
miniature obelisk, as illustrated in the margin, and are all identical
except in position and arrangement. But the resulting composite
characters are extraordinarily decisive and distinct.

  For the marginal illustration of this fine description, Figueroa's
printer saw fit to use an equilateral triangle or Greek capital delta.
This stood for over thirty years as the only published specimen of
cuneiform script.

  The first published picture of Persepolis was a composite view
of the site by the Englishman Thomas Herbert who spent two days

46

45 Persepolis. Processional stairway with the Palace of Darius in the background

there at the end of 1626.[2] Herbert and his companions 'noted above a dozen lynes of strange characters, very faire and apparent to the eye, but so mysticall, so odly framed, as no Hieroglyphick, no other deep conceit can be more difficultly fancied, more adverse to the intellect.' He remarked that the characters were arranged 'in such simmetry and order as cannot well be called barbarous', and that they undoubtedly formed intelligible writing which might perhaps 'conceale some excellent matter, though to this day wrapt up in the dim leaves of envious obscuritie', but added nothing substantial to Figueroa's account.

Between the visits of Figueroa and Herbert, Persepolis had been visited, also for two days, by the Italian Pietro della Valle, whom we have already seen as a promoter of Coptic studies (page 37): He was there on 13 and 14 October 1621, and a few days later wrote a letter from Shiraz describing what he had seen and including a specimen drawing of five characters of the script. The letter was not, however, published until 1657. Pietro pointed out that there were two types of figure, one pyramidal and one angular (which he thought thinner), and that the characters were differentiated only by the number and arrangement of these two primary components. He also dealt with the direction of the writing, saying that since the lines were all filled up with no spaces left at the end it was impossible to be certain, but the direction of the vertical strokes in the second and third signs of those he had drawn, and of the transverse stroke in the fourth, inclined him to favour a left-to-right direction. This is in fact correct. Finally,

46 The first published
example of a cuneiform
inscription. Pietro della
Valle (1657)

47 The first published
drawing of Persepolis.
Herbert (1634)

he raised the question whether the characters were letters or word-signs, that is to say phonetic or ideographic, but felt unable to answer it.

Unlike the Egyptian hieroglyphs, the Persepolis script aroused at this time little public curiosity. The newly formed Royal Society of London, in drawing up its list of scientific requirements under the heading of Persia (*Philosophical Transactions* ii 1667, p. 420) enumerated various desiderata of knowledge about the state of Persian scholarship, trade, and industrial processes, and expressed the wish to have a draughtsman copy 'the Excellent Pictures and Basse Relieves that are about Persepolis at Chilmenar', but included no mention at all of the inscriptions.

This may have been because of doubt whether they were really writing after all. In the much enlarged 1677 edition of his book, Herbert referred to scepticism of this nature, but dismissed it, saying, 'It is not to be imagined that they were placed either to amuse or delude the spectators.' That, however, was very much the view of Thomas Hyde, the Regius Professor of Hebrew and Laudian Professor of Arabic at the University of Oxford.

Hyde is an outstanding example of how wrong a professor, in his case a double professor, can be. In his book on Persia (1700) he was tetchy about the Sassanid inscriptions (see pages 97–8), regretting their survival as a triviality that was likely to waste a lot of people's time in future. He missed the point of the scene above the

48
56b

royal tombs, identifying the aerial figure as the soul of the king departing in a cloud instead of Ahura Mazda hovering on wings. He was almost absurd in his conclusions on the cuneiform inscriptions. He argued that the characters could not be letters because

49

they were each separated by a point (in fact the points are not in the original);[3] they could not be whole words after the fashion of Chinese, since the Persians never wrote like that; and they could not be syllables because Persian words, and particularly Persian names, were polysyllabic. Therefore they could not be writing. Their true purpose was revealed by the fact that the same characters were never repeated. They were therefore an experiment by the original architect to see how many different combinations and arrangements he could create from a single element.[4]

There was, however, one positive contribution which Hyde made to the study of the script – its modern name. It was he who coined the word cuneiform (pp. 517, 526 *ductuli pyramidales seu Cuneiformes*).

Further illustrations both of the carvings and of the inscriptions

50, 53

at Persepolis were soon to be published by Chardin, a Frenchman who lived in London and who had visited Persia twice (1664–70,

51, 54

1671–7), and Kaempfer, a physician who travelled extensively, and who visited Persepolis in 1686. Though Chardin did not do the drawings himself, and Kaempfer was more than usually ill-served by his engraver,[5] their illustrations were a decided improvement on what had gone before. Moreover both of them contributed observations of some importance. Chardin attempted to count the number of characters, making the total over fifty. Kaempfer, by noticing that some characters were unique to some inscriptions, was the first to suggest that different scripts might be represented.

48 Persepolis. Scene from
royal tomb. Hyde (1700)

They disagreed on the nature of the writing, Chardin thinking it
alphabetic, on the somewhat inadequate ground that hieroglyphs
would not need to be separated by punctuation, and Kaempfer,
more sensibly, but as it turned out wrongly, thought it more likely
to be ideographic, like Chinese, because of the great number of
possible different characters. Both published inscriptions of
sufficient length – Chardin approximately a hundred and Kaempfer
approximately five hundred characters – to include repetitions of
the same sign and thus rule out Hyde's fanciful hypothesis.[6]

A very much more substantial publication was soon to follow.
This was by the Dutch traveller Cornelis de Bruin, more generally known under the French form of his name, Le Brun. He had
sailed from Holland to Archangel in the summer of 1701 and
stayed for more than two years each in Russia, Persia, and the East
Indies before arriving home in October 1708. While in Persia he
spent three months at Persepolis, drawing and copying. His book
came out in 1714. The section of it devoted to Persepolis contained some sixty plates (Chardin and Kaempfer had given about
twenty each), and included copies of five inscriptions, of a total
length of some two thousand characters. In his text Le Brun was
severely critical of the accuracy of his predecessors, but his own
illustrations were by no means faultless enough to warrant his
severity (compare Ills. 50, 52 and 56a). He made no novel contribution of his own to the study of the writing, but the scale on
which he published the inscriptions made it possible for the first
time to study them with an appreciation of their context, range,
and variety.

49 Persepolis. Cuneiform
inscription. Hyde (1700)

52

55

89

50–52 Persepolis. Scene from
royal tomb. From Chardin
(1711), Kaempfer (1712),
and Le Brun (1718)
respectively

53–55 Persepolis.
Window-frame inscription,
as rendered by Chardin
(1711), Kaempfer (1712), and
Le Brun (1718) respectively

56 Persepolis. Achaemenid
sculpture. *a*, scene in the
top register of the tomb of
Artaxerxes III; *b*, Ahura
Mazda, from the east door
of the Tripylon of the
palace

a

57 Persepolis. Inscription on
right side of the window
frame in the Palace of
Darius, on which the copies
opposite (53–55) were based

b

a

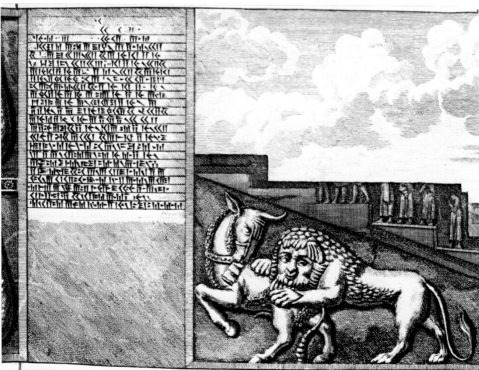

b

58 Persepolis. Inscription and bas-relief from the northern stairway of the *apadana* of the Palace of Darius.
a, photograph; *b*, as drawn by Le Brun

59 Persepolis. Detail of the inscription in ill. 58.
a, photograph; *b*, as drawn by Niebuhr

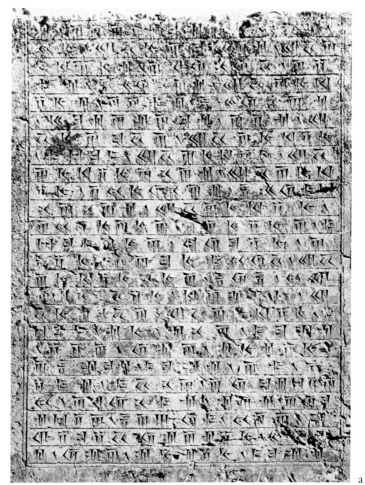

a

b

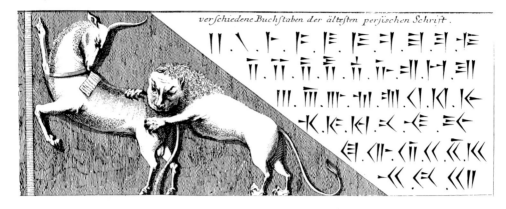

verschiedene Buchstaben der ältesten persischen Schrift.

60 Persepolis. Niebuhr's catalogue of the signs of Persian cuneiform, together with his drawing of one of the lions

It was half a century before Le Brun's work was to be super-seded. Carsten Niebuhr, whom we have already met in the streets of Cairo copying hieroglyphic, visited Persepolis too. Niebuhr's standards of accuracy were higher, and his approach was con-siderably more scientific. Not only did he do some simple excava-tion, clearing away the earth so as to be able to draw a lower register of bas-reliefs which Le Brun had omitted, but, what is much more important, he noticed that many of the inscriptions were duplicated so that he could check his readings of one against another. Comparison of Ills. 58b, 60 and 57, 58a will demonstrate Niebuhr's superiority. Niebuhr also made some firm contribu-tions in his theoretical discussion of the writing. He was able to confirm beyond doubt its left-to-right direction from the fact that the line-endings in the duplicate inscriptions did not always come in the same place. He distinguished clearly the three types of script.

60   And he attempted, with fair success, to isolate the separate charac-ters of the simplest of them.

These conclusions were to be endorsed by Sacy in 1792,[7] and ten years later were to form the material basis for Grotefend's partial decipherment of Persian cuneiform. But the tools for this decipherment had been forged elsewhere, as we shall see in the next section.

Palmyra merchants and Persian kings

In the last section we traced the history of the Persepolis inscrip-tions from their first discovery to their eventual efficient publica-tion and classification by Niebuhr. In this section we must explore the history of the decipherments of the Palmyrene and Sassanian inscriptions. Their importance for the decipherment of cuneiform was twofold. They demonstrated by example that decipherment was possible, and they generated techniques which were to be employed by Grotefend. ·

The city of Palmyra, situated at an oasis in the middle of the Syrian desert, lived in great prosperity off the caravan trade be-tween the Roman empire and the East. But in the third century of our era it became over-ambitious, attempted to proclaim its own emperor (Odaenathus, the husband of its famous queen, Zenobia), and was destroyed by Aurelian in AD 273. The ruins are well preserved and include many inscriptions in Greek, in Aramaic, and in both together. The Aramaic script is ultimately the same as the Syriac which was known from Christian manuscripts, but its Palmyra form was unfamiliar. When the inscriptions first reached Europe in the early seventeenth century they gave rise to some absurd false decipherments. For instance, in 1632 Samuel Petit in a letter to Peiresc turned the Aramaic half of a text which the Greek part showed to be a straightforward dedicatory plaque into a *cri de cœur* of the last days of Zenobia.

During the remainder of the century the number of known Palmyra inscriptions gradually grew as the result of travellers' visits, but the copies of the non-Greek part were in general so bad as to be virtually useless. Nevertheless, on the strength of them Leibnitz was able to point out the correct theoretical path to their understanding by decipherment, or decoding as he called it,[8] in a letter of January 1714:

61 Carsten Niebuhr, 1733–1815

In Palmyra and elsewhere in Syria and its neighbouring countries there exist many ancient double inscriptions, written partly in Greek and partly in the language and characters of the local people. These ought to be copied with the greatest care from the original stones. It might then prove possible to assemble the Alphabet, and eventually to discover the nature of the language. For we have the Greek version, and there occur proper names, whose pronunciation must have been approximately the same in the native language as in the Greek.

I believe this to be the first mention of the utility of proper names in decipherment. It was certainly borne out by future events. All the decipherments in this book bar one have had as their starting-point the location and identification of proper names.

The first accurate publication of the Palmyra inscriptions (twenty-six Greek, thirteen Palmyrene) was that which resulted from the expedition to the Near East of Dawkins and Wood. In the text of their book (1753) they spend less than five hundred words on the inscriptions. Even so they apologize for devoting time, space, and expense on a matter of interest to so few. The main point that they make is that the Greek and Palmyrene, when found together, must say the same thing. Their grounds for so thinking are that where words are repeated in the Greek, the Palmyrene text too shows repeated words: also that in one inscription there are erasures at the same place in both texts. The two inscriptions pointed out by Dawkins and Wood as the most certain to be bilingual are those illustrated overleaf.

62

Decipherment followed with extreme rapidity. Indeed there were two decipherments, carried out independently, one in Oxford by Swinton and one in Paris by the Abbé Barthélemy, and with identical results. Since it was Barthélemy who published first – his paper was read to the Académie des Inscriptions on 12 February 1754, Swinton's to the Royal Society on 20 June – it is Barthélemy who is always, and rightly, given the credit.

After a brief account of previous attempts (which had been so unsuccessful that in 1706 a ban had been placed on discussion of

```
CEΠT      OYOPⲰΔHN
TONKPATICTONEΠITPO
ΠONCEBACTOYΔOYKH
ΛΛΡΙONKAIAPΓAΠεTHN
IOYΛIOCΛYPHΛIOC
CEΠTIⲘIOCIAΔHCIΠ
ΠIKOCCEΠTIⲘIOYAΛE
ΞΛNΔPOYTOYHPⲰΔOY
ΛΠOCTPATIⲰNTONΦI
ΛⲰNKAIΠPOCTATHN
TEIⲘHCεNEKεNETOYC
HΘⲘHNEIΞΑΝΔIKⲰ
```
XVI

```
CEΠTIⲘION OYOPⲰΔHN
TONKPATICTONEΠITPO
ΠONCEBACTOYΔOYKH
ΝΑΡΙONKAIAPΓAΠεTHN
IOYΛIOCΛYPHΛIOCCAΛⲘHC
KACCIANOYTOY···ENAIOY
IΠΠEYCPⲰMAIⲰNTONΦIⲘON
KAIΠPOCTATHNETOYCCHOΘ
MHNEIΞΑΝΔIKⲰ
```
XVII

VIII 16

IX 17

62 Bilingual Greek/Palmyrene inscriptions published by Dawkins and Wood

the matter in the Académie until new evidence came to light) and some preliminary remarks on method (rejection of the temptation to search for a similar-looking alphabet or even worse for similar-looking letters from different alphabets; assertion of the principle that internal evidence and consistency is what matters; warning that in an oriental alphabet, at least in its monumental form, vowel-signs are likely to be lacking), Barthélemy began with the two inscriptions singled out by Dawkins and Wood. They consisted mainly of proper names, and the letter-values gained from them were enough to give Barthélemy the major part of the alphabet, which he knew from information given by Epiphanius, a fourth-century Bishop of Salamis in Cyprus, as likely to be the same as or very close to the Syriac (*adv. Her.* II ii 629). The process of matching was comparatively easy, but not automatic, as can be seen if we transliterate the part common to both inscriptions into our own alphabet, using capitals for the Greek and lower case for Barthélemy's Palmyrene:

63

SEPTIMION WORÔDÊN TON KRATISTON
sptmiws   wḍdwḍ   qḍtstws

EPITROPON SEBASTU DUKÊNARION
'ptdp'   ḍqnḍ'

KAI ARGAPETÊN   IULIOS
w   'dgpt'   'qim   iwlis

AURÊLIOS . . . .
'wdlis   . . .

The letter values in the only two Syriac words in this passage, *vau* ('and') and *aqim* ('set up') were all confirmed by their occurrences in the proper names. The similarity of the forms of *r* and *d* (transliterated above as ḍ), when unpointed, is characteristic of Syriac, and the borrowing of the Greek title *epitropos* for 'procurator' was already known to occur in it. There was in fact no room to doubt the correctness of Barthélemy's solution, and he himself made no great claims for it as an achievement, admitting that it had only taken him two days. Historically of course the inscriptions are of interest, for though the two with which we have been concerned are merely plaques for statues set up to a local grandee, the names and titles give us an extraordinary view of the mixture of influences in Palmyra life. Worod is a Persian name, Septimius a Latin one – perhaps indicating that Worod's family had received Roman citizenship from Septimius Severus. Of his three titles *epitropos* is the Greek equivalent for the Roman *procurator*, *ducenarius* a Latin word for having a salary of 200,000 sesterces, and *argapetes* a Persian rank, meaning something like commandant. From further inscriptions we know that Worod had held other offices and that he organized caravans. But for the most part the inscriptions are in Greek as well as in Aramaic, and the discovery of how to read the latter adds only, as Barthélemy said, a certain depth of flavour to our picture of Palmyra life.

Nevertheless, Barthélemy's was the first successful decipherment of an ancient script. He followed it up a few years later with work on the Phoenician alphabet, but from our point of view the most important next step was Sacy's decipherment of Sassanian Persian in 1787.

Inscriptions in Greek and two unknown scripts accompanying rock-carvings below the Achaemenid tombs at Naqš-i-Rustam near Persepolis were known from the time of Flower and Chardin, and reproduced by Hyde in his book in 1700. Hyde himself scorned them in grand academic manner. 'Travellers' graffiti . . . a monument of ill-writing and inexpert sculpture . . . late, insignificant, and scarcely worth the trouble of solving.' He thought that the unknown writing, for what it was worth, was most like the Palmyrene, and probably Phoenician. The right answer was Aramaic, but since Aramaic and Phoenician are closely related, this conjecture of Hyde's was not far from the truth.

Barthélemy (and before him Lacroze) agreed with Hyde on the affinity of the writing to that of Palmyra, but differed from him in regarding it as Persian, not foreign. For this they had the good authority of Epiphanius who, just before his mention of the Palmyrene alphabet as having twenty-two letters, tells us that 'the majority of Persians employ Syriac writing (*Surôi grammatí*) as second to their own (*meta Persika stoicheia*) just as with ourselves most peoples use Greek writing though almost all have their own local script'. But neither of them could seriously attempt a decipherment for the lack of any reliable copy.

When Sacy took up the problem (for a paper read to the Académie des Inscriptions in 1787) he had Niebuhr's copies to work on. The text of the two Greek inscriptions was in all essentials clear. I translate his French version of them (p. 62):

This is the figure of the servant of Ormuzd, the god Ardeschir, king of kings of Iran, of the race of the gods, son of the god Babec, the king.
and
This is the figure of the servant of Ormuzd, the god Sapor, king of kings of Iran and Touran, of the race of the gods; son of the servant of Ormuzd, the god Ardeschir, king of kings of Iran, of the race of the gods; grandson of the god Babec, the king.

א	א	*Aleph*
ʒ	ב	*Beth*
┤	ג	*Gimel*
ך ʒ	ד	*Daleth*
א ✕	ה	*He*
ʔ	ו	*Vau*
١	ז	*Zain*
Ⅎ	ח	*Heth*
6	ט	*Teth*
٨	י	*Jod*
コ 3	כ	*Caph*
丩ℎ	ל	*Lamed*
Ⅎ	מ	*Mem*
✓ ℐ ✓ ✓ ✓	נ	*Nun*
ℌ	ס	*Samech*
ℐ ℐ	ע	*Ain*
3	פ	*Pe*
ℐ	צ	*Tzade*
ℸ	ק	*Koph*
ℾ ʒ	ר	*Resch*
ⱶ	ש	*Sin o Schin*
ⱶ	ת	*Thau*

63 The Abbé Barthélemy's decipherment of the Palmyrene alphabet

A. Nº 3

A. Nº 4

64 Sacy's decipherment of Sassanian. *a*, the Greek text of a bilingual inscription from Naqs-i-Rustam, near Persepolis; *b*, the Sassanian text with the meaning of its parts identified by means of the Greek, and phonetic values allotted to some of its characters; *c*, (opposite) investiture of Ardashir by Hormuzd. Photograph of the Sassanian relief (detail). The inscription is on the point of this horse's shoulder

Ardashir, the founder of the Sassanid dynasty, who died in AD 240, holds the same place in the historical consciousness of Persia as William the Conqueror does in that of England. Real history begins with him. Sacy therefore had no difficulty in showing that the Greek 'Artaxaros' must refer to him, or in identifying his father and son, Papak and Shapur.

Next he turned to the titles. 'King of kings' (*schahinschah*) was still in use in Persia: Byzantine diplomatic correspondence showed that it dated back to Sassanid times, and indeed Parthian coins authenticated it for the previous Arsacid dynasty (247 BC–AD 227). Similarly 'god' was found as a title of Arsacid and Sassanian kings in the same sources. As for 'of the race of gods', Sacy could quote from a Christian martyrology a reply of Shapur's to the Christians, 'Do you not realize that I am of the race of gods?' The word *Masdasnos* which occurred in the Greek text and was not a Greek word was shown by Parsee literature to be a Persian one, 'mazdayasnian' meaning 'Mazda-worshipping': in confirmation of this it was known from Greek history that Ardashir and the Sassanids were keen restorers of Zoroastrianism.

These observations on the Greek text made the historical context of the inscriptions abundantly clear. They were Sassanid Persian. Persian should therefore be the language of at least one of the unknown scripts.

But before considering the question of language, Sacy, like Barthélemy before him and following the precepts of Leibnitz, concentrated his attention on the proper names. The first problem was to locate them. Sacy's own sketch shows which phrases of the Greek he took as corresponding to groups in the second of the two unknown texts (now known to be the Parthian one).[9] His primary aid in working out the scheme was, he tells us, the repeated word *masdasnou*, and the first name he tackled that of Papakou, whose location in the undeciphered script ought to be – and was – given away by the repetition of the letter for *p*. This yielded the characters for *p*, *a*, and *k*. The *a* recurred at the beginning of the group for Ardashir, and the *p* in the group for Shapur; the *r* and *š* in the last two names confirmed one another; *masdasnou* (already recognized as a Persian word) gave the character for *m*, which looked recognizably like the Syriac letter-form for *m*, and this in its turn gave away the location of *malcan malca* for 'king of kings', the *k* sound being confirmed by its occurrence in *Papak*.

Although the phrase *malcan malca* is Semitic, Sacy showed from a text published by Anquetil Duperron that it was used in Pahlavi. Sacy attributed the phenomenon to linguistic borrowing, but it is in fact an example of xenography. What is written is the foreign word, what is pronounced is the domestic one. A Persian reading *malcan malca* would have said 'šahinšah', just as in English when we read *lb* we say 'pound' not 'libra'.[10]

Sacy proceeded in the same manner with the second, very similar, script (now known as Sassanian),[9] identifying first the proper names and then a number of vocabulary words (seven of them genuinely Persian, five Aramaic xenograms). This was not enough in itself to shed a flood of new light on Persian, but it was enough to confirm the date and language of the Naqš-i-Rustam inscriptions, and the fact that the scripts were both a form of Aramaic.

The principal contribution of Sacy's work on the Sassanid inscriptions to the history of decipherment lay not so much in his particular conclusions, successful though they were, as in the example of his method. In particular it showed the use of a knowledge of royal genealogies and titles. The hint was taken up and was to lead to Grotefend's partial decipherment of Persian cuneiform.

c

The decipherment of Persian cuneiform

Persian cuneiform was the first script to be deciphered without the aid of a bilingual; this was accomplished, not by a sudden coup, but in three stages. The first was Grotefend's identification of the proper names and titles of the Persian kings who had caused the inscriptions to be carved, thus enabling potentially correct phonetic values to be allocated to a third of the characters. The second stage was the gradual and tentative decipherment of the remainder under the guidance of the newly born science of comparative philology. Finally, the amount of text available was multiplied many times, the decipherment was completed and confirmed, and a satisfactory translation of the whole *corpus* published by Rawlinson. We must look in turn at each of these stages.

Georg Friedrich Grotefend was not an orientalist but a Göttingen teacher who was interested in the problems of decipherment and who set himself the challenge of the cuneiform inscriptions. His progress exceeded his expectations, and in a few weeks he felt that he had arrived at some solid results. In his later years he rather tarnished his reputation by obstinately overrating their validity, but his initial publication of them was the most modest possible. It took the form of a paper read to the Göttingen literary society and an anonymous routine summary of it, followed by points of criticism, in the next number of the society's journal.[11] Grotefend himself wrote nothing until asked by A. H. L. Heeren to contribute an appendix explaining his decipherment to Heeren's book on ancient economics.

Grotefend began from Niebuhr's conclusions. He accepted that the cuneiform characters were genuine writing, that they proceeded in all cases from left to right, that there were three separate scripts represented in the Persepolis inscriptions (to which he added the Caylus vase, Ill. 42), and that the characters of the first of them were as listed by Niebuhr. The first question he tackled was whether the characters stood for letters, syllables, or words. Their limited number made it impossible to suppose that they were word-signs: the length of the sign-groups made it difficult to suppose that the characters were syllabic, or the language would have had to include words of up to ten syllables. So it had to be an alphabet. The rather large number of letters could be accounted for by long and short vowels being separately denoted.

Next, Grotefend invoked the analogy of the Sassanid inscriptions as deciphered by Sacy. This led one to expect that the content of the shorter inscriptions would be mainly the name and titles of the king or kings concerned. The inscriptions were certainly put there by the builders of Persepolis, and these almost certainly were of the Achaemenid dynasty.[12]

Taking as his pattern Sacy's Sassanian titles and making the consequential assumption that the most frequent sign-group should occur in at least two inflections and represent the word for 'king', Grotefend proceeded to set up a hypothetical formula for the shorter inscriptions:

x, great king, king of kings, son of y (the king), in race Achaemenid (?) . . .

Since the father in one set of inscriptions is in the other said to be the son of a third person who is not described as a king, it follows that we have to deal with a genealogy of three – x son of y son of z, and that the dynasty was founded by y. Given the approximate date of the Persepolis palace there are two pairs of candidates, Cyrus and Cambyses or Darius and Xerxes. Grotefend ruled out the first pair on the ground that none of the sign-groups he had provisionally located as king-names began with the same letter. This left the genealogy, known from Greek historians: Xerxes son of Darius (who founded the dynasty) son of Hystaspes (who was not a king).

It remained to discover the Persian form of these names. The ancient Greek geographer Strabo had written the name of Darius as *Dareiauês*: in Hebrew it was written *Darievesh*. Anquetil Duperron, the eighteenth-century French translator of the Zend Avesta whom Grotefend relied on for his knowledge of Persian, indicated 'Goshtasp', 'Kistasp', and 'Wistasp' as possible pronunciations for Hystaspes, and *ksch* as the sound transliterated *x* by the Greeks. Now, the sign-group for the latest of the three kings started with the same two characters as the word Grotefend had provisionally located as meaning king. This was propitious. The latest of the kings was Xerxes, and one of the words given for king by Anquetil was *khscheio*.

Up to this point Grotefend's arguments were sound and their application to the inscriptions successful. They yielded more or less plausible forms for the proper names and interlocking sound-values for some of the characters (for example, the *r* in Darius and in Xerxes). Unfortunately the knowledge of Old Persian that could be gleaned from Anquetil Duperron was not enough to give him a safe-conduct in his further progress. His translation of the Darius inscription was none too encouraging – in English it would go something like, 'Darius, mighty king, king of kings, king of

65 Grotefend's attempted decipherment of Old Persian cuneiform. From Heeren (1815 edn)

the Dahae [a rather remote Scythian tribe], son of Hystaspes, the race of the ruler of the world. In the masculine constellation of Moro of Ized'. Moreover the presentation of the decipherment was incomplete. Grotefend gave no alphabet, and no indication of how far his results were likely to be applicable to other inscriptions.

These criticisms, and more, were made in the report published in the Göttingen *Anzeiger*. In his appendix to Heeren's book in 1805 Grotefend tried to meet them. In view of the number of times he was forced to assume two values for one sign or two signs for one value, the number of mistakes he had to posit in the copies of Niebuhr and Le Brun, and his own misprints and mistakes in the specimen inscription illustrated, this publication of Grotefend's served rather to discredit than confirm his decipherment.[13]

The next attempt on the script was by St Martin in 1822. It was cursorily dismissed by Hincks (1847) as follows:

About twenty years after Grotefend M. St Martin corrected his values of two letters and sought to rob him of the credit of having discovered any. Out of France we apprehend that his labours will be but little thought of.

Indeed the case looks even worse. For the two letters whose values were altered by St Martin occur in the name of Xerxes on the Caylus vase, which is just where he had Champollion's hiero-glyphs to assist him. The rest of his results tally almost exactly with Grotefend's, though he claims to have reached them by a different and more scientific method. But since Grotefend's decipherment was only partially correct and his interpretation hardly at all, St Martin is left in the untenable position of a schoolboy who has copied the answer from his neighbour, and the neighbour's answer is wrong. However, St Martin was consulted by Champollion who speaks of him with respect, so that one is reluctant to think of him as a charlatan. The more charitable explanation is that navigators with the same chart (Niebuhr's copies) and the same compass (Anquetil Duperron's Avesta) were likely to run on to the same rocks.

But there was soon to be a new compass. In 1826 a small but important amendment to Grotefend's alphabet was made by Rasmus Christian Rask, a Danish scholar who had spent eight years travelling in the East and who was, at the time, Professor of the History of Literature in Copenhagen. By allotting the values *m* to ⊱𝍦 and *n* to ⊨< Rask was able to read both the dynastic title Achaemenis, as had been originally desiderated by Grotefend (see page 100), and the genitive plural -*anam* in the phrase 'king of kings'. 'Rask observed', to quote Hincks again, 'that this was the termination of the genitive plural in Sanskrit, and hence inferred that the language of the inscriptions was allied to that – a discovery that was the key to the interpretation of the inscriptions in fully as great a degree as that of Grotefend was to the reading of them.'

With Rask we have entered the second stage of the decipherment of Persian cuneiform, and must interrupt the story for a moment to look at the history of the Persian language. Modern Persian is as much a descendant of the Persian spoken in the time of Darius as modern Romance languages are descendants of Latin. In between lie the languages of Middle Persian – Arsacid Pahlavi or Parthian (247 BC–AD 227), Sassanian (AD 227–652), and the so-called Book-Pahlavi of the Zoroastrians in Persia and India, known from translations of parts of the Avesta and commentaries on it. The Avesta itself is earlier still and contains material of which some may go back to the time of Zoroaster – perhaps the seventh century BC. Its language (which used to be known as Zend) is a sister language to Old Persian, and was perhaps originally spoken in eastern Iran. The writing down of the Avesta as we have it is of course very much later.

These relationships were naturally not so clear at the beginning of the nineteenth century; nor was the relationship of the Iranian languages, considered as a whole, to other language groups. There had been plenty of speculation. As early as 1598 the similarity between Persian and German had been noticed by Lipsius, who lists thirty-six nearly identical words in the two languages, as well as sixteen which are nearly the same in Persian and Latin. He explained them, however, as the result of borrowings, and thought that the borrowings had probably been in both directions, maintaining the view that all languages were mixed.[14] This was the normal view: seventeenth-century theories of language and language growth were entirely vocabulary-oriented. They are clearly put by Besoldus (1632, p. 74):

Language change originates with the common people, their greater number winning. It is in markets with their indiscriminate mixture of different peoples and different languages that new words are always arising, and once born, like men, they inevitably replace their predecessors.

The theory does not rule out the concept of descent. Besoldus classed the Hebrew-like words, which he thought occurred in every language, not as borrowings, but as survivals from the original common language spoken at the tower of Babel; and he was aware that the Romance languages were descended from Latin, the Greek dialects from a common Greek, and so on. But the relationships and differences between languages were seen as matters of degree, not of kind. They were to be measured arithmetically by the number of common elements, not explained as a manifestation of organic or structural change. Even Leibnitz thought primarily in terms of vocabulary. He knew that there were words shared by Greek, Latin, German, and Celtic (he hesitated to include Persian), and in view of their very great number he was prepared to consider a common origin for them, and even for the people who spoke them, in Scythia. But the ease with which he thought words, even words for numerals, could be borrowed from one language to another, gave him pause, and he put the suggestions forward merely as a speculation.[15]

The first person to champion it as a hypothesis capable of proof was Sir William Jones (the 'Persian Jones' of Dr Johnson's club) who was by profession a lawyer and who went out to Bengal to serve as a judge in 1787. His views on an original common Indo-European language were developed in a series of presidential addresses to the Asiatic Society of Calcutta which he had founded.

Jones had been profoundly impressed on his arrival in India by the 'astonishing resemblance' between Sanskrit and both Greek and Latin. The resemblance needed explanation, and the primary principle of scientific explanation was simplicity of hypothesis. Jones quoted Newton, 'We must not admit more causes of things than those which are true and sufficiently account for natural phenomena,' and Linnaeus, 'In the beginning God created one pair only of every living species that has a diversity of sex.' For Nature does nothing in vain. Consequently there could have been at first only one pair of human beings, and Jones pointed out that arithmetically speaking there was nothing implausible about the account in Genesis. Even with a comparatively low birth-rate and making generous allowance for the depredations of war, famine, and disease, a few thousand years was ample time for the human population to have grown to its present extent. The same went for languages. Unless fixed by writing, languages multiply quickly. The families of Ham, Shem, and Japhet, migrating in different directions after the Flood, and gradually diverging in dialect, would have been enough to begin the process. There was confirmation of this in the fact that the languages of the world appeared to fall into three main groups. The two most obviously homogeneous of these were that descended from Shem (which we now call Semitic), and that descended from Ham (by which Jones meant not the languages we now call Hamitic but Indo-European, which he thought reached Europe from Egypt.[16]

The theory of an Indo-European language thus first promulgated by Jones by means of arguments that seem to belong to another world, was later to be placed on a very much firmer basis by Bopp and Rask. Bopp, who spent five years in Paris under Sacy and others studying oriental languages before becoming Professor of Sanskrit in Berlin, published a full comparison of the Sanskrit verb system with the verb systems of Greek, Latin, Persian, and German in Frankfurt in 1816, and was able to put beyond doubt their original common identity. At the same time Rask first pointed out the consistent pattern of sound-changes in the languages of the group (e.g. Latin *Pater*, *Piscis*, German *Vater*, *Fisch* – *Visch* in Old German). As a result of these discoveries that there was a predictable regularity in linguistic phenomena the study of different languages ceased to be a collector's hobby and became a science, the science of comparative philology.[17]

This is why Rask's ingenious suggestion for the values of *m* and *n* in Persian cuneiform was so important. It showed that there was a similar form of genitive plural in Achaemenid Persian and Sanskrit. But whereas on earlier linguistic ideas this could have been considered lightly as a possibly isolated 'borrowing', it had now to be taken far more seriously. Any future decipherment of the script would have to produce results which showed a consistent relationship with the language of Sanskrit and the language of the Avesta.

The practical effects of this new linguistic science showed themselves in the methods and criteria adopted by Christian Lassen, a Bonn professor, who was the most successful of the scholars in Europe who now took up the problem of Persian cuneiform.

Lassen's book (1836) is prefaced with a tribute to Grotefend for recognizing and partly reading the names of the kings and their titles. 'I wish to be his follower, not his opponent,' says Lassen. Nevertheless, he continues, the grammatical forms and most of the interpretations of words suggested by Grotefend must strike any Avestan or Sanskrit scholar as strange. Moreover the method by which he allotted sound-values to the characters was so far from rigorous that his decipherment, had it been proved correct, would have had to be attributed to luck. Approximate values are not enough. For instance Grotefend should have asked himself when considering the first letter of Darius' name whether it represented a surd *d* or an aspirated *dh*. But he never attempted accurate definition of this order.

But Lassen does. He begins the positive part of his book with the spelling of Xerxes, for which the Caylus vase (see Ill. 42) now offered a cross-check in Egyptian hieroglyphic. The first sign ≪⫪, which was also the first sign in the word for king, was clearly a 'k' sound. The question was whether it should be aspirated. In Avestan the word for king starts with *kh*, in Sanskrit (where it means 'warrior') it starts with *k*. The answer is that it should be aspirated – for not only is Avestan elsewhere closer to Old Persian than Sanskrit but the same sign occurs in the second place in the word for 'Achaemenid' where the Greeks transliterated it with a *chi*. The same question arises with the second sign. Is it *s* or *sh*? Here the second letter of the Sanskrit word and Champollion's hieroglyphic decipherment support *sh*, but the Avestan evidence is ambiguous.

And so on. The method is infinitely more meticulous than Grotefend's, and Lassen pursues it through all the recognized names, words, and grammatical terminations. He is then ready to break new ground. Applying his values to one of the longer inscriptions copied by Niebuhr he seemed to recognize the names of Persian provinces, for example *mad, ar.in, .akhtrish, çu.d.* Supply *m, b, gh* respectively for the three different unknown signs, and there emerge possible words for Media, Armenia, Bactria, and Soghdia. The trouble is that we now have two signs for *m* – ⊢⫪⫪ in *mad* and ⎰⟨⪦ . Lassen, however, noticed that the latter sign ⎰⟨⪦ never occurred except before ⌐⫔⫔, which from its use in the name of Hystaspes and elsewhere he had transliterated *i*. Further research was to show him that this was not an isolated phenomenon, and that there were other characters which only occurred before particular vowels. Thus the script was to some extent a syllabary rather than an alphabet.

This discovery of 'inherent vowels' was Lassen's major contribution to the decipherment. For though he identified correctly most of the twenty-four names of countries which the list contained, he failed to get right about a quarter of the sign-values, and – to quote Hincks (1847) again – 'his attempts at translation were as bad as could be made by one who had been put on the right way.'

The attempt was not an isolated one. Burnouf had simultaneously reached some of the same conclusions. Subsequently Beer (who discovered the proper form of the genitive singular in

-*hya*), Jacquet, and Lassen himself refined and added to the decipher-ment until it was within a sign or two of completion (see Ill. 67). But the material available was comparatively meagre, and the linguistic interpretation of it remained far from satisfactory.

In both these respects the situation was to be reversed by the dispatches of an officer of the British East India Company, Major Henry Creswicke Rawlinson. In his character and career Raw-68   linson was a model of the late Victorian ideal of manhood. His father was a country squire who once won the Derby, and his son became the best polo-player in India. He himself won distinction in several diverse fields, as an athlete, as a soldier, as a scholar, and in public life. He never went to a university, but after an education in Latin and Greek at a private boarding school at Ealing he joined the East India Company as a cadet. In 1827 at the age of seventeen he set sail for the East, where he was to remain for twenty-two years. For the four months of the voyage Rawlinson had as fellow-passenger Sir John Malcolm, the Governor of the Presidency at Bombay, and it seems to have been Malcolm who first fired him with an interest in Persia.

For the next six years Rawlinson had a sporting and adventurous life as a young army officer. Nevertheless, his time must have been in part devoted to more intellectual pursuits, since it included a momentary visit to prison for a debt of £20 contracted by book-buying, and also success in a voluntary examination in Persian. In 1833 he was seconded to Persia to help train the Shah's army, but soon after his arrival there a new Shah came to the throne and appointed Rawlinson to be adviser to the Governor of Kurdistan. While in Persia he copied, at a considerable danger to life and limb, 66   the great rock inscription of Darius on the cliff at Behistun, and qualified himself in a practical way for deciphering it by quelling a provincial revolution, as King Darius had done before him.

At this time all that Rawlinson knew of European research in the matter was that Grotefend had deciphered the names of the Achaemenids, Hystaspes, Darius, and Xerxes. He had been able to repeat the discovery for himself with the aid of two brief inscriptions from Hamadan, and now, from the first two para-graphs of the long Behistun inscription he found the names of Arsames, Ariaramnes, Teispes, Achaemenes, the name of Persia itself, and some possible vocabulary words, giving values for a total of eighteen characters. It was only now, on a visit to Teheran in 1837, that he read Grotefend and St Martin. He felt himself already more advanced than they, and sent back to the Royal Asiatic Society a draft of his translation of the first two paragraphs of the Behistun inscription.

In 1838 and 1839 he was in Baghdad, and able to read the recent work that had been done on the subject. Previously his knowledge of the Avesta had been based, like Grotefend's, on Anquetil Duperron. Now he received Burnouf and 'found for the first time the language of the Zend Avesta critically analyzed and its ortho-graphic and grammatical structure clearly and scientifically developed'. It was to this work, he adds, that he owed in great measure the success of his translations. Burnouf's own deciper-ment, however, he found less helpful – it included the value of one

character that Rawlinson had not reached, but had many more values wrong. While he was completing his decipherment (with the help of the published Persepolis inscriptions which he now possessed) Rawlinson received a letter from Lassen summarizing his latest results. He found that they 'coincided in all essential points' with his own, despite the much smaller range of inscriptions at Lassen's disposal. Since Lassen had published, and perhaps even arrived at, his results first, Rawlinson had to concede the victory. But if this disappointed him he did not let it show. The field was ample. There were still the other two classes of cuneiform writing. In the meantime, though, he still had 'one claim to originality, as having been the first to present the world with a literal, and, as I believe, correct grammatical translation of over two hundred lines of cuneiform writing.'

This was the extent of the first draft of his decipherment which he sent to the Royal Asiatic Society in 1839. It was to be enlarged in his later memoir to four hundred lines. But three years were lost. Rawlinson was transferred to Afghanistan to be political Resident in Kandahar, where, with General Nott as the only other British officer, he was cut off for the best part of the next two years by siege. On eventually getting back to India he was forced to waste another half-year because the account-books were lost at sea, and it was insisted that Rawlinson should reconstruct them from memory – a feat in which he was apparently successful. In 1843 he refused the offer of a superior post – the Residency of Nepal – in favour of returning to Baghdad as Political Agent. In Baghdad he was able to resume his cuneiform studies, working at the end of his garden in a summer-house kept cool by water poured on the roof from a great noria and with a lion and a leopard as pets. He sent his results to the Royal Asiatic Society in 1845 and 1846.

Rawlinson's decipherment, though to a large extent independent, proceeded through almost exactly the same stages and in almost exactly the same order as that carried out by the succession of scholars in Europe. It began with proper names (first of the Achaemenids, and then of the Persian provinces), and from them moved to vocabulary words and grammatical inflections, controlling them with ever-increasing regard to the new science of comparative philology. Finally, Rawlinson gave, as Lassen had begun to do, closer consideration to the orthographic principles on which the script was built. Developing Lassen's hints, he found (1846, pp. 175–86) a triple system. Different characters were used for the same consonantal sound, depending on what vowel followed. In general the system was complete for sonants (Rawlinson's word for voiced consonants), half-complete for surds, and undifferentiated for aspirates, as exemplified below:

	followed by *a*	by *i*	by *u*
t (surd)			
th (aspirate)			
d (sonant)			

This discovery (which was in fact arrived at independently by Hincks in Dublin at about the same time) removed many an apparent anomaly from the script, and incidentally made trans-

108

Comparative Table of th

No.	Character	Grotefend, from Heeren, 1824	Rask, 1826
1		é and á	
2		ô	
3		û	
4		é	
5		kh	
6		z	
7		û	
8		z	
9		ô	
10		dj ?	
11		ng	
12		m	
13		th ?	
14		i	
15		m ?	
16		n	
17		d	
18		z	
19		b or p	
20		f or ph	
21		v	
22		o	m
23		h	
24		k ?	
25		tsch	n
26			
27			
28		h	
29		r	
30		sch	
31		e	
32		g	
33		s	
34		sch	
35		gh	
36		a	
37		h	
38			
39			
40			

Saint Martin, from Klaproth, 1832	Burnouf, 1836	Lassen, 1836	Jacquet and Beer, 1837–38	Lassen 1839	Lassen 1844 (German letter values)	Rawlinson 1845	Rawlinson 1846	Kent 1950
a	â	â		â a	â	á or a (init.)	á or a	a
y	ô	i		î i	i	i	i	i
ou	u	u		û u	u	u	u	u
e	k	k		k		k	ka/ki	k^a
kh	kh	k'		kh	kh	k'h	kha/khu	x^a
h	q	a		a	q	kh	ku	k^u
?	u	g		g	g	g	ga	g^a
	gh ?	g'		gh	gh	gh	gu	g^u
e	v	î	y (J.) tch	k'	k'	ch	cha/chi	c^a
?	gh ?	g'		dj	g'	j	ji	j^i
?	h ?	ñ	(J.) j (fr.)	j (fr.)	z'	jh	ja	j^a
t	t	t		t	t	t	ta/ti	t^a
?	dh	t		th	d'h	t'h	tu	t^u
h	y	ζ		t'h	θ	th	tha/thi/tha	θ^a
?	l ?	k'		tch	k'h	t' (with i)	di	d^i
n	th ?	t'		tr or t'	thr	tř	tř	ç^a
d	d	d		d	d	d	da	d^a
?	gh	d'		dh	dh	dh	du	d^u
p	p	p		p	p	p	pa/pi/pu	p^a
?	f	f		f	f	f	fa (?)	f^a
r	b	b		b	b	b	ba/bi/bu	b^a
â	m	m		m	m	m	ma	m^a
c	î	'm ?		hm	m	m' (with i)	mi	m^i
?	gh ?	g' ?		gh ?	x	m' (with u)	mu	m^u
m	n	n		n	n	n	na/ni	n^a
						n' (with u)	nu	n^u
						ñ ?	ña (?)	l^a
e	h	h	y	y	j	y	ya/yi/yu	y^a
r	r	r		r	r	r	ra/ri	r^a
ch (fr.)	l	s'	(B.) r or l	sh ?	r	r' (with u)	ru	r^u
i	i	w		w	w	w	wa/wu	v^a
v	g	v (init.)		v ?	v	v	wi	v^i
s	ç	ç		ç	ç	s	sa/si/su	s^a
ch (fr.)	ch (fr.)	s'		s	s	sh	sha/shi/shu	š^a
e	z	z		z	z	z	za/zu(?)	z^a
ou	a	a (init.) / ng (med.)	h	h	h	h	ha/hi/hu	h^a
h				y	rp	q ?	doubtful	—
				ks	dah	dah ?	—	dahyāuš
					bu'mi	bum'i ?	—	būmiš
								word-divider

7 Table showing the history of the decipherment of the signs of Old Persian cuneiform.[18] After Rawlinson (1846) with the addition of his subsequent values (Aug. 1846) and an accepted modern system of transliteration (from Kent 1950)

literation easier. For instance the same letter *d* could be used for all
three signs, the original ones always being inferable from the
nature of the following vowel.

Though this was a novel advance, and though Rawlinson
deciphered two characters (those for *tr* and *mu*) unseized by his
competitors, his main achievement was in the field of interpretation. Nobody before him, as Hincks said, had translated
twenty lines correctly, let alone four hundred.

Their importance was immense. From the point of view of
Persian history they gave us, in the words of the title of the
admirable review by Hincks which I have several times quoted,
'Some passages of the Life of King Darius, the Son of Hystaspes,
by Himself'. From the linguistic point of view they gave us the
language of Achaemenid Persia. But their interest extended still
further. The Persian inscriptions were nearly all accompanied by
67   translations into two other cuneiform scripts. Their understanding
consequently gave a key of admission into the whole cuneiform
world.

68 Henry Creswicke
Rawlinson, 1810–95

Chapter Five

Other Cuneiform Scripts

The Babylonian syllabary and its cognates

The decipherment of Persian cuneiform provided the key to the world of cuneiform writing. This world was to prove as wide and as diverse as the European world of the Greek and Roman alphabet. But the key did not give direct access to it, for Persian cuneiform was an invented writing. Its characters were different from the characters of common cuneiform to something like the same extent that the written letters of the morse code differ from those of our own alphabet.[1] A second decipherment was therefore necessary. Luckily the great triscripts of Persepolis and Behistun offered plenty of scope for this, Darius and Xerxes having recorded their names and achievements in Elamite and Babylonian as well as Persian. The former was the language of Susa, an ancient language, but, like Basque in the context of modern Europe, unrelated to its neighbours or indeed to any other as yet known language group. The script too in which it was written, though ultimately descended from Akkadian cuneiform, was idiosyncratic. The Babylonian on the other hand was in the traditional language and the traditional script of Mesopotamian civilization. It was outwardly very much the most complicated of the three with a signary of two or three hundred different characters, but its decipherment was facilitated by the fact that the language was of the well-known Semitic group and that new documents in the same or in the closely related Assyrian script were constantly being discovered.

The descent of the cuneiform scripts as now known or deduced can be shown in the form of a table (see overleaf).[2]

The scripts were used for the writing of languages belonging to four distinct language groups, Elamite, Semitic (Akkadian, Babylonian, Assyrian), Hurrian (of which the language of the Urartian kingdom by Lake Van – which flourished from the ninth to the seventh centuries BC and used the New Assyrian cuneiform – is a distant relative), and Hittite (an Indo-European language). The relationship between the scripts is rather more complicated than simple descent suggests; for there was cross-influence as well. The Middle Babylonian or Akkadian script had international status and the Assyrian and Hittite scribes adopted many of its practices. There was also influence through time. The tradition of the scribal schools was an unbroken one so that long-disused elements could be revived and brought back into use. Finally, in the later periods, there was external influence. The

THE DESCENT OF THE CUNIEFORM SCRIPTS

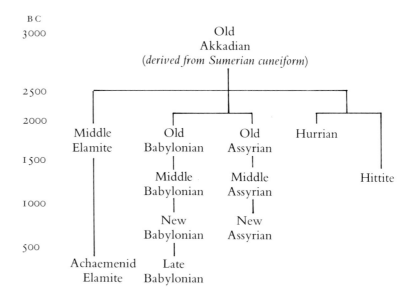

primary medium of the cuneiform writing system was clay; its primary users were officially trained scribes; its primary nature was syllabic with a more or less strongly developed repertoire of ideograms and determinatives. In all these respects it differed from the Semitic consonantal alphabet, which was certainly in existence soon after the middle of the second millennium B C, and may be much earlier. In the first millennium the Semitic alphabet became increasingly widespread, and it is possible that the frequent mistakes in the writing of vowels, particularly final vowels, in Late Babylonian are due to this. Scribes familiar with a consonantal alphabet could easily grow careless in their use of a syllabary. Since in the one system vowels are dispensed with altogether the temptation would be to discount the importance of differentiating them in the other. Furthermore the language of Late Babylonian may have been a learned one, no longer in everyday use.

These factors, together with others such as the gradual change of phonetic values in the spoken language to which the script had been adapted only intermittently or not at all, made the Late Babylonian script far from straightforward. Its position was something like that of our own writing. The English alphabet is a direct descendant through Latin of an early Greek alphabet. The Greek alphabet had a more or less one-to-one relationship between signs and sound. This efficiency has been hopelessly lost in the intervening 2500 years: *c* can stand for either a sibilant (*s*) or a palatal (*k*), *gh* for a palatal, a dental fricative, or nothing at all ('lough', 'rough', 'dough'), and so on notoriously. These are polyphones. There are also the opposite, homophones. For example, *-er*, *-ir*, *-or*, *-ur*, *-our* represent, on most occasions of their use in southern English, exactly the same sound. New letters have been invented (G in Roman times, J and V since the Middle Ages, W in the alphabets of the northern European languages). Numerous ideograms have been introduced, mainly for technical use but some general (all our numbers, %, =, +), and some xenograms (*d*, the Latin *denarius*, read 'penny' until 1970; £, the Latin *libra*, read 'pound'; and P^s corrupted to $, the Spanish *pesos*, read 'dollar'). There have been some droppings, too, mainly medieval ligatures and alternative forms of the letter *s*, but the increases have been far more numerous. The classical Greeks had some thirty different signs, we have at least a hundred in common use, as can be seen by a look at any standard keyboard. Each individual addition, adaptation, corruption has in itself been quite rational: their aggregate creates an appearance of almost complete irrationality.

Yet, given enough knowledge, we can penetrate to the underlying historical regularity. Most English signs are recognizably the same as the signs used for writing other western European languages and in many cases signs of the same appearance have recognizable phonetic similarities. So much is this the case that although, strictly speaking, French and English use different scripts it would be pedantic, were one of these languages to be lost, to use the word decipherment for the process of recovering it through its literature. Thus the recovery of Urartian (written in New Assyrian cuneiform), of Hurrian (written in an almost ideogram-free cuneiform derived from Old Akkadian), and of Hittite (written in a script derived from Hurrian but with much cross-influence from mid-second-millennium Akkadian), though feats of considerable difficulty, are not truly to be called decipherments. They therefore fall outside our scope.

Not so the decipherment of Late Babylonian; this was a true decipherment in which hitherto unknown characters had to be allocated values. But though the process was arduous in detail and though it opened the gateway to the remainder, it involved no great problems of strategy. Thanks to the decipherment of Persian cuneiform there was an extensive bilingual available, and it contained numerous proper names.

These provided the starting-point. In his paper read to the Royal Asiatic Society in 1850 when he was temporarily back in England, Rawlinson, who played a major part in the decipherment, says 68 that he had no difficulty in locating and identifying eighty of them. They yielded phonetic values for about a hundred characters. Variant spellings of some of these names added about fifty apparent homophones. Thus sound-values for about 150 characters were known. The majority of them were syllabic and of two types, which he called 'initial' and 'terminal', that is to say with the vowel accompaniment either following or preceding – what we should call 'open' or 'closed' in the pattern CV (*na*) or VC (*an*). It is clear that a double syllabary of this nature necessitates a very large number of different characters even without the presence of homophones. There were also, Rawlinson discovered, very many ideographic signs as in Egyptian, whereas in the Persian cuneiform inscriptions there had only been three or four for words or names of particularly frequent occurrence.

Besides the homophones there occurred the opposite, characters which could represent two or more quite different sounds, and Rawlinson had to confess that the phonetic signary as a whole 'defied attempt to reduce it to a definite system'. Nor did he claim at this stage a full decipherment, only 'the first outwork carried in a hitherto impregnable position'. He had in fact identified some two hundred Babylonian words ('the sound approximately, the meaning certainly', as he put it), and many of these recurred in identical or similar form in the inscriptions that were being found in the contemporary excavations in Assyria.[3] These then provided an area for further exploration. The guides were cautious use of analogy from other Semitic languages, grammatical indications, and above all extensive comparison of similar or cognate phrases with regard to the probable context. The results so far were an extra 200 certain and 100 probable words; but since there were already some 5,000 different sign-groups in the Babylonian and Assyrian inscriptions so far known, the number that could be read amounted to only a tenth of the whole. Even so the historical context of a great number of inscriptions could be recognized.

Thus Rawlinson's progress report in 1850. The next year he returned to Baghdad, this time to excavate for the British Museum, finding among other things the foundation deposits of Nebuchad-nezzar at Birs-Nimrud. But the most dramatic event was in con-nection with the annals of the Assyrian king Tiglath-Pileser I recorded on the clay cylinder which is shown opposite. It was by means of this that the validity of the decipherment was to be demonstrated to the public.

The initiator of the demonstration was Fox Talbot. Fox Talbot's major claim to fame was the invention of photography, but he was also a scholar (having won the Porson Prize for Greek Verse Composition at Cambridge in 1820), and the cuneiform decipher-ment stimulated him into becoming an Assyriologist. After Rawlinson's return to England in 1855 he was lent a copy of the Tiglath-Pileser inscription before it had been worked on by any-one else. He translated it and sent back his translation in a sealed envelope together with a proposal that independent translations should be made by others and the results compared by an impartial committee.

The principal ground occupied by the sceptics of the de-cipherment as defined in Fox Talbot's letter was the looseness of the proposed spelling system. 'If each cuneiform group represents a syllable, but not always the same syllable . . . the Assyrians them-selves could never have understood it.' Fox Talbot's answer was that this was illusory. 'Experience shows that the uncertainty arising from this source is not so great as might easily be imagined. Many of the cuneiform groups have only one value, and others have always the same value in the same word or phrase, so that the remaining difficulties and uncertainties of meaning are within moderate limits.'

Fox Talbot's suggestion of a public experiment to prove the point was taken up, and a distinguished committee appointed to decide, not directly on the merits of the decipherment, but on the amount of agreement between the translations submitted. Dr Hincks, an Irish clergyman and a more meticulous scholar than Rawlinson who had contributed substantially to the decipherment from its earliest stages, and Dr Oppert, a former pupil of Lassen's

69

▷
69 Clay cylinder bearing
inscription of
Tiglath-Pileser I, King of
Assyria. Ht 15⅜ in.

70 Biscript dedication by
Puzur-Inšušinak in Akkadian
cuneiform and the
still-undeciphered
proto-Elamite writing.
Susa. *c.* 2200 BC

who had moved to France since Jews were not at the time able to
pursue an academic career in Germany, were invited to submit
translations, as well as Rawlinson himself. When the translations
were compared, the verdict was 'a very remarkable concurrence'
with the rider that 'the closest co-incidence was found between
the versions of Colonel Rawlinson and Dr Hincks, who are understood to have prosecuted the study for the longest time and with
the greatest assiduity. Mr Fox Talbot, who was later in the field,
though on the whole mostly arriving at the same conclusions was
less positive and precise.' About Oppert the committee used polite
phrases, but it is clear that in their view he came a poor fourth.

The account of the committee's proceedings and the four independent translations were published by the Royal Asiatic Society in 1857. The gates of cuneiform were thus, as it were, officially declared open. But there was still one of the cuneiform scripts which was distinct enough to need decipherment as opposed to linguistic interpretation. This was the second of the Persepolis scripts, now known as Elamite – a name first given to it in 1874 by Sayce – but at the time generally known as Median on the assumption that it represented the language of the Medes. Rawlinson thought that it was 'unquestionably a Tartar dialect', which he conceived of (in a manner reminiscent of Sir William Jones) as the third of the 'three great lingual families' of Asia, and as ancestral to Magyar, Finnish, Turkish, and Mongolian. Indeed he somewhat romantically saw the three administrative languages of the area in his day – modern Persian, Turkish, and Arabic – as being the linear descendants of the three monumental languages of Persepolis. This is not so. Nevertheless, the Elamite language had a long history behind it. Its existence is attested in cuneiform inscriptions of the second millennium B C, the so-called Middle Elamite, and probably extended back at least a further thousand years; for it is probably the language of inscriptions found at Susa in a quite different script, which are sometimes accompanied by a text, presumably a translation, in Akkadian cuneiform. Their date 70 is approximately 2200 B C. Of an even earlier date, about 3000 B C there are several hundred clay accounting tablets written in what is probably a more ancient form of the same script, perhaps concealing the same language. The script is known as Proto-Elamite, and is still undeciphered.[4] Even Achaemenid Elamite resisted interpretation for a long time, the language being an altogether unknown one, and despite the work of Rawlinson, Hincks, Oppert, and others, its proper understanding is generally reckoned to date only from Weissbach in 1890. But the difficulty, as with Etruscan, was in the recovery of an unknown language, not in the decipherment in the strict sense of the term, for which the Persepolis and Behistun triscripts were available.

The Ugaritic alphabet

Finally, the Ugaritic alphabet. This is the most recent of the cuneiform scripts to have been discovered, and the most surprising of all since the original reports of Figueroa and Pietro della Valle. It does not figure in the genealogy on page 112 because, like the script of Achaemenid Persian, it was an artificial creation. Its discovery was due to the French archaeologist Claude Schaeffer in 1929. Excavating at Ugarit, a Phoenician town near the modern Ras Shamra on the coast of north Syria, Schaffer found documents in a twelfth-century context of which some were written in Akkadian, but others in a hitherto unknown and apparently very much simplified cuneiform script.

With exemplary generosity Schaeffer handed them over for immediate publication to a colleague, Charles Virolleaud, whose first article appeared the same year (*Syria* x 304–10). The texts in the new script were, with one exception, all written on clay tablets.

71 The starting-point established by Virolleaud for the decipherment of the Ugaritic alphabet. *a*, one of four axes inscribed with a single word; *b*, an axe inscribed with the same word preceded by one other word; *c*, a tablet whose inscription begins with the same word preceded by a single-letter word

a

b

c

As is usual in cuneiform the direction of writing was left-to-right, but the number of different signs, instead of being several hundred, was twenty-six or twenty-seven. Such a script could hardly contain ideograms, or even be a syllabary. It was almost certainly an alphabet.

71

The one inscription, or rather set of inscriptions, not on a tablet was on a series of small bronze axes. Virolleaud suggested this as a possible starting-point for decipherment, pointing to a tenth-century Phoenician arrow-head from Sidon inscribed *hets addo* ('the arrow of Addo') as a possible analogy. If the analogy was valid, the first word should mean 'axe', and the second, which occurred on all five axes, should be the name of the owner. That it represented a proper name was confirmed by its occurrence as the second word on one of the tablets. The word before it was only one sign, and therefore very possibly a preposition. Contemporary Akkadian letters written on clay tablets customarily began with the preposition *ana*, 'to', followed by the name of the person addressed. Presumably in this case the recipient of the letter was also the owner of the axes.

Apart from pointing out that the general brevity of the words, mostly of three letters and hardly ever more than four, seemed to exclude Cypriot Greek as their language, this was as far as Virolleaud ventured along the path of decipherment in his first article. But he gave drawings of the forty-two tablets in the alphabetic script and some specimen photographs. With the material thus available it was not long before others set to work on it and soon there were three separate decipherments. They were by Virolleaud himself, by Hans Bauer, a Semiticist from Halle, and by Édouard Dhorme from the French School in Jerusalem.

Let us begin with Virolleaud's own. This was read to the Académie des Inscriptions et Belles Lettres, the body which had previously heard the decipherments of Barthélemy and Champollion, on 3 October 1930, and published in the journal *Syria* the next year. Virolleaud resumed from where he had left off. The value of the sign at the start of the letter addressed to the owner of the axe might well be *l*, the consonant of the Phoenician and Hebrew preposition ל. If the language was Phoenician – and Ras Shamra was, after all, in Phoenicia – then possible words to look for containing *l* were *mlk*, 'king', and *B'l*, 'Baal'. Virolleaud found words to suit the requirements, and what was more two of them carried hopeful-looking identification certificates. For in addition to *mlk* there occurred a group which would on the same values have to be translated *mlkm*, forming the correct Semitic plural 'kings'. And the word he considered a candidate for *B'l* occurred also with an extra letter. If this was a *t*, forming the feminine Baalat, it became possible to read a disyllabic word that was to be found elsewhere in the texts as *bt*, which could be the Phoenician either for 'daughter' or for 'house'. Finally, among the words with *l* in them there was a three-letter word with the *l* in the middle and the same letter at each end. This might be *šlš* 'three'. If so, and if the previously suggested letter for *m* was correct, this made sense of another word in the texts *šlšm*, 'thirty'. Now the word *šlš*, 'three', occurred at the end of a line on a tablet of consistent format – twelve ruled lines with two words in each line. The other end-words might therefore also be numerals. On the provisional values so far assumed one of them read *šš* 'six', and it was not difficult to fill in the missing letters in three more of them to yield *ṣb'*, *ḥms*, *šmn* for 'seven', 'five', and 'eight' respectively. This was enough to convince Virolleaud that he was on the right lines, and by continuing the process of trial-and-error matching he was able to give correct values to the greater part of the letters.

In contrast to Virolleaud's empiricism the decipherment of Hans Bauer (1930) began with an ingenious piece of abstract reasoning. Setting out from the hypothesis, justified by the geographical location of Ugarit and the pattern of word-lengths already pointed out by Virolleaud, that the language would prove to be West Semitic (that is to say, closely akin to Phoenician and Hebrew), Bauer first tried to isolate the signs which appeared to be prefixes, suffixes, and the consonants of monosyllabic words. Beside them he set the phonemes to be expected in these positions on the assumption of a West Semitic language. A process of elimination should then, he hoped, produce some firm guide-lines. As can be seen from Ill. 73, two deductions emerged. The second was correct, but unfortunately for him the first was totally wrong, so that when he turned back to the texts he was worse off with his guides than Virolleaud had been without any. Taking up Virolleaud's original suggestion he made the same guess of the consonant *l* for the preposition at the beginning of the letter, and proceeded, like Virolleaud, to look for the word *mlk*, 'king'. It happened that his guide had given two alternatives for the consonant *m*, both of them false ones. He therefore chose the wrong word and derived from it two wrong values. This was to throw him badly out. But with his other, correct inference he searched for, and found, the word *bn*, 'son'. With the *b* of this he

71

72a

72b

a

b

c

72 Virolleaud's next steps in the decipherment of the Ugaritic alphabet. *a*, *mlk*, *mlkm* 'king', 'kings'. *b*, *b'l*, *b'lt*; *bt* 'Baal', 'Baalat'; 'house'/'daughter'. *c*, *šlš*, *šlšm* 'three', 'thirty'

	SIGNS observable in the Ugaritic documents	SOUNDS to be expected if the language is W. Semitic
Prefixes	[cuneiform signs]	' y m n t (and possibly also b h w k l)
Suffixes	[cuneiform signs]	h k m n t
Alone, making monosyllabic	[cuneiform signs]	l m (and possible also b k w)
A Common to all three classes	Very frequent: [cuneiform signs] — Less frequent:	w m — k
B Common to first two classes only	Very frequent: [cuneiform signs] — Less frequent: [cuneiform signs]	n t — k
THEREFORE from (A)	[sign] = *w* or *m*; [sign] = *m* or *w*	
from (B)	[sign] = *n* or *t*; [sign] = *t* or *n*	

73 Bauer's next steps in the decipherment of the Ugaritic alphabet

went on to find *B'l* in the same way as Virolleaud, and *B'lt*, the *t* of which was of course by now fixed from his second inference. He continued to identify further words and to allocate further letter values, but having set off with one foot lame he only got just over half-way.

The third of these almost simultaneous decipherments was by Édouard Dhorme (1930, 1931). Setting off from Virolleaud's starting-point he covered much the same ground but in a slightly different order. After reading a preliminary announcement by Bauer, in which Bauer had put forward his proposed transliteration of the word for 'axe', Dhorme changed course slightly. In fact Bauer's word was wrong (he read *grzn* instead of *ḫrṣn*), but at this stage it was the *n* and *r* that concerned Dhorme. They gave him *rbk.nm* for the owner of the axe, and *l rbk.nm* for the address of the letter on the tablet (whereas Bauer's alphabet had yielded

74 Dhorme's next steps in the decipherment of the Ugaritic alphabet

1. [cuneiform] = l (from Virolleaud (1929)
2. [cuneiform] = b' l = Baal
3. [cuneiform] = bn = 'son'
   [cuneiform] = bt = *bath* ('daughter') or *bayt* ('house')
4. [cuneiform] = m l k = 'king'
5. [cuneiform] = g r z n = 'axe' accepted from Bauer (4/6/1930) and step 3 retracted.
6. [cuneiform] could now be read   r b k . n m: but *rb khnm* would make sense as 'head of the priests', 'chief-priest'. Therefore [cuneiform] could be conjectured to stand for *h*.

120

	A	B	C	TRANSCRIPTION		
1.				g	t	m
2.				ṣ	p	b
3.				l	h	d
4.				z	a	w
5.				ḫ	n	y
6.				s	k	r
7.				u	i	ʾš
8.				ʿ	ġ	ṭ
9.				ḏ	q	ṭ
10.				š	z	ḥ

him an erroneous '*l rbwhnk*'). Dhorme saw that the word must be a title rather than a name and by guessing *h* for the missing value reached the satisfactory and correct interpretation of chief-priest (*rb khnm*, 'chief of the priests'). From this he progressed to further words and numerals, as Virolleaud had done, and was able to produce an alphabet of which the greater part of the values were correctly identified, and which he improved still further in a second article the next year.

At this stage there were still some characters with unallotted values in all three attempts; consecutive texts could not yet be read with confidence. But comparison of the published results, and above all an increased supply of texts from Schaeffer's continuing excavations, were soon to lead to complete decipherment.

The Ugaritic alphabet is of great interest not only for the literature it has revealed to us but also for its own sake as a writing system. The signary was evidently a conscious creation, founded on the principle of economy of strokes. This can be clearly seen if the characters are arranged by shape, as by Windfuhr. Moreover the underlying principle, alphabetic not syllabic, is unlike anything else in cuneiform. Was this too the result of independent inspiration? Such questions are tempting to ask, and normally they are unanswerable. This time, luckily, the answer was to hand. In November 1949 there was discovered at Ugarit a schoolboy tablet of the fourteenth century BC with the signs written on it in the ABC order of our own Phoenician-derived alphabet. Since an alphabetic order can hardly exist in a vacuum this can only mean that the Semitic alphabet already existed and was known in Ugarit.[5] So the Ugaritic cuneiform alphabet must have come into being as a practical compromise between two existing techniques and not as an abstract invention from nothing; it united the

75 Scheme of the Ugaritic alphabet by Windfuhr (1970)

phonetic efficiency of the alphabet with the graphic efficiency of cuneiform.

This still leaves the question of how the particular sound values were allocated to the particular sign-shapes. Here we are on more speculative ground, and there are only two certainties. One concerns the three signs of Windfuhr's seventh row. The sounds represented by them, *u*, *i*, and *s̀*, are not represented in the normal Phoenician alphabet, and moreover are placed at the end of the schoolboy abecedaria we possess. Their shapes do not fit naturally into the triple scheme of the signary. Therefore both from the phonetic and from the graphic point of view they must be later additions. The other certainty is that there is no relationship between sign-shapes and place in alphabetic order in the case of the other twenty-seven signs. The most straightforward explanation, though not readily susceptible of proof, is that the inventor tried to give the most easily made signs to the most frequently heard sounds.[6]

Our section on cuneiform may aptly close with an illustration of another one of the schoolboy ABCs more recently discovered at Ugarit, this time with the Akkadian key beside it. It is true that when it was found neither the decipherment of Akkadian, nor the decipherment of Ugaritic, nor the demonstration that our own alphabet was already in existence in the Bronze Age needed further confirmation. In a way this was a pity. Nothing could have provided it in a more convincing or more human form than this forgotten fragment of a school exercise of 3500 years ago.

76

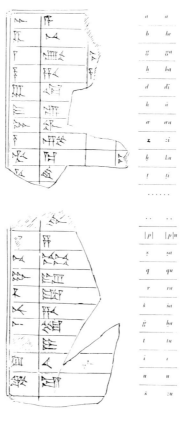

76 Drawing and transliteration by Virolleaud (1957) of a school tablet. The Ugaritic characters are arranged in alphabetic order with an Akkadian key. Fourteenth century BC

PART THREE **AEGEAN AND ANATOLIAN WRITING**

Chapter Six

The Cypriot Syllabary

The discovery of Cypriot writing

The great centres of literate civilization in the Near Eastern Bronze Age were Egypt and Mesopotamia. Egypt kept its writing system very much to itself. No other people, unless one counts the later inhabitants of Meroë, ever adopted it, and there is no firm evidence that any other writing system was ever influenced, let alone fathered, by Egyptian. On the other hand Mesopotamian cuneiform was, as we have seen, borrowed or adapted by a number of other neighbouring peoples in Syria, Asia Minor, and Persia.

But these two writing systems of the Near East, though they were the most important, were not the only ones. Other scripts were in use on the periphery of the cuneiform area (see map on pages 184/5). To the east there were the Proto-Elamite and Indus Valley scripts. These (both of which were extinct by the mid-second millennium or earlier) are not yet deciphered, and so do not concern us. To the west there was the Aegean family of scripts and Luvian Hieroglyphic, both perhaps descended from a common ancestor. It is the scripts of this group, particularly Cypriot, Luvian Hieroglyphic, and Mycenaean Linear B, which form the subject of this chapter and the next three.

The Cypriot syllabary was a script used in Cyprus between the seventh and the second century BC, with conscious conservatism it would seem, for writing the local Greek dialect on monuments and in the recording of legends on coins. It was also used for inscriptions in another language not yet understood, known as Eteocypriot. In addition there have been discovered writings of the Cypriot Bronze Age, known as Cypro-Minoan, which are presumably ancestral to it.

Luvian Hieroglyphic is known primarily from monumental rock-inscriptions and engravings on seals, found over a broad area of Asia Minor and north Syria, and varying in date from the middle of the second millennium to the seventh century BC.

Mycenaean Linear B has been found almost exclusively on clay accounting tablets baked hard by the fires which accompanied the destructions of the palaces of Knossos, Mycenae, Thebes, and Pylos where they were kept. The estimated dates of these destructions vary between about 1375 BC and 1100 BC, but since the keeping of accounts was obviously intended to serve the life of the palaces and not just to assist at their cremation, the writing system must have existed earlier than these dates. How much earlier there is no direct evidence to tell us.

77 Obverse and reverse of two of the Cypriot coins published by the Duc de Luynes in 1852

The first of these three scripts to be identified as a writing system was the Cypriot. The person responsible was the Duc de Luynes, a French collector and numismatist, whose monograph on the subject was published in 1852. It begins by drawing attention to two series of coins hitherto unassigned but represented in most Greek coin collections. Both series carried legends in an **77** unknown character.[1] Luynes observed that the character was not unique. It could be paralleled on a number of other coins known to have been found in Cyprus or on the neighbouring Turkish coast, by two or three inscriptions from Cyprus originally assumed to have been written in Phoenician, and above all on a large **78** inscribed bronze tablet found in Cyprus at Dali, the ancient Idalion, which he had bought in 1850 through an official of the French Consulate in Beirut. These varied inscriptions, all from the same area, indicated the existence of a distinctively Cypriot form of writing.

Luynes' attempt at deciphering this script was less successful than his identification of it. Largely on the basis of a gold coin of Menelaus, the brother of Ptolemy I, who was governor of Cyprus but had spent much of his tenure of office besieged in the town of Salamis by Demetrius Poliorketes, he assumed that a five-letter word on this coin and frequent on others must stand for the town, spelt in Phoenician manner SLAMS. Proceeding from this wrong assumption, following the will-o'-the-wisp of sign-recognition (he discerns 7 Phoenician, 12 Lycian, and 27 Egyptian characters in the 80 letters which he reckoned to be the total of the signary), and helping himself generously to would-be homophones (he makes 36 of the 80 letters duplicate the same sound-values), he reached the unconvincing conclusion that the language of Cyprus was Egyptian.

Others refused to follow him to this conclusion. But the Cypriot script having been recognized, Cyprus became one of the foremost centres of archaeological interest. The Comte de Vogüé led an excavating mission to the island and in 1862 found a brief biscript **79** on a tombstone, the Greek of which read simply, 'I am Karyx'. In his publication of it in 1868 Vogüé sensibly refrained from judgment, pointing out that there was no way of telling which of the five signs stood for the name Karyx, whether the *x* would take one sign or two, or whether the identification of the tomb as his would be signalled by a verb, a preposition, or a case-inflection.

The hope of decipherment was to be substantially increased in **80** the following year (1869) when a very much lengthier biscript in Cypriot and Phoenician was discovered at Idalion by Hamilton Lang.

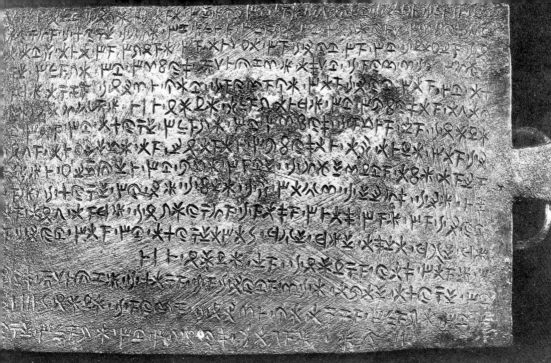

78 A contract between the city-state of Idalion and a family of physicians to secure free medical care for war casualties. Inscribed on bronze in the Cypriot script. Early fifth century BC. One side of the tablet with, *below*, the Duc de Luynes' drawing of the inscription on it

79 The top piece of a gravestone from Golgoi with an inscription in the Greek alphabet and the Cypriot script. Sixth century BC. (*Below, upper*) the drawing of the texts published by the Comte de Vogüé (1868); (*lower*) drawing by Masson (1961)

Hamilton Lang was the British consul at Larnaka, and in 1905 he published a lively account of his discoveries in Cyprus. It reads today like a compendium of archaeological vice, although its author betrays no feelings of guilt. What began his interest in antiquities was making a profit of over 1,000 per cent by compelling a peasant to part with a gold coin of Pythagoras I of Salamis for £5, and then selling it to a collector for £70. Later he was to do even better, filling five young men who had found a hoard of nine hundred gold staters with such fear of the authorities that they surrendered them for just over £1 apiece. He then sold all but a few to the British Museum at their proper valuation. From coins he progressed to the surface exploration of sites, then to their illegal excavation with workmen on a commission basis; for this purpose he chose a field near Dali where his foreman's son had found the upper part of a large statue, and which was, in fact, the site of an ancient temple. After a thousand pieces (stones, bronzes, terracottas) had been unearthed, there came the day of reckoning and a site conference to re-negotiate the terms. It was interrupted by a messenger from the Turkish Governor, who had come to arrange a date for a consultation on locust-control. Whereupon Lang pretended that the Governor was suspicious and was intending to inspect the field; the only solution, he insisted, was to move the statuary and everything else as quickly as possible to the privacy of his house in Larnaka. The frightened workmen did as they were told; but once the statues were in Lang's house the men had lost their bargaining power, and had to be satisfied with the minimum terms of the agreement.

The next year (1869) Lang bought the field (it cost him £30) with the intention of clearing it to a depth of nine feet, paying this time by the hour. No more statuary emerged, but instead there was a yield of two hoards of coins and several inscriptions – Phoenician, Greek, and the Phoenician-Cypriot biscript.

To the misdemeanours of profiteering, treasure-hunting, and illegal excavation, Lang now added that of concealment. The British Museum had advised him to let nobody copy his biscript. Nevertheless, after one scholar who had come from Constantinople especially to see it had spent what Lang considered too long a time in its presence, he denied the next visitor – the Comte de Vogüé – the opportunity to set eyes on it at all. Instead, he had an impression taken, which he sent to the British Museum, with whom he had begun to negotiate the sale of his collection.

Dispersal was his next sin. Having managed to sell a large statue to a passing Austrian admiral, Lang smuggled it on board his ship for him. Though he did not know what became of the statue, the act caused him no remorse when he looked back on it in 1905, remarking that 'the Turkish Museum would undoubtedly have been enriched by the statue except for this fortunate incident'.

Finally – illegal export. Lang laid out a number of small and comparatively valueless pieces of statuary along the quayside ready to be taken to the ship waiting in the roadstead. As soon as attempts were made to move them the customs watchman intervened. Lang's dragoman engaged him in a lengthy debate. Meanwhile the bulk of the collection, already prepared in Lang's house,

80 Inscription in Phoenician
and the Cypriot script on a
stone statue base from
Idalion, as drawn by
Hamilton Lang (1872).
Early fourth century BC

was secreted to boats and ferried out to the ship. This accomplished, Lang's dragoman yielded to the adamancy of the customs officer, and the minor statuary was carried back, with feigned regret, to Lang's house. Eventually, though the Chancellor of the Exchequer refused to make a special grant for the purchase, Lang achieved a satisfactory sale to the British Museum, and in 1905 was able after thirty years spent 'in the prosaic fields of administration and finance' to look back with nostalgia to the time when he had devoted himself to the 'old stones and ancient coins' of Cyprus in a pursuit where 'there was nothing sordid'.

Its decipherment

Lang presented his inscriptions to the world in a paper he read to the newly formed Society of Biblical Archaeology in London on 7 November 1871. He pointed out the weaknesses in the arguments of the Duc de Luynes, and made one important positive contribution of his own – that the five-syllable word which Luynes had wished to read as 'Salamis' should rather be the word for king. Lang's reasons were all good ones. First, the word was found on many different coins, which were therefore unlikely all to be of the same city. Second, it was invariably followed by another group but not always the same one: this was presumably the name of the king who issued the particular coin. Third, and most important, it was the only word to be repeated in the Greek text of the Idalion inscription, just as *mlk* was the only word repeated in the Phoenician text.

Lang's paper was followed by a paper on the reading of the inscriptions by George Smith, a cuneiformist of the British Museum, who had begun his career there as Rawlinson's assistant eleven years earlier. Smith put forward correct values for a number of signs (one or two of which had also been suggested by Lang) and a partially correct identification of the language. But his errors were too numerous for him to be given credit for the decipherment *tout simple*, as is sometimes done in England.

The first line of the Phoenician text in Lang's biscript contained three proper names and the word *mlk* for king repeated. Smith's first step was to try to locate these in the Cypriot. The first and last words were the same except for one character. Smith took this as the probable word for king, attributing the difference to case-inflection. He guessed the proper names correctly by their comparative lengths.

80

The next thing to do was to identify the values of the characters. The longest name, Milkyaton, had six characters in the Phoenician, seven in the Cypriot. The last of the seven was, however, very frequent at the ends of words, and Smith reckoned it must be a case-ending. He therefore gave the first six signs the values of the Phoenician letters *mlkitn*. The same character for *l* recurred in the word he had taken to stand for Idalion, though not in the same place. But the core of the word occurred several times on the bronze tablet of the Duc de Luynes. This enabled Smith to separate off the first character as the conjunction 'and', and the last two as inflectional endings. This left three characters, presumably a vowel, a *d*, and an *l*. In the Phoenician, however, the town-name was spelt with four letters, one of them being the vowel *yod*.

This led Smith to his next inference, which was perhaps his most important contribution to the decipherment. The vowel sound of *yod*, not being given a distinct character in the Cypriot must be 'represented by an inherent vowel in the preceding character'. 'This confirmed me', he writes, 'in an opinion I had long held, namely that the Cypriot system consisted of a syllabary, each consonant having about three forms, the whole number of characters amounting to between 50 and 60.' Though importantly wrong in detail – he should have said five forms – he was right in principle. This enabled him to explain why the character for *k* in Milkyaton was not to be found in the name of Kition: the two characters must have two different vowel values inherent in them. Here again Smith was right in principle, but went wrong in the detail. He gave them the values *ka* and *ki*: the correct ones were *ki* and *ke*.

It remained to read the word for king, already tentatively located by Lang. This is the most famous part of Smith's attempted decipherment, and the only one which yielded him values which were all substantially correct. This is how he describes it:

The other words I had to deal with were the two forms of the word king, the first of these is evidently, both from the reading of the equivalent Phoenician and from its position in the inscription, in the genitive case; now the difference between this word in the genitive and in the nominative, as seen by comparing the first and the last groups, is that the penultimate character is altered. On reviewing the words in neighbouring languages which have the meaning king, and comparing each with the conditions of the case, I came to the conclusion that the Cypriote word for king was *basileus*, the same as the Greek, and that the penultimate characters in the two forms of the word were the vowels *o* and *u*.[2]

The remainder of Lang's inscription (except for the name of Abdimelek) Smith found too mutilated to assist further progress, and he turned his attention to the coins, which he assumed would contain many proper names. He managed to identify three, Euagoras, Euelthon, and Stasioikos, transliterating them more or less rightly. But when he came to attempt the Luynes bronze tablet he found that he 'did not know a sufficient number of words to make out a fair reading of it'. He thought, however, that he could recognize some names – forms of Idalion and of 'Pythagoras' and 'Stasiagoras' – and the Phoenician first person pronoun *anuku*.

1.

לְמֶלֶךְ · מִלְכִיתן · מֶלֶךְ · כִּתִּי · וָאַדִיל
l i d A u . i t K . k l m . n t i k l M . k l m l
Idalium & Kitium king Melekyaton king of

· ⠶⠶ . ⠶⠶ . ⠶⠶
u -o -it -iK   s -un -at -i -ak -il -iM   s -o -el -is -ab
Kitium Melekyaton king of

⠶⠶ . ⠶⠶
s - u -el -is -ab   u -o -il -ad -E
king Idalium &

2. ⠶⠶ E-v-a-go-ra[s], *Evagoras.*
3. ⠶⠶ Pi-tu-a-go-ra-u, *Pythagoras.*
4. ⠶⠶ Sa-ta-si-a-go-ra-s, *Stasiagoras.*
5. ⠶⠶ Sa-ta-si-o-i-ku-u, *Stasioikos.*
6. ⠶⠶ E-v-i-l-ta-s, *Evelthon.*
7. ⠶⠶ A-pa-ti-mi-li-ku-u, *Abdamelek.*
8. ⠶⠶ A-nu-ku-u.

⠶⠶ E-da-li-o-u, *Edaliou.*
⠶⠶ E-da-li-e-i-s, *Edalieis.*
⠶⠶ E-da-li-e-i, *Edaliei.*

81 How George Smith attempted to decipher the Cypriot syllabary in 1871. *a*, section of Lang's bilingual (Phoenician text partly restored); *b*, names; *c*, case endings of 'Idalion'

Smith's harvest is given in the accompanying list. It contained some corn but even more weeds. The meaning of the biscript text is:

In the fourth year of the reign of Milkyaton, King of Kition and Idalion, on the last day of the five-day intercalation, Prince Baalrom, the son of Abdimilkon, set up this statue to Apollo Amyklos who granted him his prayer. For good fortune.

The nominative forms of the names should be Euagoras, Phil-kypros, Stasikypros, Stasioikos, Euelthon, Abdimilkon. The next word should be the Greek *anôgon* ('ordered'), not the Phoenician for 'myself'. On the forms derived from Idalion, Smith is almost correct, except for the case-ending of the first.

Thus even with regard to the proper names Smith's decipher-ment was at best approximate. He was unable to read any con-tinuous text, and indeed did not claim to have done so. Nor did he claim to have identified the language, beyond pointing out that the declensional forms seemed like Greek and Latin, and that the proper names seemed to be both Phoenician and Greek. Similarly against the Greek word *basileus*, Smith set his imagined word *anuku* as showing 'a Semitic element in the language', thus incidentally betraying a philosophy of linguistics that would have been more at home in the seventeenth or eighteenth century. His view of the structure of the syllabary was also incomplete, allowing for the full representation of only three instead of five vowels.

In general Smith's part in the decipherment of Cypriot is comparable to the part played by Grotefend in the decipherment of cuneiform. Like Grotefend he put forward correct values for just under a third of the characters. If we allow him credit for his approximation to a further nine values, his score will be higher. But of course Smith was faced with a far less formidable task.

This is evident from the speed with which Smith's partial decipherment was followed up. We need not delay over an attempt to interpret more of the texts on Smith's values made two months later by Samuel Birch, also of the British Museum. Instead we should cross the North Sea. The period was the golden age of German philology, and it was in the academic world of Germany that full success was achieved.

The first in the field was Brandis, a numismatist, whose paper was read to the Prussian Academy but who died before it appeared in print. His results were a decided improvement on those of Smith and Birch; even so, they remained on the hither side of decipherment. It is true that he added eight or so correct values and he made some sense of the conditions laid down in the last half of the contract recorded in the Luynes bronze tablet. But he missed its general purport and thought it was a deed of settlement. More important from the point of view of decipherment, at least twenty of his values were wrong; moreover he attempted to introduce a new and false principle into the structure of the syllabary by suggesting closed values of the type *-an*.

The true decipherment was achieved by Moriz Schmidt, the editor of the ancient Greek lexicon of Hesychius. Schmidt's book is unattractive, being cramped in lay-out and hand-written to boot. But in its argumentation it is a model of what a book should be, careful, systematic, and imaginative.

Schmidt began by reviewing the progress of the decipherment to date, accepting the Greek solution and finding that he could agree with twenty-eight of the proposed values, either in whole or in part, on the ground that they yielded Greek words or inflections satisfactorily spelt. He now focused on the spelling of the name Milkyaton, which is where Smith had begun, and in particular on its fourth character. This came in place of the Phoenician *yod* and could be expected to have a syllabic value rather than be a third homophone of *i* as Smith had assumed. Schmidt examined the other occurrences of the sign – fourteen in all – and observed that it always seemed to follow an *-i* vowel. So it was probable that the previous sign in Milkyaton's name was *ki*, not *ka* as Smith had thought.

This entailed reconsideration of the first sign of Kition, which Smith had naturally taken as being *ki*. Examining its other occurrences, Schmidt concluded that it should rather be *ke*.

82

83
82

78

So far Schmidt's method had been empirical, finding individual values to make plausible Greek words, though in a systematic manner. He now introduced an element of theory. He had accepted or established probable signs for *ka*, *ke*, *ki*, and *ko*. There should therefore be one for *ku*. Similarly for the vowel series. He had signs for *ti*, *ki*, *pi*, *li*, *mi*, *si*. There should be signs for *ni* and *ri*. He must have had in front of him, though he does not say so, a clearly drawn syllabic grid, showing the syllables already known with some confidence, and the gaps still to be filled. Filling each gap necessitated an initial guess, but the guess could be controlled by taking into account all the other occurrences of the sign under interrogation. For instance

> *sa–la–mi–XY–*
> *XY–ko–ta–PQ*
> *XY–ko–to–ro–se*
> *to–XY–to–i e–le–i*

Replacing the sign I have indicated as XY by the value *ni* (and, from a later argument, PQ by *mo*) Schmidt reached the following plausible Greek names and phrases:

Salamini(ôn)	'of the citizens of Salamis'
Nikodâmô	'of Nikodemos'
Nikodôros	'Nikodoros' (In fact the second sign, abraded on the original, was wrongly read. It should have been *ka* to make 'Nika(n)dros'.)
ton i(n) toi elei	'the (area) in the valley'

Those who know Greek but not its Cypriot form may like to measure their skill against Schmidt's by trying their hand at another series, remembering that the dialect is not Attic, that the article may be written together with its noun, and the other spelling conventions exemplified in the series we have just seen.

> *a–XY–to–li–se*
> *a–to–ro–XY–se*
> *to–se–ka–XY–se*
> *to–ka–XY–ne*
> *ka–XY–i*
> *to–a–XY–lo–ni*

The answer is given in the chapter notes.[3]

By methodically working through all the still-unidentified characters in this manner Schmidt succeeded in giving correct values to all but a very few signs and was able to offer a substantially correct and complete translation not only of Lang's biscript, but of other texts, including the Luynes bronze tablet, which was then and still is the longest known text in the Cypriot syllabary.

With Schmidt's work the decipherment of the Cypriot syllabary was virtually accomplished. There were still, not surprisingly, some improvements to be made and gaps to be filled. Two Strasbourg scholars, Deecke and Siegismund, had covered much of the same ground independently of him, but since Schmidt published first they were able to incorporate his conclusions as well as to put forward two or three new correct values of their own. In 1876 H. L. Ahrens, a leading expert in ancient Greek dialects, published a long review article in the journal *Philologus* giving his

82 (*Overleaf*) The stages in the decipherment of the Cypriot syllabary. In the transliterations of Schmidt, Deecke and Sigismund, and Masson the letters p, k, t are to be understood as 'labial', 'velar', 'dental' whether mute, voiced, or aspirated (for example ka=ka, ga, or kha)

Cypriot character	GEORGE SMITH 1871	JOHANN BRANDIS 1873	MORIZ SCHMIDT 1874	DEECKE & SIEGISMUND 1875	Cypriot character	MASSON 1961
✕	a	a 'mostly initial'	a	a	✕	a
✶	e (after Lang)	e	e	e	✶	e
✕	i	i	i	i	✕	i
⩊	o	o	o	o	⩊	o
Ƴ	u	u	u	u	Ƴ	ṳ
✕	a	a 'medial'	wa (?)	wa	✕	wa
I	i	ě	we	we	I	we
⅄<	i	i 'at word ends'	taken as a form of ✕	yi	⅄<	wi (first by Bergk in 1876)
↻	o	o	wo	wo	↻	wo
○	i	i/y	a following an i	ya	○	ya
					⋈	yo (first by Hogarth 1889)
≢	ba	ba/pa	pa	pa	≢	pa
⋝		-ek	pe	pe	⋝	pe
⋘	pi	pi/phi	pi	pi	⋘	pi
⌇	go	go	po	po	⌇	po
⩡	o (?)	na	pu (?)	pu	⩡	pu
⇡⇡	ka (?)	ka	ka	ka	⇡⇡	ka
⤧⤨	ki	ki/khi/gi	ke	ke	⤧⤨	ke
≋	ka	-k	ki	ki	≋	ki
⌒	ku	ko/kho	ko	ko	⌒	ko
✳	a	a 'medial'	ku	ku	✳	ku
⊦	da	ta/da	ta	ta	⊦	ta
↯		de/the/te	te	te	↯	te
↑	ti	t(i)	ti	ti	↑	ti
Ⅎ	ta	to/do	to	to	Ⅎ	to
Ⅲ	Ⅲ	an/on, sa (?)	tu (?)	tu	Ⅲ	tu
⩘		la	la	la	⩘	la

Cypriot character	GEORGE SMITH 1871	JOHANN BRANDIS 1873	MORIZ SCHMIDT 1874	DEECKE & SIEGISMUND 1875	Cypriot character	MASSON 1961
[sign]	le	le	le	le	[sign]	le
[sign]	li	li	li	li	[sign]	li
[sign]	tu	-l	lo	lo	[sign]	lo
[sign]	si (?)	ni/ne	wa (?)	lu	[sign]	lu
[sign]	pa, a (?)	g (i)	ma (?)	ma	[sign]	ma
[sign]		ou (?)	me	me	[sign]	me
[sign]	mi (after Lang)	mi	mi	mi	[sign]	mi
[sign]			mo	mo	[sign]	mo
[sign]				mu	[sign]	mu
[sign]	pe	pa, po/pho	na	na	[sign]	na
[sign]	u	u 'mostly final'	ne	ne	[sign]	ne
[sign]		ma/mo	ni	ni	[sign]	ni
[sign]	nu	no	no	no	[sign]	no
[sign]		en		ye	[sign]	nu (first by Deecke in 1881)
[sign]	lu (?)	l (o), -r (?)	ra	ra	[sign]	ra
[sign]	= 8 or ꞓ	= [sign]	re	re	[sign]	re
[sign]	ta (?)	di	ri	ri	[sign]	ri
[sign]		ra/ro, r	ro	ro	[sign]	ro
[sign]		i		ru	[sign]	ru
[sign]	sa	s	sa	sa	[sign]	sa
[sign]	final s	-s	se	se	[sign]	se
[sign]	si	si	si	si	[sign]	si
[sign]		so, s, os	so	so	[sign]	so
[sign]		en	su	su (from Schmidt)	[sign]	su
[sign]	? = [sign]	ga	ga	za	[sign]	za?
[sign]		o	o	?	[sign]	zo (first by Ahrens in 1876)
					[sign]	xa (first by Deecke in 1881)
[sign]	x	th or s	ss	xe	[sign]	xe

(a) BIRCH: vooddas depatitodou dekadekastes o-apax . . . dagathon danakto

BRANDIS: κατέστασε ὁ ἀβάθ... τὸ ἄγαλμα

SCHMIDT:
Τὸν ἀνδριάνταν τόνδε κατέστασε ὁ ϝα[?]νας... το[ι] ’Απόλλωνι
DEECKE & το[ι] ’Α-?-κόλωι
SIEGISMUND:
Τὸν ἀ[ν]δριά[ν]ταν τόνδε κατέστασε ὁ ϝάναξ... τῶ ’Απόλ[λ]ωνι τῶ
’Αμύκλῳ

(b) BIRCH: 'The ruler [Baalram] was giving an image, a tenth,
to the prince Ekatos.'

BRANDIS: 'The master [Baalram] erected . . . the statue . . .'.

SCHMIDT: 'Prince [Baalram] erected this statue to Apollo . . .'

DEECKE & SIEGISMUND: 'Prince [Baalram] erected this
statue to Apollo Amyclos'.

83 Stages in the interpretation of Lang's bilingual. *Above*, the part of the Cypriot text that, it was realized, was likely to contain the information (given in the Phoenician) that the statue had been dedicated to the god Reshef Mikal by Baalram, son of Abdimelech; *below*, how it was transcribed and translated by the early decipherers

approval to the results arrived at by Schmidt and by Deecke and Siegismund, and establishing the nature of the island's dialect. With this article the Cypriot script can be said to have passed from the sphere of speculation to that of science.[4]

Not that all the problems were solved. The Cypriot syllabary was not as precise a writing system as the Greek alphabet. For instance the Idalion bronze tablet begins, 'When [*hote*] the Medes were besieging [*katewORGON*] the city of Idalion . . .', but with a different alphabetic transliteration equally permissible by the rules of the syllabary it could run, 'Thus [*hôde*] did the Medes impose an oath on [*katewORKON*] the city of Idalion . . .'. Schmidt adopted the first, Deecke and Siegismund the second way. In this case context and linguistic probability are decisively in Schmidt's favour. But the answers are not always so clear, and there are still inscriptions in the Cypriot syllabary which have not been satisfactorily translated.

Another problem raised by the Cypriot syllabary was its origin. We have seen that the Duc de Luynes thought that this was mixed (7 Phoenician, 12 Lycian, 27 Egyptian signs). Hamilton Lang in his 1871 paper dismissed the Phoenician and Egyptian resemblances, but championed the Lycian, suggesting that the Lycians had originally possessed the same writing as the Cypriots, but had later grafted Greek letters on to it. The question was further complicated by the recognition in 1876 by Clermont-Ganneau that there was a group of Cypriot syllabary inscriptions written in a language other than Greek (these Eteocypriot inscriptions, as they are now called, are still not interpreted), and by the discovery in the seventies of the writing system now called Luvian Hiero-glyphic. This was thought by Sayce (1876) and others to be the origin of the Cypriot syllabary. Twenty years later Arthur Evans was to begin his discoveries of the scripts in use in Bronze Age Crete and to argue for their relationship with the Cypriot syl-labary. Finally, since the 1930s firm evidence has come to light of writing in Bronze Age Cyprus itself – the Cypro-Minoan script or scripts.

The interrelationship of these scripts (many of them scantily evidenced) with each other is still not clear, but interrelated they must have been and there can be no serious doubt that the Cypriot syllabary of classical times, instead of being the unique system that it originally appeared to be, was in fact the last descendant of a once more widely diffused family.

Chapter Seven

Luvian Hieroglyphic

The slow process of its decipherment

The Luvian (formerly known as the 'Hittite') Hieroglyphs and their decipherment are in almost complete contrast to Cypriot. The Cypriot syllabary was used in a limited area; the inscriptions in it are confined to a narrow period of time and are written in a dialect of a well-known language; the decipherment took less than twenty-five years and proceeded for the most part sequentially with each scholar building on the work of his predecessor. Luvian Hieroglyphic, on the other hand, is attested over a period of some eight hundred years from the middle of the second millennium to about 700 BC and through a wide area of Asia Minor and Syria. The language for which it was used was altogether unknown at the time of the first discovery of the script and was only recovered, from cuneiform texts, half a century later. The inscriptions came to light slowly, on a great number of separate occasions, and a great number of separate scholars contributed to their decipherment. Their investigations were in the nature of individual forays rather than of a combined operation, and the resulting picture grew imperceptibly, like a jig-saw puzzle being put together from various starting-points, in such a way that there was never a moment at which it could be said that it was now and for the first time clear. And as if to emphasize the exceptional nature of the decipherment of Luvian Hieroglyphic, the discovery of the only sizable bilingual text came not at the beginning but at the end and its main service to the decipherment was to confirm the results which had already been arrived at.

The blessing given to the Luvian Hieroglyphic decipherment by this, the Karatepe, bilingual can be considered as the epilogue of a three-act play. The first act began as far back as 1812, when the traveller Burckhardt, describing the Syrian town of Hama, or Hamath as it used to be spelled, on the Orontes, wrote: 'In the corners of a house in the Bazaar is a stone with a number of small figures and signs, which appear to be a kind of hieroglyphic writing, though it does not resemble that of Egypt.' This was before Champollion, and by hieroglyphic Burckhardt must have meant in the broad sense pictographic or ideographic (see Zoëga's definition of hieroglyphic on page 59). But his mention of the script was not accompanied by an illustration, and it stirred no immediate curiosity.

The first illustration of a Luvian Hieroglyphic inscription, and also one of the earliest archaeological photographs, was published

in Georges Perrot's account of his 1861 expedition to Asia Minor. It was a rock inscription near Boghaz-köy, consisting of ten lines, each almost 20 centimetres high and some 6·5 metres long. Perrot had no doubt that it was writing, and could therefore in theory be deciphered.

Ten years later detailed drawings of the Hama stones which had been described by Burckhardt were published in *Unexplored Syria* by Richard Burton (the famous Arabist and explorer) and Tyrwhitt Drake. These drawings, and other more accurate ones sponsored by the newly formed Palestine Exploration Society, opened the script for serious study.[1]

At first progress seemed rapid. In an essay on the inscriptions which he contributed to the Burton and Drake book, Hyde Clarke showed by the 'simple statistical method' of counting the signs that the inscriptions were genuine writing and not 'vagaries

84 The earliest photograph of a Luvian Hieroglyphic inscription on a rock face near Boghaz-köy. Perrot (1862)

85

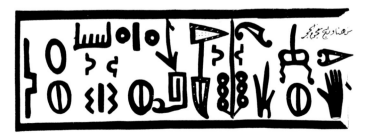

85 The Hama Stones Reproduction by Richard Burton (1872) of one of the inscriptions built into a shop wall in the Hama bazaar

137

of ornamentation'. There were about 300 characters in the text or texts, but only 59 different types. Moreover their distribution pattern – the most frequent character being used 27 times, the next most frequent 26, then 24, 21, 15, 11, 11, 9 and so on, finishing with 17 characters used once only – was of the kind which, according to Hyde Clarke, was to be expected of an alphabet (though he was prepared to allow it to include some punctuation signs or determinatives). To the best of my knowledge this is the first occurrence of such an argument in the history of undeciphered scripts. It is interesting for that reason, even though the manner of its use was rather unsophisticated.[2]

Four years later A. H. Sayce, a young Oxford scholar whose lifetime was to cover a major part of the history of the decipherment of the script, reviewed all the evidence available on the Hama inscriptions and concluded that the script was more likely to be a syllabary, though probably with an ideographic element as well. He deducted this from the lengths of the individual words as far as these could be judged, and the close similarity between the total number of signs (fifty-six on his count) and those of the recently deciphered Cypriot syllabary.

In the same article Sayce suggested that the inscriptions belonged to 'the great Hittite race'. This was a direct hit on the truth, though fired from an unlikely gun. Barnett calls Sayce's argument on the point a curious one. In fact it is not so much curious as antiquated, being the argument used by Sacy in his letter to Dr Young in 1816 (see page 65). Sayce begins by saying that the script of the Hama stones must have been hieroglyphic before it became syllabic, and continues, 'It is difficult to understand a hieroglyphic system of writing being invented by a people who spoke an inflexional language. The first requisite of such a system is that the same sound should represent different parts of speech . . . another that the grammatical terminations should be easily separable from the roots. . . . So in China, in Turanian Chaldaea [Sayce means Sumer], in Egypt, in Central America. . . . The probability is that the North Syrian inventors of these Hamathite characters did *not* speak a Semitic or inflectional tongue.' The Hittite people, whose existence was known from Greek and Biblical sources, seemed a suitable candidate for the vacancy. The Hittite language, which was to prove to be Indo-European and inflected, was at the time a completely unknown quantity.[3]

During the next few years further discoveries in Asia Minor, particularly that of Carchemish by George Smith, seemed to support Sayce's guess by showing the presence of a uniform art over a wide area of Anatolia, in most cases accompanied by inscriptions in the new hieroglyphic script. In a paper read to the Society for Biblical Archaeology in July 1880 Sayce set out what was known of the Hittite empire, its extent and history, and collected from Assyrian and other sources a tally of Hittite proper names, reaching a total of over a hundred. He also suggested that the script be no longer called Hamathite but Hittite Hieroglyphic, the name by which it was to be known until recently.

The only complaint against fortune that Sayce could make in his July paper was the lack of a bilingual to enable the script to be

86 Copy (much enlarged)
of the biscript known as
the 'Tarkondemos seal'

read. Even this lack was to be made good. A seal, in the form of an
embossed silver roundel the size and shape of half an orange, that   86
had been on the Smyrna market and subsequently published in a
German numismatic journal, was brought to Sayce's attention,
and he hoped that it would prove 'the Rosetta Stone of Hittite
decipherment'. Round its edge was a cuneiform legend which
Sayce transliterated *n Tar-rik-tim-me šar mat Er-me-e* and interpreted as, 'Tarkondêmos, King of the Land of Erme', Tarkondêmos being a Cilician name known from later Greek sources. It
was borne by a king of Cilicia at the end of the first century B C, and
there was a later Christian bishop of Cilicia called Tarkodimatos.
As for the Hittite Hieroglyphic part of the biscript, Sayce pointed
out that it was doubled, being written once on each side of the
central figure; he established the likely direction of reading (down
from the goat's head to the pointed triangles, and then upwards
again to finish with the four strokes and tang: thus the king's name
will appear to be coming from his mouth, the single and double
triangular signs will be the ideograms for 'king' and 'land' respectively, and the four strokes appended to the second sign and
independent as the last will in each case stand for the phonetic
value *me*), and proposed *tarku-timme* KING of-the-LAND
er-me as the reading of the whole.

But the inscription was too short to give a chance for a convincing decipherment.[4] It gave probable enough meanings for two
ideograms and one phonetic value (*me*), but Sayce's three other
identifications were too speculative to carry much weight. The

Sign	before 1931	Forrer 1931/2	1931	Gelb 1935	1942	before Karatepe bilingual	Laroche 1960	Morpurgo Davis/ Hawkins 1999	No.
	aʔ 1917 Cowley; a 1929 Meriggi	a	a				a/e	i	209
			ā	ā			difference from 209 uncertain	ia	210
				'a			á	á	19
				e			no significant function	a	450
	i 1892 Peiser; i 1893 Halevy; i 1917 Cowley; i 1929 Meriggi	i	wa	i			i	zi	376
			wā	ī			difference from 376 uncertain	za	377
			u				u (wa)	u	105
				he		ha 1934 Meriggi	ha	há	196
	hi 1912 Thompson	ha	hi	ha			ha/he	ha	215
							hi	hi	413
				hu			hu	hu	307
	ka 1894 Jensen; ka 1903 Sayce; ka 1923 Frank; ka 1929 Meriggi	ka	ka				ka	ka	434
				kc					
					ki		hù (ʔ)	kwi/a	329
			r.	ri		l. 1933 Meriggi	ki	ki	446
	ku 1912 Thompson	ku	ku				ku	ku	423
				la		la 1932 Bossert	la	la	175
	li 1912 Thompson	li	li				li	li	278
				le		là 1937 Meriggi	lá/lu (perhaps ll)	la/i/u	445
	ma 1912 Thompson; ma 1923 Frank; ma 1929 Meriggi	ma	ma				ma	ma	110
	me 1880 Sayce and all thereafter	mi	mi				mi/ma/m	mi	391
	mu 1917 Cowley	mu		mu			mu	mu	107
	n 1893 Sayce; n 1912 Thompson; n 1929 Meriggi	na		na			na	na	35
	n 1917 Cowley	n	n	ne		na 1933 Hrozny	ná	ní	214
				ni			nà/niʔ	ni	411
				nu		nu 1934 Meriggi	nu	nú	395
			ʔ	nu	ʔ	nú	nú	nu	153
	p 1917 Cowley	pi		pa		pa/ba 1932 Bossert	pa	pa	334
		ne	pi			pa 1933 Meriggi	pi	pi	66
					pu 1937		pu	pu	328
		ri		ra			ra/ri/-r	ra/i	383
		hi	ru			ru 1932 Bossert	ru	ru	412
	'affix' 1876 Sayce; es 1894 Jensen		si			sa 1932 Bossert	sa/s	sa	415
	s 1917 Cowley	si	sa				sá	si	174
	s 1894 Jensen and all thereafter	as	si				sa/s	sá	433
	s 1912 Thompson and all thereafter	sa		sc		si 1933 Meriggi	sà	sà	104
		sʔ		su			sa_4	sa_4	402
		si			la 1933 Hrozny	li 1933 Meriggi	sa_5	sa_3	327
		mi		lu	su 1950	lu 1933 Hrozny; lu 1934 Meriggi	su	su	370
	t 1917 Cowley			ta			ti/te/taʔ	ti	90
							tá	–	40
					za		tà	tà	41
		ta		ti			tá	tá	29
	ta	ta		te			ta_4	ta	100
		tu		kiʔ	zi		te/ti	ta_4	319
		te		keʔ	zc		tì	ta_5	172
	tu; tu; tu	ti		tu			tu	–	80/1
	tu 1903 Sayce; tu 1912 Thompson; tu 1929 Meriggi			piha 1953		tu 1937 Meriggi	tú	tú	325
	u/w 1920 Cowley	wa	i	wa			wa/wi	wa/i	439
							wa	wà/i	165
			w.	wc			wa_4	wa/i	207
				š		i 1933 Bossert	i	wa/î	335
								wa/i$_4$	

Tarkondemos seal was hardly a Rosetta Stone, and the realization of this may be said to mark the end of the first act, or honeymoon phase, of Hittite Hieroglyphic research.

The second act, which now began, lasted fifty years. It was characterized by a steady growth in the material available for study, and by the number of scholars, working for the most part independently of each other, who contributed interpretations and decipherments. The correct, and near-correct, proposals of syllabic values made during those years are shown in the table opposite. They are very few compared to the wrong guesses made. For instance Sayce in 1903 published phonetic values for sixty-five syllabic signs: only one or two were right. Many others did little better. It was not easy to separate the grain from so much chaff, but nevertheless, a small nucleus of agreed values gradually came into being.

Main events in this second act included a collected edition of the known inscriptions by L. Messerschmidt (1900–06: over forty sizable texts), and the discovery of the cuneiform archives of the Hittite capital in the excavations at Boghaz-köy by Hugo Winkler and Makridi-Bey in 1906–07 and 1911–12. The total number of tablets and fragments of tablets amounted to some twenty thousand. They were being worked on by Friedrich Hrozny, the Professor of Semitic Languages at the University of Vienna, when the First World War broke out and he had to return home. Nevertheless, he had copied enough to enable him to identify, in 1915, the language as a branch of Indo-European on the grounds both of vocabulary (for instance *wa-a-tar*, 'water') and inflection (for instance the present tense of the verb for 'I make', *i-ya-mi, i-ya-si, i-ya-zi, i-ya-u-e-ni, i-ya-at-te-ni, i-ya-an-zi*). The reading of the documents (which date to between 1450 and 1200 BC) presented no serious problem of decipherment since the great majority of the syllabic signs were used with their expected values. As a result the language of cuneiform Hittite came to be known with considerable certainty. Moreover in the Boghaz-köy documents there were occasional passages and quotations in other languages, one of which was the closely related dialect known as Luvian. This was to prove the language of the so-called Hittite Hieroglyphs.

The third act in the story of the decipherment can be said to have begun at a clearly defined point in time, the International Congress of Linguists held at Leiden in September 1931. At this congress two major, independent, papers were read on the subject of Hittite Hieroglyphic. One was by Emil Forrer, the other by Ignace Gelb. Forrer's interest was focused on the interpretation of the texts, and Gelb's on the structure of the script; but despite this difference of approach there was a substantial amount of agreement in their results, as can be seen in the table opposite.

The measure of this agreement and the fact that it had been reached independently was a most encouraging sign. The progress of the decipherment became quicker, with contributions being made from many quarters – see Ill. 88.

At last came the discovery of what had been so long hoped for, a substantial bilingual. It was made in 1947 by H. T. Bossert, then

87 Ignace J. Gelb, b. 1907

◁
88 The stages in the decipherment of the syllabary

141

a

b

89 Bilingual monument at the entrance-way to the hill-fortress at Karatepe. a, general view showing the panels with the Phoenician inscription; b, detail of the wall opposite, with Luvian Hieroglyphic inscription

Director of the Department of Near Eastern Studies at Istanbul University, in the excavation of an eighth-century hill fortress at Karatepe in eastern Cilicia. The biscript is in Luvian hieroglyphs and in Phoenician and occurs twice, on the sides of two of the entrance ways into the citadel. The author of the inscription is Azatiwatas, a local prince, and its purpose is to announce that he was the founder of the citadel and the bringer of security, peace, and prosperity to his countrymen.

The bilingual brought security to the decipherment too, in that the greater part of it was clearly confirmed. But some was erroneous, and unravelling error is notoriously more difficult than finding the right solution to begin with.

The credit for the reform, like that for the decipherment itself, belongs to no single person. Gelb and Bossert himself made initial suggestions, and the major work was done by Neumann, Hawkins, and Morpurgo-Davies. Ill. 88 shows the extent of the improvement. It mainly concerned two pairs of signs, ⋂ ⋒ and ↑ ⫯, but they are of frequent occurrence, and the effect of understanding them more accurately has been profound.

It began with new evidence. Pithoi excavated in 1969 carried a hieroglyphic inscription in which ↑, hitherto transliterated *i*, seemed to correspond with a cuneiform syllabogram that began with a sibilant (*s*, *š*, *s*, or *z*). Now the relationship between the four signs had always been a puzzle. Only the simple forms occur in the second millennium, or Empire, period. So what was the purpose of the innovation? Meriggi had thought it might indicate a long vowel, Gelb a nasal one. But if ↑ was after all not a pure vowel but a syllabogram of the normal CV type, then this opened a new possibility. Hawkins *et al.* (1974, pp. 155 ff.) showed that the double stroke distinguished the vowel, whereas in the early period the one sign served for both *(i)i* and *ia*, and the other for both *zi* and *za*.

The new values clear up many points both of vocabulary and of grammar. A simple layman's example is that the Luvian for sheep, which had previously been *hawas* (viz. *ha-wa-a-sa*) is now *hawis* (*ha-wa/i-i-sa*) with the same −*i* stem as its cousins, Greek οϛ, Latin *ovis*, and Sanskrit *avih*. Each such improvement is a small thing in itself, but their cumulative effect for the understanding of Luvian and its place in the Indo-European family of languages is great.

Decipherment techniques

We have now surveyed the history of the decipherment from its first beginnings to its present state. Let us now look at the techniques employed in it. An unknown language written in an unknown script with virtually no bilingual aid should by all the rules have been undecipherable. So how was it done?

First of all, as we have seen, there was never any serious doubt that it was a script, and very little doubt about what sort of a script it was – a syllabary with an ideographic element. Thus the case was very different from that presented by the Egyptian hieroglyphs. But, of course, it was the decipherment of them and of the cuneiform scripts and of the Cypriot syllabary, that made it possible to arrive so quickly at this basic conclusion.

Then there was the so-called 'Tarkondemos' seal. The value of this lay mainly in the corresponding confirmation it offered, though it also gave one plausible phonetic value and the meaning of two ideograms.

Third, the ideograms. It was these which contributed most to the decipherment. To a large extent they supplied the place that in other decipherments was filled by a bilingual. Thus the sign ⊕ was recognized by Sayce as indicating GOD as early as 1880, 'a solid starting-point for ascertaining the values and meanings of the Hittite Hieroglyphs'. His reasoning was that on the rock-carvings 'the divinities are all given their appropriate symbols, and Hittite characters are attached to each of them, evidently expressing their names. Each group of characters begins with the same hieroglyphic, which must therefore be the determinative prefix of divinity.' The use of this ideogram is illustrated below.[5]

a

b

90 Beginning of an inscription from Carchemish. The names of Carchemish (KAR-ka-mi-si-za-sa) TOWN

[symbols] and of Tarhunzas (DEITY STORMGOD – sa [symbols]) occur in each of the lines illustrated. *a*, photograph of the original; *b*, a squeeze reproduced by Hogarth in 1914

Another two ideograms, those for KING and COUNTRY, were given by the Tarkondemos seal. Later the ideogram for TOWN (which had at first been confused with that for KING [6]) was identified.

Now there were plenty of contemporary names for gods, kings, towns, and countries available in the cuneiform records. In theory these gave a hope of reading the sign-groups accompanying the ideograms that occurred in the texts. However there was still the formidable problem of finding the right group for the right name. Success was most likely with places. When a particular sign-group was unique to inscriptions from a particular site, and was always accompanied by the ideogram for TOWN, then it was a reasonable guess that the sign-group gave the town's name. Ill. 90 shows an example of such a group. It was unique to inscriptions from Carchemish, for which the most usual Assyrian spelling can be transliterated Karkameš. The identification, first made by Six and adopted by Jensen in 1894, was generally accepted thereafter, though the sound-values were not always allocated in the same way. Nevertheless, there could be no disputing the confirmation offered by the third sign for the *me/mi* of the Tarkondemos seal.

Another instance among many, this time assisted by the remarkable durability of Syrian place-names, was the allocation of the value *hi* to sign 413.[7] This was identified by its being the middle sign of a town-name on an inscription built into the wall of a church at Andaval. This was near the modern village of Nakida, whose name is spelt Naḥita in cuneiform Hittite texts.

However, as this sort of reasoning is inevitably somewhat precarious, mistakes were made. Cowley, a careful scholar, felt reasonably confident in 1917 about reading a sign-group found only at Marash as *murkaš* (the Assyrian name of the town being *markašu*). But in fact he was wrong, and Forrer was later to show that the name ought to be read Muwatallis, a king of Marash known from Assyrian and Hittite records.

The fourth tool was positional analysis. Experience with syllabaries, such as the Cypriot, had made it clear that frequent signs which occurred predominantly or uniquely at the beginning of sign-groups were likely to be pure vowels; this was the main argument for giving the value *a* to sign 209 (now read as *i*). But there are not many signs for pure vowels in a syllabic script, and so this particular argument is of limited utility. More useful on a wider field, but also more risky, is the argument from interchange. If the same word can be spelled in different ways (for example in English *enquiry, inquiry; synchronise, synchronize; inflexional, inflectional* in the passage quoted from Sayce on page 138), it is pretty well certain that the interchanging letters carry the same, or much the same, sound-value – provided of course that the word is the same. If not, there will be a disastrous mistake, and not even context is an infallible guide. For instance, 'the issue was debated' and 'the issue was debased' are both letter-sequences that may be found in English, but it does not follow from them that *s* and *t* are pronounced alike. During the course of the decipherment the interchange argument was used successfully several times (for instance, for the signs 19, 29, 41, 100, 103, 196, 207) and once or twice fallaciously (for instance, Gelb's initial assignment of *u* to sign 215).[7]

Finally, after the recovery of the Hittite and Luvian languages from the cuneiform archives of Boghaz-köy, it became possible to use language arguments to help the decipherment. Thus the Luvian enclitic word for 'and' (*ha*) gave Forrer the phonetic value *ha* for sign 215, the context of whose occurrences showed it to be used for writing such a particle, and the value was confirmed by its occurrence as a verb-ending (the first person singular of the Luvian past tense ends in -*ha*. However the values of *a* and *i* for signs 209 and 376 were thought to be confirmed by the frequent word beginning *aia*- interpreted as Luvian for 'make' (cf. Hittite *iya*-). This was dangerously misleading because when it became an orthodoxy it took courage as well as clear-sightedness to gainsay it.

These instances, which could of course be multiplied, may serve to give an idea of the principles on which the decipherment progressed. None of them was novel; none by itself led to a breakthrough. Indeed, as we saw at the beginning of the chapter, there never was any moment of breakthrough. The decipherment of Luvian Hieroglyphic was thus the least dramatic of all. What made it unique was the comparatively equal contributions made to it by so many different scholars and by means of so many different avenues of approach.

Finally the script. As it has come down to us it may seem less than genuine writing, used not for communication so much as for display on seals and on rock-inscriptions, which, as Laroche put it, are essentially seals writ large. However there do exist letters of the late period written on lead, and there are also accounting documents. Furthermore the script not only survived from the Bronze Age into the first millennium (as Mycenaean failed to do) but underwent improvement. The creation of 𝕝 and 𝕥 out of 𝕟 and ↑ is analogous to the way in which our own *u* and *v*, *j* and *i* were differentiated in modern times, and is not the kind of thing one would expect to happen in a script that was dying or being artificially preserved.

However die it did. If the main purpose of the hieroglyphs was to perpetuate the glory of local rulers they were sadly ineffectual. The Greek historian Herodotus, writing in the fifth century BC of a Luvian Hieroglyphic inscription in the Karabel pass, could mistake it for an Egyptian one. Worse than that, Homer, writing or singing at a time when the script may still have been in use and was certainly not long dead, makes his hero Achilles refer to rock-carvings near Smyrna as Niobe and her people turned to stone by Zeus. Neither the poet nor any of his subsequent commentators had any memory of the existence, let alone the meaning, of the Luvian Hieroglyphic writing.[8]

Chapter Eight

Evans and the Aegean Scripts

Early intimations of Cretan writing

The script of Mycenaean Linear B, which was to become the subject of the most dramatic decipherment since Champollion's, was discovered and identified together with two of its cognate Aegean scripts by Arthur Evans, the excavator of Knossos.

99

Evans had begun adult life as correspondent of the liberal newspaper, the *Manchester Guardian*, at Dubrovnik, the Balkans being then very much a centre of national liberation movements, but by the time his career becomes relevant to us he had made a name for himself as a numismatist and antiquary and was Keeper of the Ashmolean Museum in Oxford. In this capacity he had his attention drawn, in the early 1890s, to sealstones from the Aegean area engraved with unfamiliar characters of a hieroglyphic appearance. This made him interested in the possibility of the existence of an Aegean writing system, for his mind, he tells us, had for some time been exercised by the apparent contradiction between the high artistic and material level of the civilization unearthed by Schliemann and the lack of any evidence of literacy in the excavated sites.

91

What is surprising about this is not so much Evans' surprise as the form it took. One might have expected him to argue on the lines that the social organization needed to maintain a Mycenaean palace must have required written records or that the Mycenaeans could hardly have failed to acquire a technique of such convenience which was already in use in Egypt, Mesopotamia, and Syria. Instead he talks of 'Man before Writing', a concept that carries the implicit assumption that technological development is evolutionarily determined – as if there were a certain stage at which normal societies become literate just as there is a stage at which normal jaws grow teeth.

But though this evolutionary preconception was to have a strong influence on Evans' subsequent interpretation of the facts, it did not stop his objective and energetic pursuit of them. In Athens in 1893 he was able to buy a number of sealstones engraved with designs similar to those he had been shown in Oxford, and which were said to have come from Crete. The next year he travelled in the island, and purchased, or took casts of, many more. The stones, he found, were often still in use, being worn by women as milk-charms. By April 1894 he was already in a position to send a letter to the *Athenaeum*[1] narrating his discoveries and making most of the points he was to include in his first main article in the *Journal of*

91 'Was it possible that such masterpieces as the intarsia designs of the daggers from the Acropolis tombs at Mycenae, the intaglios of the signets, the living reliefs of the Vapheio vases, were the work of "Man before Writing"?' Evans (1909)

Hellenic Studies later in the year. In the article he published seventy-three sealstones, together with a number of potters' and masons' marks. The whole was enough to put the existence of some sort of Cretan Bronze Age writing beyond reasonable doubt.

Evans was not content just to publish the objects; his article contained a full discussion of the new writing in its historical and evolutionary perspective. Since Evans' views on Cretan writing were to carry more weight during the next fifty years than those of everybody else put together, we must look at their formative period with particular care.

The first sentence of the first article is a strange one. It invites us to keep our eyes on a fact for which it tells us there is no evidence. 'In the absence of abiding monuments the fact has generally been lost sight of, that throughout what is now the civilized European area there must once have existed systems of picture-writing such as still survive among the more primitive races of mankind.' All that remains now of these perished systems is the occasional pictograph painted or scratched on rock or megalithic monument in Denmark, Lapland, the Maritime Alps, and the Dalmatian coast. But 'if we had before us the articles of bark and hide and wood of early man in this quarter of the globe or could still see the tattoo marks on his skin we should have a very different idea of the part once played by picture-writing on European soil. As it is, it is right that imagination should supply the deficiency of existing evidence', particularly in the case of 'the great Thraco-Phrygian race' which inhabited south-east Europe. 'It is impossible indeed to suppose that this European population was so far below even the Red Indian stage of culture as not to have largely resorted to pictographs as an aid to memory and communication.'

Pictographs, then, according to Evans, were widely diffused. With them was diffused a readiness for writing proper. This matured first in the older civilization areas of Egypt, Babylonia, and China. Elsewhere 'the same development from the simple pictographic to the hieroglyphic or quasi-alphabetic might naturally be expected to have taken place in more than one European area had it not been cut short by the invasion of the fully-equipped Phoenician system of writing'. Indeed this maturation had already begun to take place in Anatolia and the Aegean, as is shown by Luvian Hieroglyphic and Cypriot. Some, but only some, of the Cretan signs show a striking resemblance to signs in one or other of these systems. This can 'best be explained by supposing that the systems had grown up in a more or less coterminous area out of still more primitive pictographic elements'. What could be more natural than that certain common features should have been preserved when each area 'began independently to develop' its share of the original substrate of pictographs into 'a more formalized hieroglyphic script'?

In this way Evans fitted his new Cretan writing very neatly on to his scheme of the evolution of human writing in general. But one more element was needed to complete the join. If writing was a sort of evolutionary process with an innate tendency to move from the pictographic towards the alphabetic, then the development should not have stopped dead but have continued within the body of Cretan writing itself. Evans thought that he could detect evidence for this continued growth. The script he had discovered seemed to him to be classifiable into three overlapping stages. The earliest of them, the pictographic (Ill. 92), 'often exhibits somewhat earlier versions of the same designs that reappear among the "hieroglyphs" of the later class'. The 'hieroglyphs' (Ill. 93) were conventionalized, almost linear, signs selected from the repertoire of pictographs, and amounted in total to some eighty-two characters. The 'linear signs' (Ill. 94), which were sometimes the same as the 'hieroglyphs', numbered thirty-

92–95

92–95 The evolution of
Cretan writing as conceived
by Evans in 1894.
92, genuine pictographic: a
sealstone whose 'owner
was evidently a master of
flocks and herds'. Steatite.
From Praesos.
93, conventionalized
pictographs or
'hieroglyphs'. Carnelian.
From eastern Crete. 94, the
signs further reduced to
'linear symbols'. Blocks
from the (then still
unexcavated) palace of
Knossos. 95, these different
stages on a single stone.
Steatite. From Siteia
province.

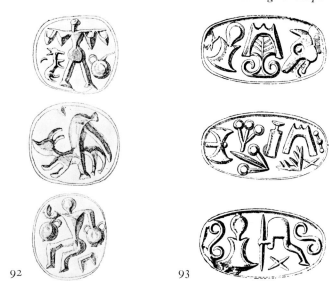

92

93

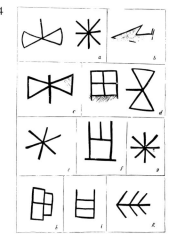

94

95

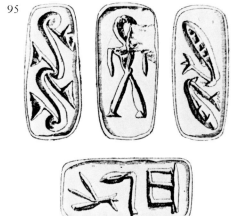

two on twelve inscriptions, including sealstones, vase graffiti,
potters' and masons' marks. All classes might be represented on a
single stone – for an example see Ill. 95, where the purely decora-
tive signs on faces *a* and *c* showed up the significant nature of the
others, the figure on face *b* (though analogous to the pictographic
sign on Ill. 92) was so conventionally drawn as to be considered
a 'hieroglyph', and face *d* contained three signs of which the two
on the left were purely linear while the one on the right belonged
to both the hieroglyphic and the linear class.

It is clear from this how very subjective were Evans' criteria for
distinguishing his three classes of sign. The difference between a
pictograph and a hieroglyph depended on how conventionalized
he considered the picture to be. The difference between a 'hieroglyphic' and a 'linear sign' depended on whether he could recognize
a picture in it.[2]

The subjectiveness of his criteria was to lead him into difficulties.
Further travels in Crete brought him more material, including the

96 Libation table from the
Dictaean Cave with an
inscription in 'the
prae-Phoenician script of
Crete'. Drawn by Evans
(1897)

97

first inscription in the script that was later to be distinguished as
Linear A. Publishing these in 1897 (and attributing the far too
early date of 2000 B C to the Linear A inscribed libation table) Evans
had second thoughts both on the independence of Cretan writing
and on the direction in which it had evolved. Evidence for pre-
dynastic Egyptian writing gave 'some warrant for inferring that
the proto-Egyptians were ahead of the Aegean peoples in the
evolution of their Aegean script'. The latter may therefore have
been 'partly derived' from Egypt. Evans was looking at the signs
on the libation table as if they were items in a museum rather than
as constituent members of a coherent system, comparing them
with his Cretan 'linear' or 'pictographic', with Egyptian, Libyan,
Cypriot, Semitic, and even with early Greek letters. But he did
not go the whole way along this road. 'That the Cretan linear
forms are wholly of exotic origin it is impossible to believe. Simple
as these signs are, and early as they appear, we are entitled by all
analogy to suppose that the linear characters are themselves only
the worn survivals of a primitive system of picture-writing, in
which, like the first drawings of a child on a slate, various objects
are depicted by a series of lines.'

   This view of primitive pictures is decidedly different from that
taken in his 1894 article. He had begun to feel that 'the linear
characters of the Cretan and Aegean scripts go back to a very early
period and may be rather derived from the primitive school of
engraving in which the objects are indicated by mere lines, like
the first drawings of a child on a slate, than from the more developed
pictographic style. The conventional script [that is what in 1894 he
had called the 'hieroglyphic'] derived from this more advanced
style must therefore in the main be regarded as parallel with the
linear characters rather than as their immediate source.' On this
ground he now decided that the seal shown in Ill. 95 pre-dated

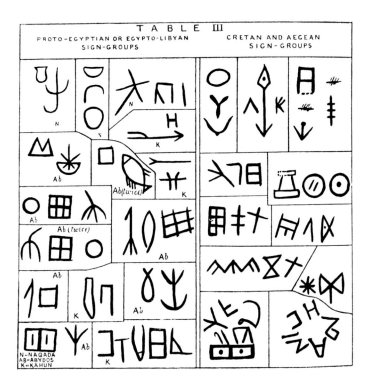

TABLE III

PROTO-EGYPTIAN OR EGYPTO-LIBYAN SIGN-GROUPS	CRETAN AND AEGEAN SIGN-GROUPS

97 Far-flung comparisons. Evans (1897)

the evolution of the conventionalized pictographic or 'hiero-glyphic' class, saying that it 'illustrates the fact that linear signs had already been evolved from linear drawings in this primitive period'. Moreover the direction of sign evolution might be reversed. In 1894 Evans had illustrated the theoretical degradation of an eye into a circle. In 1897 he envisaged development in the opposite direction. 'A wholesale revival of the pictographic style . . . took place in Crete during the Mycenaean period. . . . The linear figures assume a more realistic aspect in keeping with an age in which the engraver's art and the artistic sense were more highly developed. . . . A mere circle completes itself as the human eye. The upright and cross lines that seem to have stood for a tree take again a more vegetable shape. . . .' It should be stressed that at this date Evans had no evidence other than stylistic for dating his material. His argument therefore was to a large extent circular.

98

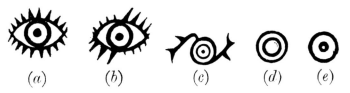

(a)   (b)   (c)   (d)   (e)

98 Sign-evolution – but in which direction? From Evans (1894)

Excavation and speculation

What Evans wanted was evidence from excavation, and he was soon to get it. The site of Knossos, the great city in Crete where Homer tells us Minos ruled, had long been known. To excavate it had been among Schliemann's plans, but Schliemann had died before he could realize it. Evans staked his claim to the site in 1894, during his first visit to the island, by buying a quarter-share in the land from one of the Moslem brothers who owned it. With the liberation of the island from Turkish rule and its establishment as an independent republic, he acquired the whole. Excavation began with the new century. Within a week he had found the first fragment of a tablet, and a few days later on 5 April 1900 'an entire hoard of these clay documents, many of them perfect, was discovered amidst a deposit of charred wood in a bath-shaped receptacle of terracotta set close against the wall' (Evans 1900, p. 18). He at once sent a description of the discovery together with a drawing of one of the tablets to the *Athenaeum* under the title 'The Palace Archives of Mycenaean Cnossus'. At the time he naturally thought that what he was discovering was another Mycenaean palace: only later did he realize that Cretan civilization was earlier and distinct, and coined the word Minoan to describe it.

100

Many more of these tablets and also a deposit of the 'Hieroglyphic Class' were to be found in the next few weeks. When he published his account of the season's work in the *Annual of the British School at Athens* for that year, Evans still maintained his 1897 view that the 'hieroglyphic class' represented a later development. Indeed, he thought it was supported by the stratification of the respective deposits. The new inscriptions enabled him to expand his list of 'hieroglyphic' signs to over a hundred. Surveying it in the light of the tablets in the 'linear' script which he had discovered, he was able to make the still valid observation that 'although a small proportion of the signs of the hieroglyphic Cretan series are common to the linear group, as a whole it contains surprisingly few common elements and clearly represents an independent system'.

100, 101

He assigned the script of the tablets to his previously determined 'linear' category, and made about it a large number of remarks which have stood the test of time. Among them were the left-to-right direction of the writing, the decimal system of numeration, the existence of ideograms and of metric signs, the word-divider, the nature and number of the syllabic signs (about seventy in common use). Where Evans was weakest was on the sign-forms. Eager as ever to detect their evolutionary origins he saw among them 'the human head and neck, the hand, the crossed arms, a pointed cup, a bird flying, three- or four-barred gates, a fence, a high-backed throne, a tree, and a leaf'. This is a perilous type of argument as one can see if one imagines a future anthropologist using it to analyze the script of our own motor-car culture: he could identify symbols derived from the wheel (O), the spring (C), the gear-lever gate (H), a popular cylinder-arrangement (V) and so forth. The identifications would lend support to each other and it would not be easy to prove him wrong without a knowledge of the prior history of the letter-forms. In the case of the Cretan script such knowledge was, and still is, lacking.

But though Evans believed that he could detect the ultimate pictorial origins of a number of signs, he felt that the script as a whole belonged to an advanced stage. 'The letters are of free up-right "European" aspect, far more advanced in type than the cuneiform characters. They are equally ahead of the Egyptian hieroglyphs.'[3]

The reader will have noticed that so far Evans has talked simply

99 Sir Arthur Evans,
1851–1941

100 The first publication of a
Linear B tablet. From Evans'
dispatch in *The Athenaeum*,
18 May 1900

The tablets themselves are oblong slips of hand-moulded clay, flat on the engraved side, with almost adze-like ends, but thickening towards the centre of the back. They vary in length from about two to nearly seven inches, and in breadth from a half to three inches. As in the case of the Chaldæan tablets, lines are ruled at intervals for the convenience of the scribes, and one of the largest examples shows eighteen of these, a certain proportion of them left blank. The most usual type consists of two lines, or even a single line of inscription, written from left to right lengthwise along the tablet, but some of the broader tablets have the lines arranged across their narrower diameter. The subjoined copy reproduces a good specimen of this latter class.

101 'Letters of a free,
upright, European aspect' –
the first photograph of a
Linear B tablet, published by
Evans in 1900

of 'the linear script' or 'the advanced linear script'. But in 1902 the Italian archaeologist Halbherr discovered a large number of very different-looking tablets at Hagia Triada in the south of the island; and in the year after, at Knossos, Evans himself found similar inscriptions in the 'Temple Repository' datable to an earlier period than the other tablets. As a result Evans now divided his linear system into two classes, 'A' for the script found in the Temple Repository, on the libation table, at Hagia Triada, and at some other sites in Crete, 'B' for the main deposits of clay tablets at Knossos. The two scripts shared 'a large common element', but the distinguishing features, though minor (e.g. different forms of what was evidently the same sign; some signs present in the one and absent in the other; the alternative use of dots as well as dashes for 'tens' in Linear A), were regular and consistent. Evans concluded that Linear B, though attested in a later stratification at Knossos, was 'fundamentally a parallel rather than a derivative system . . . of more or less equal antiquity' which had come to the fore at Knossos in the latest Palace period at the expense of the other, 'owing to some political change' (1903, p. 53).

In the same year Evans found cause to reassess his dating of the Knossos 'hieroglyphic' documents and to assign them to a period earlier than that of the linear scripts (1903, p. 20).

Evans' classification of the scripts he had found into three types, namely 'hieroglyphic' or 'conventionalized pictographic', 'Linear Script of Class A', and 'Linear Script of Class B', has stood the test of time and is still employed. It was no inconsiderable achievement.

The flaw in his thinking about the scripts was, as I have indicated above, his desire to see a significance in the form of each individual sign and to trace their origin back to a hypothetical seed-bed of very primitive picture-writing. Evans continued to take this seriously, and devoted the whole of the first of his three lectures delivered to the Royal Institute in 1903 to its elaboration. These lectures, only published in note form (Evans 1903 *b*), began with the astonishing headings:

Articulate language of relatively late development
This fact increases importance of pictorial records in primitive times
Man drew before he talked

These ideas are expanded in an essay Evans wrote for R. R. Marett's book *Anthropology and the Classics* (1908). After some lyrical praise of the fine features of the men of the 'proto-European race', akin to the men of Cro-Magnon who were responsible for the art of the Reindeer Period, he asks whether, in addition to the gestures attested in Reindeer Art, they had also a fully developed speech. His answer is that they may not have had. For in North America there are more than sixty language families, each with up to twenty distinct languages, yet there is a unity of race and a unity of gesture-language. 'Is it conceivable', he asks, 'if the original forefathers of these tribes had brought with them a fully developed articulate speech that the languages of their descendants should be so radically different?' The example of deaf mutes among other things shows the baselessness of the idea that 'oral language is necessary for the expression of abstract ideas', and it is therefore quite possible that men drew before they talked.

We can see too in this essay that Evans, despite his 1903 re-dating of the Cretan 'conventionalized pictographic' at Knossos had not abandoned his 1897 ideas of evolution. He still stresses the possibility of its proceeding in either direction. Picture may give way to Linear ('degeneration', 'stylization', 'linearization'); but there also exists a less generally recognized process of 'elaboration', in which, starting with the 'slate-pencil style' of children, line gives way to picture. 'Art begins with skeletons, and it is only a gradual proficiency that clothes them with flesh and blood.'

Finally these contradictory concepts of evolution are reconciled in a remarkable passage of Romantic Anthropology, all the more remarkable for being inspired by the prosaic problem of the development of the alphabet.

It is strange indeed that in the very infancy of its art mankind should have produced the elemental figures which the most perfected alphabetic systems have simply repeated. The elements of advanced writing were indeed there, but the time had not yet come when their real value could be recognized. It has only been after the lapse of whole aeons of time, through the gradual decay and conventionalization of a much more elaborate pictography, that civilized mankind reverted to these 'beggarly elements', and literature was born. Yet it is well to remember that the pre-existence of this old family of linear figures, and their survival or re-birth, the world over, as simple signs or marks, were always at hand to exercise a formative influence. There may well have been a tendency for the decayed elements of pictographic or hieroglyphic writing to associate themselves with such standard linear types.

Evans' final views

I have quoted at length from these lesser-known passages of Evans' philosophy of writing, partly for their own intrinsic interest, partly because they illustrate a way of thinking then fashionable and still alive, and partly because Evans himself took them seriously. Unless we suppose that his theorizing was just an irrelevant foible or disease of the mind, we must suppose that it somehow affected his more practical and empirical work on the problems of the script. I prefer the latter supposition and would see the manifestation of his theory in the strange inability he always exhibited to accept the consequences of his conclusion that the seventy or so most common signs of the 'advanced linear scripts' were syllabic. He had reached this conclusion in 1900 and did not subsequently retract it. But he could never rid himself of a belief in the simultaneous importance of the assumed pictorial origin of the signs. For instance, he thought that the sign now deciphered by Ventris as *a* represented a double-axe and had a religious connotation in the inscriptions where it occurred; and that the sign now deciphered by Ventris as *o* depicted a throne and was a symbol of dominion, or at any rate of royal lineage, in the names where it occurred as a phonetic sign.[4] This confusion was obviously a major barrier to his own prospects of success in decipherment. Moreover it helps to explain, and even to excuse, his delay in publishing. For though his main discoveries of the Linear B tablets were made between 1900 and 1904, Evans had still not published them when he died forty years later, nor did he allow anyone else to do so. This has generally been considered a possessiveness hard to forgive, and so perhaps in part it was. But it is made understandable by the nature of Evans' general theory. This implied that the writing system of the tablets was not an isolated technical problem which could be usefully worked on piecemeal by others, but an integral part of Minoan civilization, only intelligible in the light of the whole body of the archaeological evidence.

However this may be, Evans' plan was that he should publish the documents himself under the title *Scripta Minoa*, and the first volume of the series, the only one to be completed in Evans' lifetime, was issued in 1909. Its subject was the 'hieroglyphic' or 'conventionalized pictographic' script, though Evans was tempted by the recent discovery of the Phaistos Disk into a long digression on its unique (and still undeciphered) writing. *Scripta Minoa I* is an admirably full publication, giving photographs and drawings of each document and a detailed discussion of each of the 135 signs that Evans now identified in the script, but in the way of general theory it contained nothing new, merely re-stating the ideas that Evans had already put forward elsewhere.

After this the *Scripta Minoa* project seems to have yielded its priority in Evans' mind to that of the more general *Palace of Minos* (4 vols. 1921–35). Nevertheless, he did not altogether cease to think about the problems of Minoan writing; aspects of the subject come up for discussion several times in the *Palace of Minos*, particularly in the first and last volumes.

The first volume (1921) contains an important section on 'Linear Script A and its Sacral Usage'. Here Evans observed that whereas the Linear B script was almost exclusively attested on clay tablets, the script of Class A was employed also for inscriptions on other objects, most, if not all, of which were of a religious nature. This observation is still valid. He also pointed out various more detailed differences between the scripts, for instance the greater fondness of Linear A for ligatured signs. He settled its numeral system and tabulated its signary. But he made no attempt to analyse the structure of the sign-groups which he regarded as phonetic.

In regard to the 'hieroglyphic' script the volume contained only one addition of significant theoretical import. This was an instance 102 of how he supposed the ideographic element of the script to work. It is a clay sealing, equivalent to a piece of used sealing-wax in the world of a few generations ago. The impression on it is that of a

102 *Export oil* was Evans' tentative interpretation of this sealing (OLIVE SPRAY + SHIP)

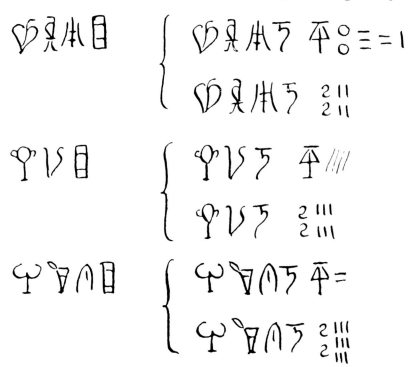

103 Linear B inflection
recognized by Evans in 1935

sealstone carved with an olive-spray and a ship. Evans interprets
the whole as a sort of label meaning 'export oil'. But it is an isolated,
almost random, interpretation. Before accepting it one would
have to see it related systematically to other evidence. It would
have to be shown that there were other sealstones which looked
as if they identified classes of document rather than individual
owners, and plausible explanations of their commercial use
would have to be given. But Evans did not attempt any of this.

However, in his final discussion of the scripts in the fourth
volume of the *Palace of Minos* (1935), Evans, now over eighty years
old, was to take some preliminary steps in the sort of internal
analysis that was later to prove so fruitful in the hands of Alice
Kober and Michael Ventris. The ideas of it may have been suggested by Cowley, for in the interim period in a volume of essays
presented to Evans on the occasion of his seventy-fifth birthday
Cowley had contributed some extremely well-reasoned remarks
on the subject of Linear B. He observed that if one looked at the
later, but almost certainly related, Cypriot syllabary one could see
six signs that were practically identical in form to Linear B
characters. In Cypriot these stood for the sign-values *ta, to, lo, pa, u,
se*. The obvious thing to hope was that these signs carried the same
values in the Knossos script as well as having the same shapes. The
question was, how could one find out. Cowley thought he had
found a way. A long tablet, a copy of which had been given to him
by Evans, appeared, from the way in which each listed item was
followed by a particular determinative and the figure '1', to be a
list of men's names. If the sign-groups preceding each determinative
carried syllabic values, as was generally believed, and if the language

104 Linear B sign-groups
for 'boy' and 'girl'
recognized by Cowley in
1927

was an inflected one, then it was reasonable to suppose that many of the final syllables in the listed names would share the same vowel. Now eleven of the sixty-four names ended with the sign that had the same form as the Cypriot *lo*, and an equal number ended with the sign that looked like the Cypriot *to* (and eleven more with what Cowley thought might be the Cypriot *po*). So it seemed that a significant proportion of men's names ended in *-o*. If so, then the language was probably an inflected one in which terminations were significant, and the signary was close enough to the Cypriot for useful comparisons to be made. This was a most ingenious argument.

Another proposal made by Cowley in the same article was that two groups which occur in a tablet listing women might stand for 'boy' and 'girl'. Cowley suggested two ways in which the signs might bear this meaning. Either they could be ideographic, in which case the first would mean CHILD and the second MALE or FEMALE respectively; or they could be syllabic 'as if κοῦρος and κούρη' (Greek words for 'boy' and 'girl'). Cowley preferred the first alternative, but it was the second which was confirmed by Ventris' decipherment, though with the sexes reversed and some important differences of spelling (see page 174).

In 1935 Evans accepted Cowley's interpretation of 'boy' and 'girl', and followed up his suggestions on the terminations of male and female names by bringing into consideration a wider range of material. His conclusion was that 'an examination of the names followed respectively by the male and female figures showed that in each case there was a preponderance of particular terminal signs.' He also pointed out the frequent alternation of the signs ⧈ and ⧧ at the end of otherwise identical sign-groups, commenting 'We have here, surely, good evidence of declension.' He was quite right.

It is pleasant to reflect that Evans, who had discovered and classified the Minoan scripts, and who had spent so much of his life and fortune in pursuit of Minoan facts, succeeded at last in pointing to the path that was to lead to Ventris' decipherment.[5]

105
104

103

105 Linear tablet apparently listing women. From Evans (1935)

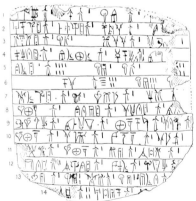

Chapter Nine
Kober, Ventris, and Linear B

Alice Kober

Though the only example recounted in this book of a decipherment which is not yet absolutely certain, that of Linear B is unquestionably the most brilliant considered purely as an intellectual feat. To understand it we shall have to go into rather more technical detail than we have had to with the others, and at rather greater length.

The credit for its accomplishment belongs to Michael Ventris, and the path to it was, as we have seen, pointed out by Evans, aided by Cowley. But the first and most difficult steps along that path were taken by an American, Alice Kober. It was one thing to suggest that the writing on the Linear B tablets might conceal an inflected language. It was quite another to establish definite patterns of inflection. This is what Miss Kober did. Her work on the script is contained in a series of firm and penetrating articles which appeared from 1943 to 1950.

Let us start with her survey article 'The Minoan Scripts: Fact and Theory', published in 1948. In it she set out what was known of the various Aegean scripts,[1] argued that Linear B almost certainly represented a different language from Linear A (since it had a different word for 'total' and a number of inflectional patterns lacking in A), and concluded that because of the presence of this inflectional evidence as well as the greater quantity of known texts and their more homogeneous nature, the Linear B script offered the better prospect for decipherment. Not that the prospect was encouraging. 'Let us face the facts. An unknown language written in an unknown script cannot be deciphered, bilingual or no bilingual. It is our task to find out what the language was, or what the phonetic values of the signs were, and so remove one of the unknowns. . . If, as seems probable, the language of Linear B was highly inflected, it should be possible to work out some of the inflection patterns. Once this is done two possibilities exist. The inflection pattern may prove a clue to the language or to the language group. In that case we have a more or less known language written in an unknown script. . . . Or the inflection patterns . . . may give information about the phonetic relationship of the signs. . . . In that case we should have an unknown language written in a more or less known script.' In theory, therefore, there was hope. But in practice very little advance had been made towards its realization. The preliminary work had not been done. How could the signs be deciphered when it was not known how many were used with

a

	(a)	(b)	(c)
Case I	𐀀	𐀀	𐀀
Case II	𐀀	𐀀	
Case III	𐀀	𐀀	𐀀
?			𐀀

b

Case I	Case II	Case III
𐀀	𐀀	𐀀
𐀀	𐀀	𐀀
𐀀		𐀀
	𐀀	𐀀

106 Examples of Alice Kober's analyses of Linear B made in 1946. *a*, sign-groups that may represent the same words in different forms; *b*, the three 'cases' identified; *c*, partial paradigms for a second type of noun

c

1	2	3
𐀀	𐀀	
𐀀	𐀀	
𐀀		𐀀
𐀀		𐀀

phonetic significance, or which these were? And this information was still lacking for all the Minoan scripts.

In a previous article in 1945 Miss Kober had assessed the difficulties of discovering inflectional patterns in a syllabic script. 'If a language has inflection, certain signs are bound to appear over and over again in certain positions of the written words, as prefixes, suffixes, or infixes. No matter how much these changes may be obscured (. . . and with syllabaries they are bound to be obscured . . .), the fact that they occur regularly must reveal them if the amount of material available for analysis is large enough, and the analysis sufficiently intensive.' But caution was needed. For instance the written words berry/merry, heavy/heaven would, if English were an unknown language, look like indications of inflection, which they are not. So similarity or identity of context are essential controls. On the other hand words genuinely inflected from the same stem, such as the Latin fecit ('he did'), fecerunt ('they did'), might be scarcely detectable. On a Cypriot-type open syllabary the only common sign in these two forms would be the first, the sign for *fe*. The problem would be how one could find out that the quite different-looking signs for *ci* and *ce* shared the same consonant. One would need a number of instances of the final signs or sign-groups (those for *t* and *runt*) interchanging in other words. Only then could one be confident that the forms *fe-XY-t* and *fe-PQ-runt* belonged to the same word. Consider again the Latin alphabetic spelling avus ('grandfather'), atavus ('forefather'), where the *at* is clearly seen as a prefix. In a syllabically written script, what would appear would be a false infix *ta*: a–vus, a–ta–vus.

These considerations seem simple enough. But somehow it is difficult to hold in the mind the true relationship between language and writing. Unsuspecting people, asked how normal plurals are formed in the English language, will generally reply that they are formed by adding an 's'. A moment's reflection will show that this cannot be right. If by 'an "s"' is meant 'the written letter "s"', then the answer fails because a language has nothing to do with the written signs that may be used to represent it. On the other hand if 'an "s"' means the sound of an 's', then this is the way to form certain feminines (poet, poetess), never plurals. The proper answer of course would be 'by adding the sounds ez, z, or s'. If the distinction causes difficulty in one's own language and in alphabetic writing, how much more so in an unfamiliar syllabary? We have seen Evans confused on a similar, equally elementary, point (page 155). Kober's clear warning of the possible booby-traps ahead was far from unnecessary.

As a sample of Kober's method in practice it will be best to take her most rigorous, and most famous, 1946 article. Its purpose was to set up noun paradigms. Its assumptions were that the language was inflected and must therefore show paradigms of some kind; that in tablets of the form

> *word* IDEOGRAPH numeral
> *word* IDEOGRAPH numeral

the words must be nouns; and that in any one list all the nouns must be in the same case, though they may belong to different declension patterns and so have different forms.

Kober began with Evans' 'woman' tablets, especially the one here reproduced. Twelve names ended in the same final sign, two or three of them having the same penultimate sign as well. From the rest of the inscriptions then published (amounting in all to about seven hundred words), there were eight words ending in these same two signs. We could provisionally suppose that these were all nouns in the same case. Moreover, if this two-sign termination regularly interchanged with another type of ending, we might have another case. The occasion does occur – see the second column of Ill. 106a. The instances in the third column, being unique, could not be relied on, and would have to be discarded. Now if one looked again through the known Linear B words, one could find a further six ending in the same two signs as those in column 2. This was therefore another plausible case-ending. There was still a third to be discovered by combining the two lists and going once again through the seven hundred available words. The same process failed to yield a fourth case-ending. Nevertheless, to have discovered three was satisfactory enough, especially as applying the same process through a different set of terminations gave a similar paradigm. These were presumably nouns of the same declension whose stems ended in a different consonant. The evidence available for the second set was less complete than for the first. On the other hand sign-groups of the two sets, but with the termination of 'case 1', occurred together on the same list on a tablet-fragment now in the Metropolitan Museum. *Ex hypothesi* these were in the same case, an important confirmation of the rightness of Kober's reasoning.

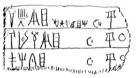

107 Proof that the - ᚷᚺᛒ and - ᚪᛒ endings can represent the same grammatical case. Tablet in the Metropolitan Museum, New York, drawn by Alice Kober (1946)

106a

106b

106c

107

Consonant	Vowel 1	Vowel 2
1		
2		
3		
4		
5		

108 'Beginnings of a tentative phonetic pattern'. From Kober (1948)

But this was not all. There was an equally important rider. If the syllabary was an open one of CV type like the Cypriot, it became possible to say something about the phonetic values of four of the signs. Two of them must share the same consonant, and two of them must share the same vowel, as in the first two rows of Ill. 108. The other three rows in this figure were deduced from further paradigms discovered by Miss Kober after the publication of her 1946 article.

The conclusions were not perhaps very many; but they were reached from the small amount of evidence to be gathered from the specimen tablets and discursive essays published on different occasions mainly by Evans. There had been no full publication of any excavated deposit of tablets. Yet every one of Kober's inferences in Ill. 108 has been supported by Ventris' decipherment, the signs reading *ti/to, si/so, ni/no, mi/mo, wi/wo*. This was remarkable enough. Even more remarkable was the originality of the method. Miss Kober herself claimed (1945, p. 144) that her study was of a kind almost unprecedented. She could have legitimately left out the 'almost'. All but one of the decipherments we have considered up to now began with the location of proper names. The only exception, that of the Ugaritic alphabet, began with the location of a preposition. Thereafter all of them proceeded immediately to the trial-and-error allocation of phonetic values. Kober's method of trying first to establish the interrelationship of the phonetic values of particular signs on an abstract level was as unique as it was fruitful.

Michael Ventris

Among those who were at the time working on the Aegean scripts almost the only one, in Europe at least, who recognized the full importance of Kober's method was Michael Ventris. Ventris was by profession an architect, but while he was still a schoolboy he had had his interest aroused in the scripts by hearing a lecture given by Sir Arthur Evans in 1936 at the fiftieth anniversary celebrations of the founding of the British School at Athens. Four years later he published an article in the *American Journal of Archaeology* in which he argued for the probability of the Minoan language being related to Etruscan. It was generally held in antiquity that the Etruscans had originally come to Italy from Lydia, and in modern times inscriptions have been discovered on the Aegean island of Lemnos written in what is apparently a cognate dialect to Etruscan. Also many Greek place-names (such as Hymettos, Halicarnassos, Corinthos) and some Greek words (such as *kuparissos*, 'cypress'; *terebinthos*, 'terebinth', 'turpentine') were generally thought – because of the non-Greek terminations of their stems – to be survivals of a language spoken in the area before the arrival of the Greeks. This language was therefore a not unlikely candidate for the language of the Bronze Age tablets, and Ventris' argument was that it was also likely to be related or directly ancestral to Etruscan.

After the Second World War, in which he served with the Royal Air Force, and after qualifying as an architect, Ventris returned to the problem of the Minoan scripts. It was now fifty years since

109

their discovery, and he decided to prepare a progress report. He sent a detailed questionnaire to a dozen scholars in the field, ten of whom replied. Their replies, which Ventris translated into English where necessary and circulated back to them, are on the whole not very illuminating. But, as John Chadwick (1958, p. 48) comments, they 'show at least how little agreement there was on the basic issues'. They also show how little anybody then expected the language to turn out to be Greek.

Throughout the next eighteen months (January 1951 to June 1952) Ventris continued writing 'Work-Notes' and circulating them to the same group of scholars to whom he had written for his mid-century report, as it came to be called. The group gradually grew from the original dozen to three times that number. This method of semi-publication had a decided practical advantage at the time in that the Minoan signs under discussion could be drawn on stencils very much more readily than they could be reproduced by the conventional processes of printing. It also has the contingent advantage for the historian looking back on the decipherment that he has before him the whole process, false starts as well as ratified conclusions – though this has its drawbacks too. The Work-Notes run to nearly two hundred foolscap pages. A summary of them that is confined to the dimensions of half a chapter must be highly selective.

109 Michael Ventris, 1922–56

Ventris' chief tool was the concept of the 'syllabic grid', a table showing which signs share the same consonant, and which the same vowel. There was nothing new in such a table itself. It goes back to the seventeenth century (see page 41), and played an important part in Schmidt's decipherment of the Cypriot syllabary (pages 130–1). Kober's innovation, followed by Ventris, was the idea of constructing such a grid in the abstract, that is to say without settling what particular consonant or vowel it might be that a particular set of signs had in common. Ventris, commenting on his first 'experimental grid' in his first Work-Note (28 January 1951),   110 put its purpose very clearly. 'It is risky to guess what the consonants (or vowels) actually are: but one can predict that when at least half the signs of the syllabary have been securely fixed on the grid, it will need only a small number of inspired pieces of linguistic deduction to solve the whole "simultaneous equation".'

The Work-Notes contain three experimental grids at varying stages of improvement. The first full publication of the decipher-   110, 112, 114 ment contains a fourth, drawn up after the allocation of phonetic   116 values to the signs on the hypothesis that the language is Greek. It is clear from just looking at the fourth grid that it differs considerably from the third grid of the Work-Notes. The amount of difference can be quantified in an approximate manner by adding up the number of signs correctly aligned for their consonant and vowel values, and then subtracting the first in each series (which obviously has no meaning in itself before the allocation of specific phonetic values), and measuring the results against the values now generally allotted to the signs. This will give the number of correct equations made.[2]

	signs placed on grid	correct alignments	correct equations	score (%)
Kober (Ill. 108)	10	20	13	100
Work-Note 1 (Ill. 110)	29	29	15	33
Work-Note 15 (Ill. 112)	51	74	54	67
Work-Note 17 (Ill. 114)	51	80	60	75
1953 grid (Ill. 116)	65	123	(105)	(90)
1970 grid[3]	72	144	(123)	(100)

This comparison of the grids raises an important question. In the final state of the abstract, value-free, grid, a quarter of the signs were wrongly placed. If Ventris used the grid like an automatic pilot it must have led him off course to a solution that was three-quarters wrong. If not, how did he recognize which were the rightly placed and which were the wrongly placed signs except by the same sort of trial-and-error guessing of phonetic values as all previous decipherments had depended on? In this case the concept of an abstract grid will have been no more than an illusion, giving a comforting colour of scientific method to a solution that was really reached in quite a different way.

Now, it is plain that after the initial launching of the decipherment the predictions of the grid had little part to play. Phonetic values were arrived at empirically on the basis of conjectured Greek words and names, and the grid was re-tailored to accommodate them. The real question, however, concerns the initial launching. Here it is legitimate to argue that the grid played not only a genuine but an indispensable part. If we look at the words tentatively transliterated by Ventris on the brink of the decipherment in his final Work-Note 20 – the place-names Amnisos, Knossos, Tylissos, and the Greek words for coriander, total, boy, girl, together with forms inflected or derived from them – we find that of the nineteen different signs used, all but two are entered on this third grid: thirteen of them interlock as predicted in regard to both vowel and consonant, three as regards the vowel, two as regards the consonant. Not one conflicts with the predictions of the grid. Nor could these words have been reasonably guessed without the grid. In Virolleaud's decipherment of the Ugaritic syllabary his first seven words contained only six different characters, of which four recurred six times, to make an almost completely self-interlocking pattern. In the nineteen different characters of Ventris' first words two recurred four times each and a further four twice each. The other eleven only occurred once each. They could certainly not have been guessed if the grid had not given clues to nine of them.

72

To understand Ventris' decipherment it is therefore necessary to see first how he constructed his grid, and then, since the grid was no longer enough after the original launching, to see what further tools he was able to use.

110

The first grid must be regarded as a failure. Admittedly the material was still scanty (it was drawn up just before the preliminary publication of the Pylos tablets), and it contained more correct equations than Kober's had done; but it also included, unlike Kober's, a number of placings made on insecure evidence

▷
110 Ventris' first grid, circulated 28 January 1951

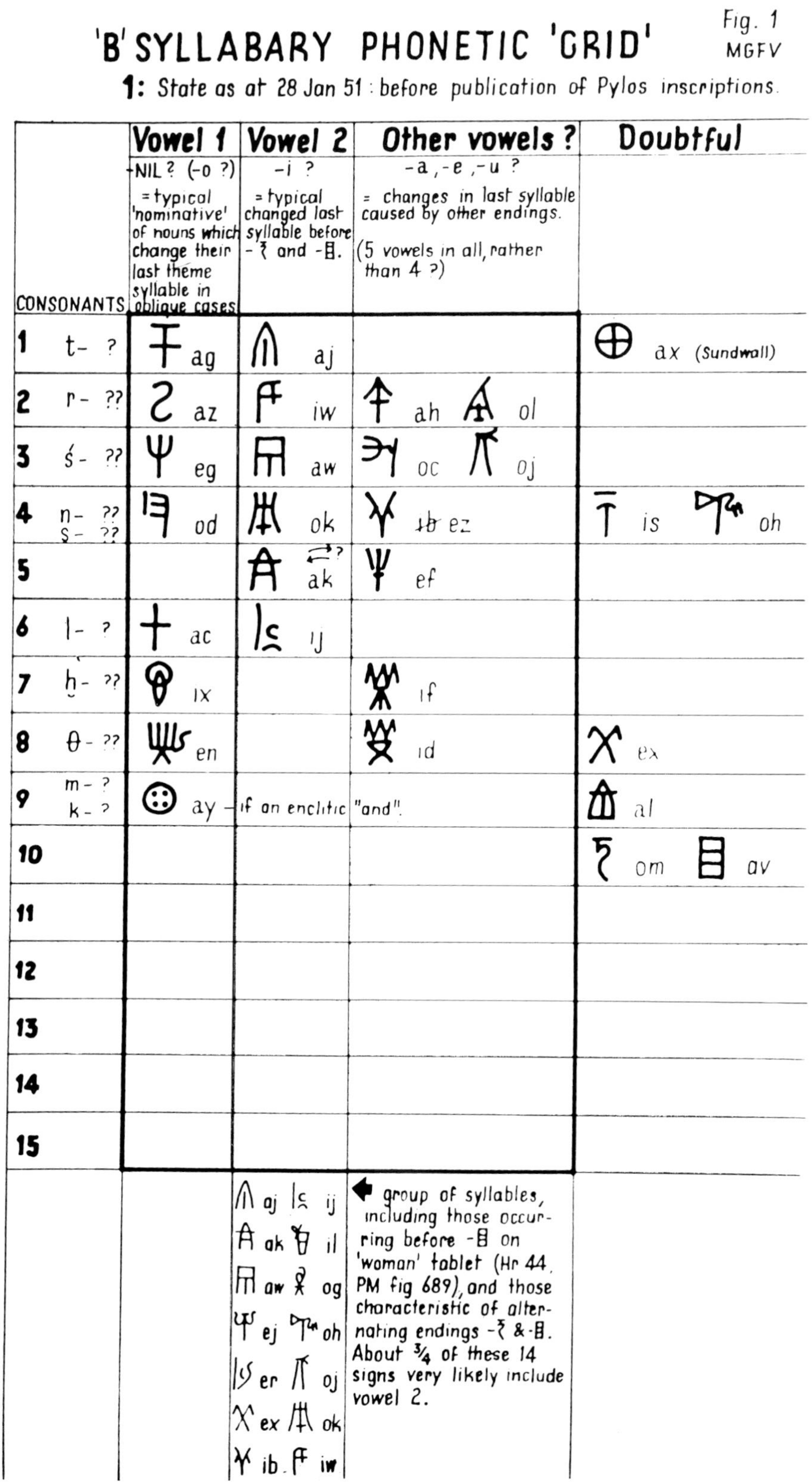

'B' SYLLABARY PHONETIC 'GRID' Fig. 1 MGFV

1: State as at 28 Jan 51 : before publication of Pylos inscriptions.

CONSONANTS	Vowel 1	Vowel 2	Other vowels ?	Doubtful
	NIL? (-o ?) = typical 'nominative' of nouns which change their last theme syllable in oblique cases	-i ? = typical changed last syllable before -ʒ and -ᗺ.	-a ,-e ,-u ? = changes in last syllable caused by other endings. (5 vowels in all, rather than 4 ?)	
1 t- ?	⟊ ag	⋀ aj		⊕ ax (Sundwall)
2 r- ??	Ƨ az	Ƒ iw	⟰ ah Ⱥ oi	
3 ś- ??	Ψ eg	Ⱈ aw	⇥ oc Ⱔ oj	
4 n- ?? ṣ- ??	彐 od	业 ok	Ⴘ ɪᵇ ez	Ʇ is ▷ᴙ oh
5		Ᾱ ak →?	Ψ ef	
6 l- ?	✝ ac	⧏ ij		
7 ḫ- ??	Ꙩ ix		Ⱳ if	
8 θ- ??	Ⱳ en		Ⱳ id	Ⱪ ex
9 m- ? k- ?	⊕ ay ─ if an enclitic "and".			Ⱌ al
10				5 om 目 av
11				
12				
13				
14				
15				

		⋀ aj ⧏ ij Ᾱ ak ⱶ il Ⱈ aw ⅄ og Ψ ej ▷ᴙ oh ⧏ er Ⱔ oj Ⱪ ex 业 ok Ⱳ ib Ƒ iw	◀ group of syllables, including those occurring before -ᗺ on 'woman' tablet (Hr 44, PM fig 689), and those characteristic of alternating endings -ʒ & -ᗺ. About ¾ of these 14 signs very likely include vowel 2.	

which had later to be abandoned. The principles of its construction were for the most part ones with which we are already familiar.
Two long sign-groups, which are the same except for the last
sign or signs, are likely to be forms of the same word, and there is
a good chance – though not a certainty – that the last syllable in
each case will begin with the same consonant (as in English
radia*tor*, radia*ting*, but intermedia*cy*, intermedia*ry*). One of
Ventris' examples in this class was the pair of words now transliterated *wa-na-ka-te-ro* and *wa-na-ka-te-ra*, 'royal', which gave
him the two signs in the sixth row. The same argument could be
used for short words if they occurred in exactly parallel contexts.
For instance, the disyllabic words for child, of which the final
signs are entered by Ventris in the third row, and the disyllabic
word for total (final signs entered as the second and third signs
of the fourth row). Ventris also tried to identify case-endings on a
more extended scale than Kober had done, and to consider what
signs occurred with particularly high frequencies *before* particular
signs (see bottom of Ill. 110). This innovation was later to prove
valuable, as we shall see.

The first grid was especially weak in its allocation of vowels.
This was partly because Ventris, still thinking that the language
would prove to be Etruscan, was reluctant to assume gender-
differentiation. In Work-Note 11, however, he accepted the
view that gender might be differentiated, and that one way in
which this revealed itself was by the nature of the final vowel.
This criterion, together with the results of a much more intensive
analysis of possible noun-declensions carried out on the now-
111   published Pylos tablets (see page 170), resulted in a more satisfactory treatment of the vowel columns in the second grid,
particularly the second and fifth columns (which were to become
112   *-o* and *-a*). But the success of the second grid was not limited to the
vowels. It contained several consonant series which were to be
vindicated in their entirety.

114   The third grid, produced just before the long-awaited publication of the Knossos tablets (by Sir John Myres from Evans' papers)
is, as far as the consonant series go, almost the same as the second.
But in regard to the vowels it incorporates the consequences of
Ventris' most important original observation. One of the noun-
declensions he had deduced in his Work-Note 14 was expressed
by the endings ⌐ , 𝑙, and 𝜋² (today transliterated as *u*, *we*, and *wo*).
He now noticed (Work-Note 16) that the previous sign was
always one of twelve, and that of these twelve signs the nine that
were placed on his second grid all belonged to a different consonant. The observation was a difficult one, but its implication was
clear. He must have discovered an almost complete vowel series.
This was to become the major part of column three of the third
grid, and to be eventually transliterated *-e*.

Let us now leave the grids and look as briefly as possible at the
other analyses that Ventris conducted. They can be considered
under three heads: grammar, context, and spelling.

The grammar gave Ventris great trouble. Had there been only
one declension-pattern with distinct endings for each case or
gender (domin*a*, domin*ae*; domin*i*, domin*o*), the syllabic spelling

▷
111 Ventris' diagram
summing up the evidence
for the interrelationship of
sign-values used for the
construction of his second
grid

SUSPECTED CONSONANT EQUATIONS IN PYLOS INFLEXIONAL MATERIAL

WORK NOTES
FIGURE 9
KNOSSOS, 27 SEPT 51

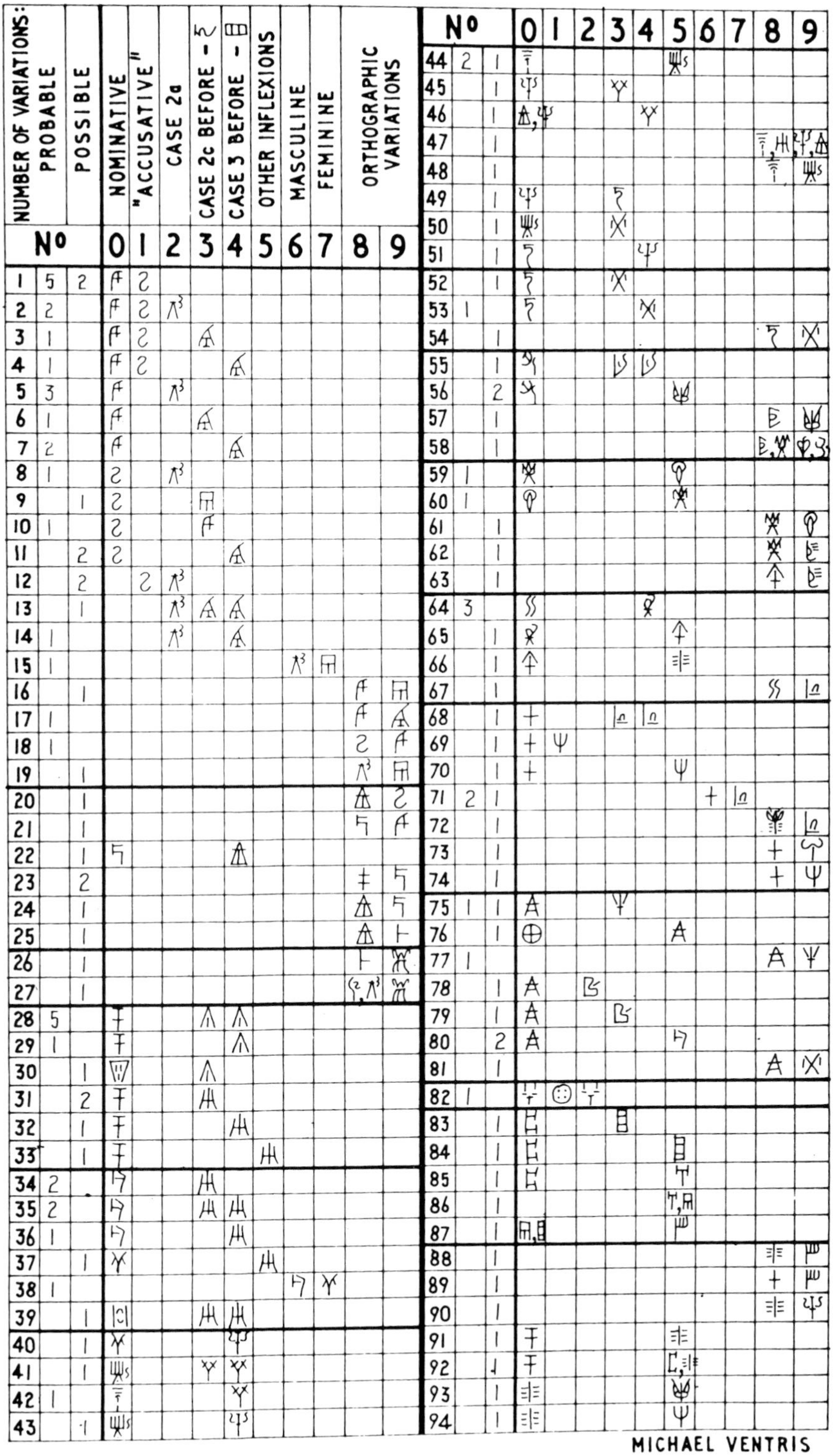
NUMBER OF VARIATIONS: PROBABLE
POSSIBLE
NOMINATIVE
"ACCUSATIVE"
CASE 2a
CASE 2c BEFORE –
CASE 3 BEFORE –
OTHER INFLEXIONS
MASCULINE
FEMININE
ORTHOGRAPHIC VARIATIONS
No
0 1 2 3 4 5 6 7 8 9

MICHAEL VENTRIS

LINEAR SCRIPT B SYLLABIC GRID
(2ND STATE)

DIAGNOSIS OF CONSONANT AND VOWEL EQUATIONS
IN THE INFLEXIONAL MATERIAL FROM PYLOS:

WORK NOTE 15

FIGURE 10

ATHENS, 28 SEPT 51

Left margin (vertical): THESE 51 SIGNS MAKE UP 90% OF ALL SIGN-OCCURRENCES IN THE PYLOS SIGNGROUP INDEX. APPENDED FIGURES GIVE EACH SIGN'S OVERALL FREQUENCY PER MILLE IN THE PYLOS INDEX.

	vowel 1	vowel 2	vowel 3	vowel 4	vowel 5
	"Impure" ending, typical syllables before -ʔ & -目 in Case 2c & 3	"Pure" ending, typical nominatives of forms in Column 1	Includes possible "accusatives"	Also, but less frequently, the nominatives of forms In Column 1	
	THESE SIGNS DON'T OCCUR BEFORE -ß-	THESE SIGNS OCCUR LESS COMMONLY OR NOT AT ALL BEFORE -目-			
	MORE OFTEN FEMININE THAN MASCULINE ?	MORE OFTEN MASCULINE THAN FEMININE ?			MORE OFTEN FEMININE THAN MASCULINE ?
	NORMALLY FORM THE GENITIVE SINGULAR BY ADDING -ʔ	NORMALLY FORM THE GENITIVE SINGULAR BY ADDING -ß			
pure vowels?	30.3				37.2
a semi-vowel?			34.0	29.4	
consonant 1	14.8	32.5	21.2	28.1	18.8
2	19.6	17.5			13.7
3		9.2		3.3	10.0
4	17.0	28.6			0.4
5	17.7	10.3		4.1	10.2
6	7.4	20.5		14.8	14.4
7	4.1	44.0			
8	6.1	6.1		13.5	15.2
9		33.1		32.3	2.4
10	22.2		38.2	3.5	2.2
11	31.2	33.8	34.4	8.3	0.7
12	17.0			37.7	24.0
13		9.4	14.2		
14	5.0				
15	12.6				

MICHAEL VENTRIS

112 Ventris' second grid ◁

would have made it difficult enough to sort out the quite different-looking final signs. But it soon became apparent, not only that there were different declensions, but that the same ending might disguise different cases and genders (as in Latin *-a* may be among other things the termination of the feminine singular, the neuter plural, and even the masculine singular of proper names; *-i* the genitive singular or masculine plural of one declension, the dative singular of another). Ventris realized that he was up against a problem of great complexity (stated in Work-Note 13). Nevertheless, aided by the assumption that nouns listed together would be in the same case, by the fact that ideograms often indicated gender (demonstrated by Kober in 1949), and by the discovery (made also by Bennett and by Ktistopoulos) of a preposition which was always followed by one of the cases, he managed to work out an inflectional pattern for three different declensions (Work-Note 14 of 28 August 1951).

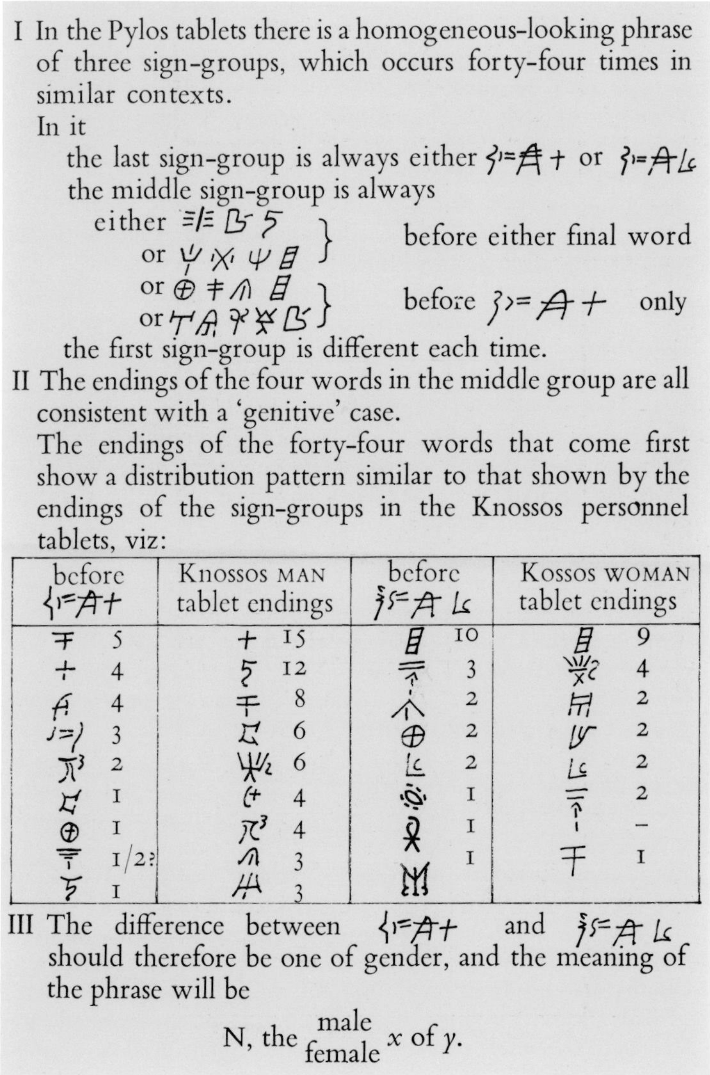
I In the Pylos tablets there is a homogeneous-looking phrase of three sign-groups, which occurs forty-four times in similar contexts.

In it

the last sign-group is always either … or …

the middle sign-group is always

either … or … } before either final word

or … or … } before … only

the first sign-group is different each time.

II The endings of the four words in the middle group are all consistent with a 'genitive' case.

The endings of the forty-four words that come first show a distribution pattern similar to that shown by the endings of the sign-groups in the Knossos personnel tablets, viz:

before …	Knossos MAN tablet endings	before …	Kossos WOMAN tablet endings
5	15	10	9
4	12	3	4
4	8	2	2
3	6	2	2
2	6	2	2
1	4	1	2
1	4	1	–
1/2?	3	1	1
1	3		

III The difference between … and … should therefore be one of gender, and the meaning of the phrase will be

N, the male/female *x* of *y*.

113 An argument from Ventris' Work-Note 11 (27.5.51) in abbreviated form

Context analysis was now possible on a much more comprehensive scale than before owing to the publication of the Pylos tablets. These, the first Linear B tablets to have been found outside Knossos, were excavated by the American archaeologist, the late Carl Blegen, just before the war broke out in 1939. With the same exemplary generosity that had been shown by Schaeffer at Ugarit, Blegen delegated their publication to others. The war, however, and its aftermath imposed an inevitable delay. In addition the processes of cleaning, photographing, joining broken fragments, classifying, transcribing, and checking were all laborious and time-consuming in themselves. In the event it was not until 1951 that Bennett, who had undertaken the actual publication, was able to put out a preliminary transcription. The full edition, including material later discovered, was published in 1955. The total number of sign-groups that the Pylos tablets contained was in the region of five thousand. The work was therefore difficult for its scale as well as for its complexity. It was admirably done, and Bennett's contextual analysis of the tablets, particularly as regards their ideograms, and the consequent orderly arrangement of their publication, formed the most solid part of the foundations on which Ventris worked. It was this which enabled the homogeneous lists, on which so many further suppositions depended, to be identified.

A minor, though important, result of Ventris' analysis of the sign-groups was the discovery of the sign for 'and', apparently a one-syllable enclitic word like the Latin -*que*. But this was not in itself a key to decipherment since such enclitic conjunctions occur in many languages. Another, and more complicated, piece of contextual analysis was that which I have tried to show in abbre-

113   viated form in the diagram on page 169. I hope that the three stages of the argument are clear enough to need no further commentary. For the word *x* in the phrase elucidated in the final stage Ventris tentatively suggested a meaning of the type 'servant', and still more tentatively suggested that the phonetic reading might be *do-we-lo* (the sign that looks like a cross being *lo* in the Cypriot syllabary), and the word the original of the Greek *doulos*, 'slave' (i.e. Mycenaean *do-we-lo* with the Greek termination -*os*).

Why did he not at this stage think of the word as being itself Greek? This brings us to our next problem, that of spelling convention. In the Cypriot syllabary, the deciphered script that was closest in appearance to Linear B, the word *dowelos* would have been written *do-we-lo-se*. Indeed nearly all masculine nominatives would have ended with this same sign -*se* to indicate the pronounced termination -*s*. But if anything was obvious in Linear B it was that masculine nominatives had a great variety of final signs (see Ill. 113, second stage). It was this, as much as any historical preconceptions, that ruled out Greek from consideration as the language of the tablets. Provided, of course, that the Mycenaean spelling conventions were the same as the Cypriot.

The possibility that the final consonant, instead of being written with a 'dead' vowel as in Cypriot, might be simply omitted was one that had not been previously entertained. It was a new idea, perhaps indeed the only major innovation of theory made by Ventris in the whole course of the decipherment. And as so often

LINEAR B SYLLABIC GRID

THIRD STATE : REVIEW OF PYLOS EVIDENCE

FIGURE II
WORK NOTE 17
20 FEB 1952

SMALL SIGNS INDICATE UNCERTAIN POSITION. CIRCLED SIGNS HAVE NO OBVIOUS EQUIVALENT IN LINEAR SCRIPT A.

POSSIBLE VALUES	VOWELS	-i ? / -a ?	-o ? / -e ?	-e ? / -u ?		-a ? / -i ?	VOWEL UNCERTAIN
CONSONANTS		v 1	v 2	v 3	v 4	v 5	
PURE VOWEL ?	–						
j- ?	c 1						
s- ? v- ? θ- ? c- ?	c 2						
z- ? p- ?	c 3						
s- ?	c 4						
t- ?	c 5						
t- ?	c 6						
θ- ? r- ?	c 7						
n- ?	c 8						
f- ?	c 9						
h/x ? θ- ?	c 10						
r- ? l- ?	c 11						
l- ?	c 12						
v- ? r- ?	c 13						
c- ?	c 14						
m- ?	c 15						
OTHER CONSONANTS							

171

with the right ideas that we have seen in the course of this book, it was originally put forward for a wrong reason. In Work-Note 9 (24 July 1951) Ventris discussed briefly the language of Hittite Hieroglyphic. He decided that it was not promising for his purposes. For one thing, there was no formal distinction of masculine and feminine visible in proper names or other words, and he had now recognized that there was such a distinction visible in Linear B. For another, all personal names ended in -*s* both in the nominative and in the genitive, though this was an objection, he says, that could be got round. Noting, from a recently published article by the Finnish scholar Sundwall (1948) that Lycian – a language descended from, or at least related to, the language of Hittite Hieroglyphic – had lost the -*s* ending of the nominative, Ventris suggested that there might have been a Minoan spelling convention whereby the -*s* of the nominative was unwritten, the -*s* of the genitive written.

The idea was twice removed from the truth. Linear B, as Ventris deciphered it, was not Luvian, nor does it go out of its way to express grammatical distinctions in writing more clearly than they were expressed in speech. Nevertheless, it lit the path to success.

Two or three weeks later Ventris found a more serious reason to question the transferability of the Cypriot spelling rules. He had discovered a class of affixes which were added to the nominative forms of words. He now realized (Work-Note 14 of 28 August 1951) a further significance in this. For, according to Cypriot spelling rules an affix would in most circumstances inevitably impose a change of spelling on the stem.[3] Since the Linear B stems were unaffected by the affix it followed that the Cypriot rules could not apply.

Success

We now come to the justifiably famous Work-Note 20 (1 June 1952) entitled 'Are the Knossos Tablets Written in Greek?'. It begins and ends with an apology for venturing on such a perilous speculation. It may seem strange to a layman that any apology should have been necessary when suggesting that written documents found in Greece in the very cities described in ancient Greek epic might perhaps be written in the Greek language. Strange indeed it is. But orthodox opinion had long favoured dating the arrival of the Greeks in the Aegean at or after the fall of the Mycenaean palaces. There were also perhaps other factors of a kind less easily expressed. If the tablets were really written in such a well-known language as Greek it would have been natural, though illogical, to suppose that they would have been already deciphered. There could even have been a hidden fear of being identified with earlier would-be decipherers who had published insecure attempts to make Greek out of the Minoan texts.

In any case Ventris felt the need for a historical justification, and argued, sensibly enough, that if the language of Linear A was different from the language of Linear B (as Kober and Bennett thought it was), then Linear A could represent the much discussed

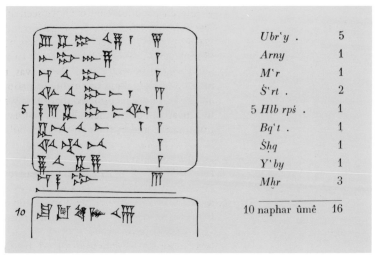

115 Ras Shamra tablet (RŠ 11850) listing nine towns which are to furnish a total of sixteen work-days. The entries are in the Ugaritic alphabet, the total in Akkadian. Drawing and transcription by Virolleaud (1940)

Ubr'y .	5	
Arny	1	
M'r	1	
Š'rt .	2	
5 Hlb rpś .	1	
Bq't .	1	
Šḫq	1	
Y'by	1	
Mḫr	3	
10 naphar ûmê	16	

pre-Hellenic language (or one of them), and the ground would be clear for Linear B to represent Greek. Moreover Linear A was attested throughout Crete, but in Crete alone: Linear B had been used on the Greek mainland, and in Crete only at Knossos in the Late Minoan II period where Evans and others had detected mainland influence. There were thus geographical and historical differences in the usage of the two systems as well as the internal differences of the writing.

All this was of course justification for a hypothesis otherwise arrived at. Our main concern is how Ventris arrived at it. It was, as in all the decipherments we have dealt with except that of the Ugaritic alphabet, through the recognition of proper names. But there was no bilingual, as for Champollion's Ptolemy and Cleopatra; there was no reliable historical king-list as for Grotefend's Hystaspes, Darius, and Xerxes; there were no recognizable place-name determinatives as for the decipherers of Hittite Hieroglyphic. How, then, did Ventris locate proper names which he might have a chance of recognizing?

In Work-Note 12, entitled 'Functional Classification of Pylos Sign-Groups', he had specified a category of sign-groups (also to be found on the Knossos tablets) which occurred in both introductory and itemized positions on the lists. It was the words of this category which had yielded the most material for Kober's three cases. It did not look as if they were ordinary personal names, and at the time Ventris thought that they seemed 'to indicate an attribution to a wider group, department, clan, or area rather than to a single individual' (Work-Note p. 32). The question of what these words might be stayed at the back of his mind. Now, among the more or less contemporary Ugaritic tablets there was a category of list figuring the names of local 'towns and corporations'. 115 A specimen of one of them is reproduced on this page. Though there was nothing compulsive about the parallel, it suggested to Ventris that local place-names might be the answer he was looking for, with one of the inflected forms being the ethnic and corresponding to the Ugaritic forms in -y.

173

The names of towns near Knossos were fairly well known from classical sources. One of them, the harbour town of Amnisos, would probably begin with an *a*, and he was almost sure he knew the Linear B character for this from its great initial frequency. He also thought that he knew the sign for *ni* (see Ill. 114, eighth consonant series) – the *n* being suggested partly by the Cypriot sign for *na* and partly by a now irrelevant Etruscan-based argument, the *i* partly by the Cypriot for *ti* and partly by the frequency of the signs of the series before ⫫ , which Ventris already suspected of being *ya* (i.e. a glide followed by *a*). One of the sign-groups in the category showed the desired pattern *a-..-ni..*; the grid immediately filled this out as *a-.i-ni-.o*, and so made it comparatively easy to guess the remainder: *a-mi-ni-so*. The word was in fact one of those used by Kober in her demonstration of Linear B decelensions Ill. 106a, column c).

A second word of the same type could now, thanks to the grid, be read for two-thirds of the way: *..-no-so*. This, being in the same context category as *a-mi-ni-so* and therefore on the hypothesis the name of a town, was easily read: *ko-no-so*, 'Knossos', the *o* of the first sign being supplied by the grid.

The next town identified in Work-Note 20 was less certain: *..-.i-so*. If supplemented as *tu-li-so*, it could render 'Tylissos'. There was no evidence from the grid for the first, somewhat infrequent, sign. But a new tack gave plausibility to the *li*. There were on the Knossos and Pylos tablets two words differently spelt, but associated with the same ideogram, which yielded according to the values so far tentatively identified: *ko-li-ya-.o-no* and *ko-li-..-.a-na*. The spice coriander (used for flavouring bread) is variously spelled in classical Greek as koliandron, koriannon, koriandron, koriamblon. If this was the word here it confirmed the *li* of Tylissos, and further gave *do* and *da* for two signs predicted by the grid as sharing the same consonant.

So far there was nothing to define the language, coriander not having a Greek etymology. But if the sign for *ya* belonged to the fifth instead of to the second row of the grid, then the sign ⫯ would have the value *-yo*. The effect of this would be (from context analyses carried out in Work-Note 14) to create a class of genitives ending in *-oyo*. This, despite its faintly comic ring in English ears, was in fact very plausible. The old form of the Greek second-declension genitive, known from Homer and the Arcado-Cypriot dialect, ended in *-oio*. But there was still a difficulty: *a-mi-ni-so*, *ko-no-so*, and *tu-li-so* could only be Greek forms for Amnisos, Knossos, and Tylissos if the last consonant was unwritten.

This surprising requirement would probably have been enough to stop Ventris and the decipherment then and there if he had not previously foreseen that there was likely to be something unexpected in the spelling rules as far as they affected final consonants. As it was, Ventris was prepared to accept provisionally that the final *s* and purhaps other final consonants might be omitted.

This was the crucial step. Once it was taken, the way ahead was plain. The sign-groups for 'boy' and 'girl' identified by Cowley could be read:

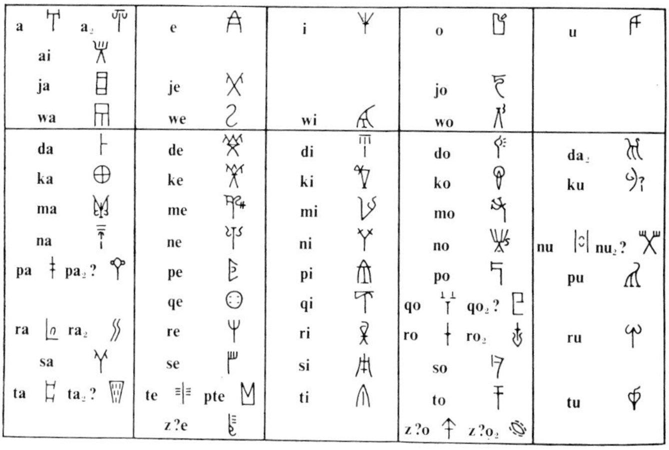

116 The 'experimental syllabic grid' published by Ventris and Chadwick in the article explaining their decipherment in *Journal of Hellenic Studies*, lxiii (1953)

ko-wo = ko(r)wo(s) 'boy' (Homeric Greek κοῦρος)
ko-wa = ko(r)wa 'girl' (Homeric Greek κούρη)

The declensional endings identified in earlier work-notes came out as *-o*, *-o*, *-o-yo* (-os, -on, oio of the Greek second declension) and *-e-u*, *-e-wa*, *-e-wo* (-eus, -êwa, -êwos of the Greek nouns of the type βασιλεύς), and the two signs universally recognized as meaning 'total' came out as *to-so* and *to-sa* (toso(n) and tosa, the neuter singular and plural of the Greek tosos, 'so much').

There was one further step needed. The writing of *-o* and *-a* had to be able to stand also for the diphthongs *-oi* and *-ai* in order to explain why the singular and plural of the word for child were written the same – *kowo(i)* and *kowa(i)* – and why *to-so* and *to-sa* could be used for totalling lists of men and women respectively – *tosoi* and *tosai* being the Greek masculine and feminine plurals.

Ventris had now suggested decipherment values for nineteen different characters such as led to the identification of three place-names and the interpretation of three vocabulary words (two of them indisputably Greek), as well as several patterns of Greek case and gender inflection. All the interpretations corresponded well to predictions previously made on grounds of context. The only stumbling block was the method of spelling that had to be assumed. But even this was not as lax as it might seem – at least from the point of view of the writer. It can be comprehended under the simple rule that what was felt as one syllable was expressed by one sign.

Though these initial steps had been more firmly prepared and more cautiously taken than those of most other decipherments, when Ventris posted Work-Note 20 to his correspondents he still felt that the apparent Greek words and forms might be a mirage. But he continued to investigate it, and in a talk which he gave on the BBC Third Programme at the beginning of June 1952 he felt confident enough to announce his provisional conclusion. John Chadwick, a classical philologist then at Oxford, heard Ventris' broadcast. He saw Sir John Myres, one of those who had corresponded with Ventris, borrowed a copy of the most recent form of the grid, and began to check its applicability for himself. He was convinced that it was on the right lines, and wrote to Ventris congratulating him and offering his help. Ventris, who, as we have seen, was an architect and not a professional philologist, accepted Chadwick's offer, and together they prepared a detailed article, 'Evidence for Greek Dialect in the Mycenaean Archives', which was completed in November 1952 and appeared in the 1953 issue of the *Journal of Hellenic Studies*. In it they presented sixty-five signs. Since then the values of six of them have been amended, and values have been found for seven further signs. Substantially therefore the decipherment was already completed.

116

While the Ventris and Chadwick article was still in the press there came a dramatic confirmation of the decipherment. This was a newly excavated tablet from Pylos. Immediately recognizable words on it included *ti-ri-po*, *ti-ri-po-de* (Greek *tripous*, *tripodes*, 'tripod', 'tripods') at the beginning of the tablet, and at its end words for cup (Greek *depas*) in the singular and the dual, for larger and smaller (Greek *meizone*, *meion*), and a series of words for different numbers of ears or handles. These were particularly convincing. They contained good Greek adjectival forms for 'eared' (from *ouas* 'ear') and good Greek prefixes for 'without', 'three', and 'four' (*a-*, *tri-*, *qetr-*). Moreover the descriptions were accompanied by ideograms of the vases showing in each case the correct number of ears. A further confirmation was given by the word for 'four'. Its initial sign was the same as that for the enclitic word for 'and', previously identified (see page 170). In classical Greek the words for 'four' and 'and' are normally written *tettares* and *-te*. But the related Latin *quattuor* and *-que* and Sanskrit *catur*, *ca*, as well as Greek dialect spellings for 'four' like *pettares*, indicate that at one time the words were pronounced with a different initial consonant, called a labio-velar, whose existence had been predicted by comparative philology long before the decipherment.

117

Blegen, the excavator of Pylos, had at once recognized the importance of the tablet.[4] He allowed Ventris to quote it in his lectures, and gave it advanced publication. Though it contains phrases that still cause difficulty and one apparent spelling mistake of the scribe (a dual for a singular) the positive evidence it offers in favour of the correctness of the decipherment is so striking that it has convinced the majority of those qualified to express a judgment. But not all. There are still some who either reject the decipherment or who consider it not proven.

In theory there can only be three grounds for outright rejection: that the decipherment was arbitrary, that it was based on false principles, or that it has been ousted by a better. Since there has been no subsequent rival decipherment and since nobody wants to revive the earlier attempts, the last ground is untenanted. The thoroughness of the argumentation of the Work-Notes makes the first ground untenable. This leaves only the middle ground, and there are some who occupy it. Their stronghold is a denial that the script is syllabic, their chief weapon the undoubted fact that many of the signs which occur in the sign-groups and to which Ventris allotted phonetic values, also occur standing alone before numerals with an evidently logographic significance.

di-pa-e me-zo-e ti-ri-o-we-e	3-HANDLED VASE	2
di-pa me-wi-jo qe-to-ro-we	4-HANDLED VASE	1
di-pa me-wi-jo ti-ri-jo-we	3-HANDLED VASE	1
di-pa me-wi-jo a-no-we	HANDLE-LESS VASE	1

117 Confirmation of the Ventris/Chadwick decipherment: the 'tripod tablet' from Pylos, and Bennett's drawing of the text and transliteration of its final part

Instead of accepting the usual explanation, that on such occasions the signs are conventional or standard abbreviations (like *c* for cents), they argue the other way round – that the signs must still be ideographic when they occur in groups. What is not easy to discover is how they suppose that such a writing system would work: the only analogies they can point to are scripts like Linear A, the so-called Cretan Pictographic, and Proto-Elamite. These are not only undeciphered but less well attested than Linear B. The argument therefore proceeds from the worse to the better known. In addition it creates an otherwise unnecessary problem about how, when, and why the Cypriot script altered its nature and became syllabic. Above all, it depends on an abstract theory about the pictographic origin of writing, which is by no means necessarily true; nor, if it is true, is it likely to be relevant to documents as late as the latter half of the second millennium BC.[5]

On the other hand those who say that the decipherment is still unproven not only have a case, but are perhaps right. No independent bilingual has yet been found. The ideograms, and the contexts of words such as those for 'child' and 'total' give us a bilingual of sorts, but not an independent one. And though it is scarcely conceivable that the many words which aptly describe their accompanying ideograms (such as *i-qo*, *o-no*, *po-lo* beside sketches of horses' heads – Greek *hippos*, 'horse', cognate to Latin *equus* and Sanskrit *aśvas*; *onos*, 'donkey'; *pôlos*, 'foal' – and those on the tripod tablet) were all taken into account by Ventris when first allocating the phonetic values (for this would make him a Machiavelli of Machiavellis), it is just possible that they are an illusion sired by the compliant spelling system of the syllabary out of the size of the known Greek vocabulary. For instance in his early 'experimental vocabulary' circulated in July 1952 Ventris interpreted the word accompanying sword ideograms as *sphagnai* (presumably to be connected with *sphazô*, 'I slaughter'): it is now interpreted as *phasgana* (a Homeric word for 'swords'). The decipherment, *pa-ka-na*, allows both interpretations. Those who argue 'not proven' suggest that on these spelling rules any scheme of decipherment, however false, could offer as many hits on target. Or perhaps even more. For on Ventris' decipherment there still remain many words not interpreted.

It is hard to calculate the probabilities involved in this argument. Until this is done, or until some genuinely independent external confirmation appears, it is perhaps best to consider Ventris' decipherment as a theory. Theory, however, not in the sense of an interesting suggestion thrown up almost at random, but in the sense of a solidly constructed argument which is not yet capable of a logically convincing proof.

But when this has been said, there remain two further points. One is the distinction between interpretation and decipherment. Although some of the interpretations made, especially in the first year or two of the decipherment, have been over-enthusiastic and have even verged on the absurd, and although many words and phrases still resist interpretation, nevertheless criticism on this score no more invalidates Ventris' decipherment than Klaproth invalidated Champollion's by pointing out that the *Précis* contained no translation of the Rosetta Stone. Between the Mycenaean tablets and the earliest alphabetically written Greek there is not only the gulf of several hundred years but also the gulf which separates the situations of an administrative accountant and an epic poet. Major difficulties of understanding are therefore exactly what one would expect. The other point is a more superficial one. If we forget for a moment the question of internal validity and look on Ventris' decipherment as a historical phenomenon, we shall see a striking resemblance of pattern between the attacks on it and the attacks made in the last century on the decipherments of Champollion and Rawlinson. Disregarding the elements of personal attack and without going into technical detail one can point out as common to all three cases the allegation that the proposed decipherment allows too much laxity of interpretation, the assertion that the scripts are not really phonetic at all but symbolic or ideographic or in some way different from anything we can readily conceive, and finally a sort of death-wish denial that the key to their proper understanding can ever be recovered. We shall also observe that no decipherment which has been based on rigorous argument and which has won independent approval from scholars of repute – and not even the most resolute opponents of Ventris' decipherment can deny this description of it – has subsequently had to be abandoned.

Neither of these points has anything to do with proof; but that does not mean they are unimportant. What the layman, and that includes most classical scholars and prehistorians, needs to know is whether he can accept the decipherment as a working hypothesis, and these are considerations he can legitimately take into account in making his judgment.

I close with an illustration of how difficult it is to get proof. It relates to a gallery running round the mortuary temple of the Pharaoh Amenophis III, who died in about 1372 BC. On the face of it the discovery, long subsequent to the decipherment, of this gallery recording place-names which include several that can be plausibly identified with ones on the Cretan Linear B tablets, among them Knossos, Amnisos, and Lyktos next to each other, and which also includes the name Keftiu, previously thought to be the Egyptian name for Crete, might seem to offer just the

118 Cartouches representing three foreign place-names from the Mortuary Temple of Amenophis III, perhaps to be read (r. to l.) as Knossos, Amnisos, Lyktos. *Below*, drawing from Kitchen (1965)

independent confirmation for the correctness of the decipherment that has been required.[6] But it is not so easy. The Egyptian spellings (Knš, 'Imnš, Rkt) are not conclusive, and do not necessarily support each other. In assembling a list of foreign places which 118 acknowledged the glory of his Pharaoh the Egyptian scribe need no more have felt himself bound to keep a geographical order (even if he knew it) than an auctioneer in arranging his catalogue of sale need feel obliged to preserve the order of provenance of its items. Nor is there any proof on the other side. Even if the Egyptian readings of the names is correct, it does not follow that their reading in the Linear B texts is. The Cretan place-names are attested in classical sources and could be accepted as having been the same in the second millennium BC even if the decipherment had never been made.

But when all is said and done, it is hard to believe that such an apt discovery does not confer some further degree of probability on Ventris' decipherment, even if it is hard to put an exact value on it. It is fitting too that an inscription which can be read thanks to the earliest of the three great decipherments should be the first to give an independent blessing, in however wavering a tone, to the latest.

A GENEALOGY OF WRITING IN THE OLD WORLD

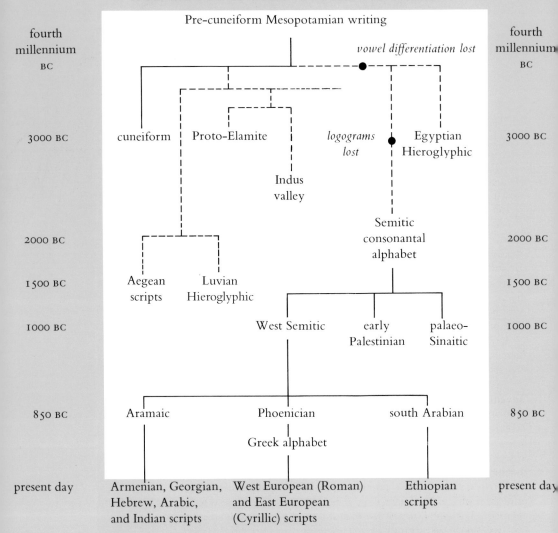

| fourth millennium BC | Pre-cuneiform Mesopotamian writing | fourth millennium BC |

vowel differentiation lost

| 3000 BC | cuneiform   Proto-Elamite   *logograms lost*   Egyptian Hieroglyphic | 3000 BC |

Indus valley

| 2000 BC | Semitic consonantal alphabet | 2000 BC |

| 1500 BC | Aegean scripts   Luvian Hieroglyphic | 1500 BC |

| 1000 BC | West Semitic   early Palestinian   palaeo-Sinaitic | 1000 BC |

| 850 BC | Aramaic   Phoenician   south Arabian | 850 BC |

Greek alphabet

| present day | Armenian, Georgian, Hebrew, Arabic, and Indian scripts   West European (Roman) and East European (Cyrillic) scripts   Ethiopian scripts | present day |

The history of writing

Readers of this book may like to have a brief conspectus to show how the various scripts discussed in it are related to each other and to the main writing systems that are in use in the modern world.

Establishing paternity requires very complete evidence. The evidence for the early history of writing is far from complete; so we have to make do with probabilities, a subjective matter. Broadly speaking there are two approaches, one optimist, the other pessimist. The optimist approach, with its eye on the intelligence and adaptability of mankind, is ready to believe in writing systems being independently invented or consciously improved. The pessimist approach, impressed by the difficulty of persuading societies to accept innovations in an established system, let alone replace them with whole new ones, prefers to account for the variety of scripts by faulty copying and occasional improvisation.

This latter approach is the one I favour. It has the important advantage that it accords with all known analogy. In other words it assumes that what happened in the early history of writing, which we do not know, was much the same as that which later happened in the history of the scripts, which we do know. For example Cyrillic and Coptic, Armenian and Georgian, the missionary scripts for previously unwritten languages in America and Africa, have all been close copies of the most prestigious script of their time and place (Greek, Aramaic, western European) with adaptations of detail to suit the requirements of the new language, but with no innovations of principle. The vernacular languages of western Europe took over the Latin script, Latin took over (either directly or through Etruscan) an early Greek script, and Greek itself took over the Phoenician script – all with slight alterations of detail but no intended alteration of system. It is true that a new system, the alphabetic, resulted from the way in which the Greeks used the Phoenician 'alep, he, yod, 'ayin, and waw to represent a, e, i, o, u. But, as Jeffery (1961, pp. 2, 22) argues, this is much more likely to have been accident than design. For these five Phoenician consonants are precisely the ones that would have been meaningless to a Greek ear, and the Greek who first used these signs as vowels almost certainly thought that he was using them in the same way as his model.

It is therefore a fair assumption that if neighbouring scripts operate on the same general principles, this is likely to be the result of borrowing. The question remains whether the scripts of the Early Bronze Age did share the same general principles. Since some of them are undeciphered, and some are only known to us from a later period, we cannot be sure. But since they all have the same system of writing numbers (and, where it can be checked, fractions too), and since they probably all contained a signary of phonetic signs (as I have tried to show in *Antiquity*, March 1966), the hypothesis of a common origin is a legitimate one. Nevertheless, it remains a hypothesis. Those who prefer the theory of independent evolutions may still use the genealogical table on page 180 by excising the dotted lines. They will then start the history of Near East writing from seven points instead of from one.

In any case the table, as they say in auditors' reports, should be read in conjunction with the accompanying notes.

NOTES

1. *Pre-cuneiform Mesopotamian writing* seems to have already possessed phonetic signs, according to Falkenstein (1936). Although it cannot on present knowledge be asserted to have possessed an ordered syllabary, the hypothesis that it did is not an irresponsible one, since theories of independent evolution require equally hypothetical explanations repeated separately for each script.

Chinese writing, which appears in China with the Shang dynasty simultaneously with other Middle East cultural influences, may be a cousin of this pre-cuneiform script, the common ancestor of the two perhaps being purely logographic. It would be possible to account for a syllabary arising from this if we apply the same principle of loss as for the other innovations on the table. For if the meanings of the word-signs were forgotten (perhaps by being borrowed to serve another language) one would be left with just their sounds. But here we are in the realm of pure speculation. The total independence, however, of Mesoamerican writing seems now to be beyond question (see Postscript, pp. 192–194). The date of its first appearance (final centuries BC) and its *modus operandi* would both rule out any likelihood of foreign influence in this even if it could be shown that in other matters there had been contact between America and the Old World.

2. *Cuneiform* describes not a script but a technique of writing on clay developed by the Sumerians and Akkadians around 3000 BC, and which became for the succeeding 2500 years thereafter the standard means of writing in the Mesopotamian civilization and the civilizations derived from it. A conspectus of the cuneiform scripts is given in chapter 5 (page 112).

3. *Aegean Scripts* include the First Cretan Palace Script (the so-called Cretan Pictographic), Linear A, Linear B, Cypro-Minoan, and the Cypriot Syllabary of classical times. The script of the unique and still undeciphered Phaistos Disk may be provisionally thought of as a third member of the broad family that includes Aegean and Luvian Hieroglyphic.

4. *Egyptian Hieroglyphic* remained in use as the monumental script of Egypt throughout the three millennia of ancient Egyptian civilization. The cursive hieratic and demotic scripts derived from it, and the latter even contributed a few letters to the Coptic script of Christian Egypt.

The primary phonetic signs of Egyptian Hieroglyphic are consonantal in value and about twenty-four in number. It has therefore
often been thought that the ancestors of the Semitic scripts was
consciously created from Egyptian by borrowing these signs and
these alone. This is by no means impossible, though I prefer the
alternative here outlined.

In the developed Egyptian phonetic signary there are some
eighty bi-consonantal (as well as some tri-consonantal) signs. On
the monogenesis theory these present a certain embarrassment and
must be explained either as elaborations made within the tradition
of Egyptian writing after its establishment or as derived from
CVC-type syllables of pre-cuneiform writing. On the other hand
the champions of logographic-to-alphabetic simplification are not
without embarrassments of their own. For the simple unicon-
sonantal signs are already present in full force in the earliest
Egyptian writing that we have.

5. *West Semitic, early Palestinian, palaeo-Sinaitic* are names given
to the scripts of various inscriptions found in the Sinai peninsula
and in the Levant coastal area; they are of dates ranging from the
sixteenth to the eighth century BC. Some can be read. Others from
their small signary, their geographical proximity, and their
similarity of general appearance can be reasonably assumed to be
of the same family, though neither the precise affiliations within
it nor even the precise number of different scripts can yet be
determined.

6. *South Arabian*'s descendants include Thamudic, Lihyanic, and
Safaitic. It seems to have diverged from Phoenician by the
thirteenth century BC (see page 201, note 5).

7. *Phoenician* is the ancestor of Punic, Iberian, and Numidian
(whence comes the still-used Tamachec); also of Old Hebrew
(and the still-used Samaritan).

8. *Aramaic* and Aramaic-derived scripts spread through most of
the cuneiform-using world in the first millennium BC and eventually replaced cuneiform. The family includes the scripts of the
Sassanian inscriptions, of Palmyra, of Petra and other Nabataean
cities, Pahlavi, Sinaitic, and Syriac, as well as the surviving
descendants listed in the table.

9. *Greek.* The Greek alphabet probably originated from Greek
colonists living in north Syria in the middle of the eighth century
BC (see Jeffery 1961, p. 21). Its use spread rapidly through the
Greek world, taking a variety of local forms. Eventually the
Ionian form became standard, being officially adopted in Athens
in 403 BC.

Descendants of the Greek alphabet that are no longer in use
include Etruscan, Runic, Gothic, and Coptic.

On the origin of the separate vowel notation that is characteristic of Greek and Greek-descended writing, see the brief remarks
at the beginning of this chapter.

Lake
Van

URARTIAN

RIAN

Nimrod
ASSYRIAN

Hamadan

Behistun

PERSIAN

Euphrates

Tigris

ELAMITE

Susa

PROTO-
ELAMITE

Persepolis

Babylon
AKKADIAN

almyra

Uruk
SUMERIAN

C
BETS

Cuneiform	PERSIAN
Non–Cuneiform	/// AEGEAN

The scripts of the Near East.
Hatching shows the areas of
usage of non-cuneiform
writing systems, stippling
the central area of usage of
cuneiform. Cuneiform
scripts were used to write the
languages whose names are
underlined

Morals

All good stories end with a moral. The natural thing to ask at the end of our survey of decipherments is whether there is any single pattern to which they can be reduced. So let us look at them again with this question in mind.

Every decipherment is ultimately a substitution cipher. If we are told that *xyz*, *xypqrs*, *trp* spell out the English names for farm animals, we could by trial and error arrive at the answer DOg, DONkEy, hEN. The interlocking of the letters in capitals would give it a high measure of probability, though only an exhaustive search through the English dictionary could convert this into certainty.

Now consider what made this problem easy. First, we knew it was solvable. Second, we had a limited target (English farmyard animals). Third, we knew the rules (letter for letter English spelling). The last of these requirements is less simple than it sounds. Suppose the ciphered script, like the Cypriot syllabary and some of the Bronze Age ones, had not distinguished between voiced and unvoiced stops. Then the *k* and the *g* would have been represented by the same sign. Or suppose the ciphered script had been a truly phonetic alphabet. Then the *n* and the *e* would not have recurred in it. In either case the answer would have been more difficult both to reach and to confirm. Among other things we would have needed to know how the English words spelled 'donkey' and 'hen' were pronounced.

It has been the same with the historical decipherments. These are the three preliminary conditions that have had to be satisfied. The first of them, confidence in the ultimate solubility of the problem, being of a psychological nature, is the most difficult to be specific about. But it was clearly the lack of such confidence that led to the almost total neglect of the hieroglyphic part of the Rosetta Stone for the first ten or fifteen years after its discovery. Had Hyde's view of the nature of cuneiform (page 88) prevailed, no sane person would have devoted his time to it. It was only the belief in its decipherability that led Le Brun and Niebuhr to spend so long copying the inscriptions. It was perhaps partly despair at the prospect of trying to solve an unknown language written in an unknown script that delayed the publication and analysis of Linear B.

The most effective way to fulfil the second condition, a limited target, was that proposed by Leibnitz in 1714 – the location and identification of proper names (page 95). This has been the line taken by all the decipherments in this book except that of the Ugaritic alphabet. The proper names have been known either through biscripts, or through historical and geographical information variously acquired, in most cases through ancient Greek authors. The means for locating the names have been various, and have differed in their degree of precision. Where there was a biscript, it was generally possible to ascertain that 'this sign–group must represent that name', in the other cases only that 'this sign-group must represent one of those names'.

Finally, the discovery of the rules of the script. This, to adopt a metaphor once used by Medawar in describing scientific research, has been the side of the drawer that has most often stuck. The direction of writing must be determined; the different signs must be recognized and counted. This is not so straightforward as it sounds, even with the aid of good copies. For instance, in our own script, having observed that R stood in the same relation to P as Q to O, E to F, and L to I, you might count these as four letters plus a modifying stroke instead of eight. After this the signs must be classified by function. They may be all phonetic, or they may include ideograms and determinatives. The phonetic signs may be alphabetic or syllabic. If alphabetic, they may or may not include separate signs for vowels. If syllabic, the syllables they represent may be open only, or both open and closed, or even more complicated. That is to say they may be of the type CV, or CV and VC, or both these together with CVC and even CVCV. There do not seem to be any scripts with a syllabary of the type VC only, though theoretically there could be. Then the script has to be accommodated to the language it is used for. The phonetic representation is likely to be both prolix and insufficient (as in English the letters *c* and *x* are superfluous to requirement, while a frequent sound like *sh* has no letter to represent it), and these anomalies may necessitate artificial spelling devices (as in English 'brag' adds a *g* to make 'bragging', while 'page' drops an *e* to make 'paging', and as syllabaries adopt different conventions to denote consonant clusters and consonantal endings). This list of difficulties is not exhaustive, but it will serve to indicate the range of possible problems, many of which had to be solved without there being at the time any precedent to work on.

Where the limits set by the target have been relatively easy and the nature of the script readily recognized, the drawer has not stuck. Barthélemy in Paris and Swinton in Oxford in January 1754 independently solved the decipherment of the Palmyra script within hours of setting to work on the newly published transcriptions of Dawkins and Wood. The decipherment of the Sassanid and Parthian inscriptions in 1787 caused Sacy no great trouble. In 1929 Virolleaud showed the gateway to the decipherment of the Ugaritic script immediately after its discovery; and despite the absence of either a bilingual or known proper names he and two others independently passed through it with great rapidity. The fact that the inscriptions were in a known language, coupled (in the first two cases) with the presence of a biscript giving proper names, limited the target. The alphabetic nature of the script was clear in the first two, and highly probable in the third, from a counting of the separate signs.

The same technique of sign-counting showed that the Cypriot script must be an open syllabary. Since this conclusion was generally accepted and was in fact correct, and since there existed a biscript with proper names recorded in it to provide a means of access, it is perhaps surprising that the script was not deciphered more quickly than it was. This was no doubt partly due to the accident that George Smith, who made the first attempt on it, did not know Greek. Nevertheless, within three years there appeared two independent decipherments, both of them almost totally correct.

In the case of the slowest of the more recent decipherments, that of Hittite Hieroglyphic, the side of the drawer that stuck was not that concerning the nature of the script – this was early recognized as syllabic with an ideographic element – but the problem of limiting the target. Until Karatepe there was only one brief bilingual. The crucial determinatives for KING and CITY were long confused. The language was not known until after the recovery of cuneiform Hittite and Luvian. The back of the decipherment was then very quickly broken, independently, by Gelb and Forrer.

The three decipherments that are generally recognized as having presented the most formidable tasks and whose accomplishment merits the greatest admiration, those of Persian cuneiform, Linear B, and Egyptian, were not in essence different from any of the others. In the case of Persian cuneiform the lack of a bilingual was made good by Grotefend's location and identification of the names of Hystaspes, Darius, and Xerxes, and his justified expectation that they would have used the title King of Kings. The reason that Grotefend's success was only partial was because his Persian – indeed the Persian philology of his day – was insufficient. He was also wrong about the nature of the script, thinking it alphabetic, not syllabic. The former defect was repaired by Rask and Burnouf, the latter by Lassen and Rawlinson. All that was now needed for full decipherment was a wider range of text, and this Rawlinson himself supplied with his copies of the great Behistun inscription.

In the case of Linear B there was no bilingual aid either. Since the only Linear B documents we have are palace inventories, it was not likely that the lack of a direct bilingual could be made good by finding royal names in them, even if we had any reliable knowledge about what Mycenaean kings were called. Ventris did, however, succeed in identifying a category of words on the tablets which might represent place-names. Various place-names in the Knossos area were known from classical sources, and it was these, together with some acute analysis of the grammatical inflections of the language and some few vocabulary words whose meaning was certain or probable from the contexts of their usage, that provided the necessary limited target. From the size of the phonetic signary it could be deduced that the script must be a syllabary, and probably an open one like the Cypriot. This might have been enough for decipherment if the spelling rules had been the same as for the Cypriot. The first person to question the universal, and reasonable, assumption that they would be, was Ventris in his Work-Notes 9 and 14. This was the indispensable step. But what made the Linear B decipherment unique and caught the imagination of the world was the abstract phonetic grid, initiated by Kober and greatly extended by Ventris. Its effect was to define the employment of the syllabic signs more closely than before. Instead of saying 'sign x stands for a syllable' it became possible to say 'sign x stands for a syllable sharing one element with the syllable represented by sign y'. So the writing rules were known more precisely, and this made up for the smallness and imprecision of the target area.

Lastly, Egyptian. Why did the decipherment of the hieroglyphs take so long? More than twenty years after the discovery of the

Rosetta Stone, over three hundred years since the discovery of the script. Looked at from another point of view one could say, however, that the decipherment was remarkably quick. The possibility of the cartouches spelling proper names was first suggested in 1811. Though many cartouches were known, the only one firmly attributable to a particular king was that of Ptolemy on the Rosetta Stone. The first cartouche to be identified through the number of signs it had in common with Ptolemy's was that of Cleopatra. Though recognized by Bankes and known to Young in England some years earlier, no copy of it reached Champollion until January 1822. This was only nine months before he announced the first stage of his decipherment. And the reason that it took months not minutes was largely the homophones. The *t* of Ptolemy was a different sign from the *t* of Cleopatra. The interlocking could be accomplished, but only by calling on a much wider range of evidence. This is what Champollion was capable of doing, while Young was not.

So there is a pattern to which all the decipherments have conformed; but there is also a moral of another and more general sort which concerns the introduction of new ideas. Consider for example the decipherment of Linear B, a feat of intellect if ever there was one. It was made possible by a multitude of ideas. Among them were Leibnitz's suggestion of the utility of proper names, made in 1714; the syllabic grid, which dates from at least the seventeenth century and was used for decipherment purposes by Rawlinson, Hincks, and Schmidt in the nineteenth; the realization that grammatical inflection could be used to draw up a grid in the abstract (Kober 1945–48). The only equivalent idea of this nature contributed by Ventris was the realization of how the Linear B spelling rules must differ from the Cypriot. Everything else was application, brilliant though it often was, of ideas that had been introduced by others.

If this should seem strange, let us remember that it is difficult to credit other decipherers with even one new idea of comparable magnitude. We might perhaps allow Sayce's discovery of the use of determinatives in Hittite Hieroglyphic and Schmidt's use of the grid principle to help in discovering the values of Cypriot signs; certainly Lassen's discovery of the 'inherent vowel' in Persian cuneiform qualifies. But not Grotefend's use of Persian history and Persian royal titles, which had been suggested by Olaf Tychsen, nor Champollion's use of cartouches, which had derived from Sacy's conjecture.

The paradox lies in the use of the word 'idea'. Structural ideas differ from ideas of application in the same way as, in a building, structural walls differ from partition walls. Partitions can be erected and taken down more or less at will. To erect a new structural wall on the other hand is a different matter altogether, in fact it cannot really be done as an isolated operation; while to knock one down is disastrous unless you have previously made other arrangements to distribute the load.

This is the primary reason why the decipherment of the hieroglyphs took so long to start. The structural framework of theory was quite wrong, and it is this which was difficult to remodel. We

can see why if we try to put ourselves in the position of the Abbé
Barthélemy in 1762 making for the first time (albeit for two wrong
reasons) the correct suggestion that the cartouches might contain
the proper names of kings. Why did he not add 'written phonetically' or 'perhaps written phonetically'? The statement 'The cartouches spell the names of kings' would not have been nonsense
like 'music smells green', nor would it have been contrary to
perception like 'wood is liquid'; so why could the statement not
have been made? Certainly not because it would have been
original. The eighteenth century was no foe to originality. But
there is a difference between originality and folly, and to have
made such a statement in 1762 would have seemed the arbitrary
act of a fool. It would have been demolishing one of the supports
of a fully structured theory without putting anything in its place.
It was not owing to neglect that Egyptology took so long to arrive
at a point where decipherment was possible; the subject was on the
whole energetically pursued. Nor was the necessary intellect
lacking: on the whole those pursuing it were clever men. It was
the great difficulty of altering a stable and coherent theoretical
structure.

Egyptian writing was regarded as direct philosophical or
theological communication by symbols and not by language. This
edifice of ideas was erected in Graeco-Roman antiquity and re-
inhabited in the Renaissance. Many supplementary ideas arose to
furnish and equip it, including the whole literature of emblem
books and the accompanying codes of artistic practice. The
existence of Mexican and Chinese writing, the Hebrew Renaissance, the discovery of Egyptian texts in a cursive script all called
into question the uniqueness of the hieroglyphs, the quality of their
wisdom, and their sphere of use. Though each of these new factors
demanded minor alterations in the original Neoplatonist theory,
none of them caused any weakening of belief in the ideographic
nature of the script. Indeed they strengthened it, particularly
the last. For if the cursive texts were alphabetic, the hieroglyphic
must be symbolic, or why the two? Even Sacy's conjecture
in 1811 that the signs in a cartouche were to be read phonetically was intended to support the original structure. Its purpose
was to explain, on supposed Chinese analogy, how an ideographic script could write proper names while remaining for
the most part ideographic. This led directly, and fairly quickly, to
the decipherment of the 'phonetic hieroglyphs' in the cartouches.
The realization that these phonetic values were valid outside the
cartouches too could perhaps not have been long delayed. But it
is worth noticing that when it came, the general theory of Egyptian writing had been badly weakened by the demolition of what
had now become one of its major supports – the distinction
between the cursive script (supposedly phonetic) and the hieroglyphs (supposedly ideographic). This distinction was demolished
by Young and Champollion independently between 1814 and
1821. On the positive side too an all-clear had been given to the
wider application of phonetic values. For Chinese and Egyptian
were considered capable of illuminating one another, and
Rémusat had argued in 1822 that phoneticism was an important

factor in ordinary Chinese writing apart altogether from the notation of names.

In the case of the other decipherments in this book, with the partial exception of Linear B, the available theoretical structures were as much of a help as they were a hindrance to the solution of Egyptian writing. This is no cause for surprise. The decipherment of Egyptian hieroglyphic had shown what could be expected in the way of determinatives and ideograms, and to some extent greater familiarity with various Eastern writings in the modern world had helped by suggesting other possible conventions that could exist. Where the right theoretical structure has been available the path from the discovery of a script to its decipherment has generally been short, and sometimes has been taken independently by two or more people.

There are two other morals, one of which I find embarrassing, the other congenial. The embarrassing one is the frequency with which right ideas have been entertained for the wrong reasons. The outstanding example of this is Barthélemy's original suggestion that the cartouches contained proper names (see page 53), but Sacy's conjecture that they were spelled phonetically (based on Chinese analogy), and Champollion's discovery of species-signs or determinatives (based on the supposed philosophic nature of Egyptian writing) are cases in point. So is Cowley's recognition of the Linear B sign-groups for 'boy' and 'girl' (which seems to have been suggested by the similarity of the sign for -*wo* to the ideogram of 'woman'), and Ventris' identification of the *n* series from which his decipherment began (at least half-based on the assumption that the language of Linear B would turn out to be Etruscan). Minor instances are Sayce's attribution of the Hama inscriptions to the Hittites (on the basis of arguments about 'hieroglyphic language') and Virolleaud's identification of the preposition *l* (on the ground that the word following it was a proper name). While it would be dishonest not to mention this phenomenon, it seems hardly sane to suggest that fallacies should be cultivated as the best seed-bed for truth.

The last moral, and the one that I find most congenial, is that though the individual decipherments, being difficult, dramatic, and demonstrable, deserve their reputation as the summit achievements of literary scholarship, none of them has been the achievement of inexplicable genius. Whether the ideas that have led to them have been structural ideas and come slowly, or supplementary ideas and come in rapid succession, they have come, as everything in this book shows, one after the other. The sudden *gestalt*, the lightning flash of insight that illuminates the whole landscape, has not occurred. There have been surprises, but there has been no magic. For those who prefer a rational world to a romantic one, this is a comforting conclusion.

POSTSCRIPT

The Decipherment of Carian

The nature of the problem

The Carians lived in the south-west corner of Asia Minor. They are best known today for their fourth-century BC king, Mausolus, or rather for the Mausoleum, which was built in his memory and which was as famous in the ancient world as the Taj Mahal is in ours. Homer mentions them as speaking a barbarous (i.e. non-Greek) language, as does Herodotus. They also had their own alphabet. Inscriptions in it were first recognized in 1844. They had been written far from home, at Abu Simbel, by mercenaries in the service of the pharaoh Psammetichus. Since then more inscriptions have come to light, mostly in Egypt (about 150), some in Caria itself (about 40), and one or two elsewhere. They are all brief and the sum total of words they contain barely exceeds five hundred.

There are over forty letters. This is on the high side for an alphabet, but what is rather more strange is its mixed character. About half of the letters look Greek, but the rest are *sui generis*. This is a much higher proportion of new signs than most borrowed scripts show. Nevertheless the early investigators, led by Sayce (from 1887) did the obvious thing and tried to understand the inscriptions by giving the Greek-looking letters their Greek values. The result was unsatisfactory. However there seemed no alternative, and for the best part of a century the Carian inscriptions remained opaque.[1]

A way forward

But in 1975 T. W. Kowalsky suggested a new approach – that Carian should be tackled from scratch like any other undeciphered script, and that since there existed a dozen or so biscripts where the Egyptian or Greek text contained proper names the first step should be to identify them in the Carian. This worked much better. A particularly good match, since it occurred on more than one inscription, was that between the name of the pharaoh

119 A Carian word from Buhen in Egypt, Read as *psmaśk* by Kowalski (= Psammetichus). On the traditional values it would have been read as *msnalb*

Psammetichus and a Carian sign-group of six letters. Kowalsky transliterated it *psamšk*, the *k* (a non-Greek letter form) being suggested by an inscription in Caria where it appeared to begin the Carian word for the city of Kildaros. But the match was surprising too. The *p* was a letter that looked like a Greek *m*, and the *š* one that looked like a Greek *r*.

A few years later John Ray, an Egyptologist from Cambridge who did not know of Kowalsky's article, made an attempt on similar lines. But it was more discriminating and therefore more successful. Ray observed that there were two distinct types of biscript, one in which the Egyptian text had good Egyptian-type names and another in which it had names which did not look Egyptian at all. The probable reason for this, Ray suggested, was that the Carians, being an immigrant community, often had two sets of names, one official 'Egyptian', the other their own. In that case the 'Egyptian' name was unlikely to be reproduced in the Carian text except of course for Psammetichus. The pharaoh of that name was their patron and protector, and it was natural enough for them to adopt it. Further confirmation of this was that the name was confined to Egypt and not found even there in the later inscriptions: after the Persian conquest of Egypt towards the end of the sixth century the name would have become politically undesirable.

Ray's narrowing of the field resulted in identifications, which though not immediately obvious become convincing on reflection. For example the Egyptian 'Iwrsz and *Arlis*, an extremely frequent Carian name known from Greek inscriptions in Caria (Αρλισσοσ). And as for the objection that Greek-looking letter forms should have their Greek sound-values, Ray pointed out that this was an unsafe line of reasoning – in our own script, for instance, despite its being a close relation of both Greek and Russian there are many changed values. (Our H is *e* for a Greek and *n* for a Russian, our C is a Russian *s*, our P a Greek *r*, and so on.)

Ray had confined himself to Carian inscriptions in Egypt, and in 1982 was able to claim 20 or so consistent values. And when they were applied to Carian inscriptions in Caria itself they proved successful. One example will show how the decipherment progressed. Kowalsky in 1975 had cited a name written in Egyptian *šzrkbym* as a match for a Carian sign-group which he transliterated *šarkbr°om*. His reason for the vocalic *r* was that it was the second letter in what he had identified as the Carian for Kildaros. But Ray (1987) had a more satisfactory value for the third sign, which implied that the second should be a pure vowel. He gave it the value *e* and transliterated the name as *šarkbeom*. Three years later a Carian personal name Κεβιωμοσ (Kebiomos) from Mylasa was published by Wolfgang Blümel. This enabled Adiego (1993, p. 242; 1994, p. 38) to point to a pattern. *Šar* when prefixed to a personal name could clearly make another personal name. Examples were *Šarusol/Usol, Šrquq/Quq, Šaruliat/Uliat, Saryassis/Panyassis*. And it was also true of *šarkbiom* (as Adiego transliterated it) since *kbíom* itself occurs twice at Saqqara and once at Thebes. But Adiego did not depend on one example. He found 52 certain matches (and another 18 less certain) between Carian names written in Carian and the five

No.	Sign	Value				No.	Sign	Value				No.	Sign	Value			
		A	R	K	Š			A	R	K	Š			A	R	K	Š
1	A	a	a	a	a	1	A	a	a	a	a	1	A	a	a	a	a
3	CϽ	d		g	g	3	CϽ	d		g	g	3	CϽ	d		g	g
4	Δ	l	d	d	d	4	Δ	l	d	d	d	4	Δ	l	d	d	d
5	EΛ	ù	é	e	í	5	EΛ	ù	é	e	í	5	EΛ	ù	é	e	í
6	Fꓱ	r	r	r	v	6	Fꓱ	r	r	r	v	6	Fꓱ	r	r	r	v
7	↕	λ/r		z	z	7	↕	λ/r		z	z	7	↕	λ/r		z	z
9	⊕	q	q	ĭ	t	9	⊕	q	q	ĭ	t	9	⊕	q	q	ĭ	t
10	ꓥ	b	b	b	n	10	ꓥ	b	b	b	n	10	ꓥ	b	b	b	n
11	N	m	m	m	n	11	N	m	m	m	n	11	N	m	m	m	n
12	O	o	o	o	o	12	O	o	o	o	o	12	O	o	o	o	o

120 The progress of the Carian decipherment. A = Adiego 1994 with the values confirmed by the Kaunos biscript of 1996 picked out in bold lettering. R = Ray 1987, K = Kowalsky, S = the traditional values as presented by Severovskin, 1994

hundred or so Carian names known from Greek inscriptions. This enabled him to assign phonetic values to thirty-two letters (see illustration above).

Confirmation

Despite a few doubters, most scholars had accepted the decipherment in principle by 1993 when Adiego published his full-scale book and when an International Congress was held in Rome (Giannotta 1994). Then, in 1996, a Greek/Carian bilingual was discovered at Kaunos in modern Turkey (ill. 121) which, on the scale of Carian epigraphy, can be called substantial. It was a decree granting privileges to two resident Athenians. Their names can be recognized, or reconstructed, on both parts of the stone despite its incomplete state,[2] and their verdict is incontrovertible. Nine letter-values of which the great majority could not have been predicted from their outward form, are confirmed and none is upset. This put the general correctness of the decipherment beyond question. The exact phonetic values will no doubt be given more precision by further discovery and debate, the Carian language remains little known, and the question of the origin of the script – when it was taken over and whether from Greeks or Phoenicians or from some intermediary – has scarcely been broached.[3]

So there is work still to be done, and it will undoubtedly give us further insights into what it meant to belong to a minority community in the ancient world. But though it has been a great achievement of scholarship, the decipherment of Carian cannot be expected ever to raise the Carians to a leading part in the pageant of world history.

In this last point it is quite opposite to the Maya glyphs whose decipherment has been the other triumph of recent scholarship.

The Maya Glyphs

Rumour of American literacy first reached Europe in 1516. An Indian, who claimed to be a refugee from a distant inland city, saw a Spanish official in the settlement of Darien reading a book and was astonished. 'You have writing too?' he exclaimed. 'So you too can talk to people when they're away!' He then asked to be shown the book, but could not read it as the writing was different from his own. The Spaniards could not discover his religion, but he was apparently circumcised. He also said that his people lived in walled cities, had laws and wore clothes.

The story is told by Anghiera[1] who three years later could add substance to it. Actual books had been brought back to Spain. The paper was bark, made into a single long sheet, sized with a kind of plaster, then folded like a screen and placed between wooden boards. The overall appearance was therefore booklike in our sense. The writing too was like ours in that it proceeded by lines, but the actual characters were very different, dice, hooks, loops, strips 'resembling Egyptian forms'. Anghiera adds that among the subjects for which the system could be used were history, law, religion, astronomical and agricultural tables.

These views would now be considered close to the mark. But the belief that won the day was that writing, as opposed to memory-jogging by pictures, did not exist. The main authority on the subject at the end of the century was Acosta whose *Historia natural y moral de las Indias* was published in 1590 and rapidly translated into five languages. In it he asserts, to quote the 1604 English translation, 'No Nation of the Indies discovered in our time hath had the use of letters and writings,' only of 'images and figures'. In a previous publication he had stated even more firmly 'Since the Indians do not have the use of letters they have no fixed history.'[2] So Francis Bacon made no mention of literacy when detailing the degree of civilisation attained in America, nor did the Royal Society when drawing up its list of subjects worth investigation.[3] The same orthodoxy continued throughout the eighteenth century. Warburton (p. 49) and Zoega (p. 59) both knew about Mexican and classified it as pictures, not as genuine script. About Mayan they knew nothing.

◁
121 The biscript from Kaunos discovered in 1996 (after Frei and Marek, 1997)

Rediscovery began with the great von Humboldt. In 1810 he reproduced pages of a manuscript from the Dresden library that

122 A page from the Dresden
Codex similar to some of
those illustrated by von
Humboldt in 1810, showing
the Aztec-like drawings, the
numerals, and the glyphs,
which were then new to the
world

had been up till then completely forgotten.[4] He introduced them as Aztec because the large-scale drawings resembled those in Aztec manuscripts, but he was aware that the glyphs were something new, 'like Egyptian hieroglyphs or Chinese characters'. The codex was evidently a kind of almanac, and Humboldt knew a surprising amount about its likely background. Counting by fives was common throughout America. Five, thirteen, twenty and fifty-two were 'favourite numbers'. There was a ritual cycle of 260 days (20×13), and the civil year consisted of 18 months of 20 named days plus five 'empty' days. Humboldt even printed (from Boturini) a list of the Toltec day-names from Chiapa, and knew that they were different from the Aztec names.

Humboldt was therefore on the brink of recognizing Maya as a distinct culture. Twelve years later came the first published Maya stone inscriptions. These were from Palenque and had been copied on Guatemalan government orders by a Spanish army officer, Antonio del Rio, in 1787. Del Ro's report was sent to Madrid, but first saw the light of day in an English translation published in 1822.

The availability of samples of Mayan writing together with the fact that this was the exact period of Champollion's decipherment fired an American with an ambition to do likewise. This was Constantine Rafinesque.[5] He wrote two open letters to Champollion. The task, as he saw it, was similar. As Egyptian was to Coptic, so pre-conquest Mayan must have been to the Maya languages still spoken in the area. Similarly Humboldt's book script must stand to the script on the monuments as Demotic to Hieroglyphic. The letters were 'nearly the same', and so was the numeral system – 'strokes meaning 5 and dots meaning unities, as the dots never exceed 4'.

All this was on the right lines. But Champollion died before Rafinesque could write him a third letter and Rafinesque himself died not many years later. In any case it was soon to be eclipsed by the dramatic discovery of an actual alphabet, taken down from a genuine Maya using genuine Maya signs. This should have solved all the problems at one go. Unhappily, however, it was not to be so easy.

The discoverer was well qualified to exploit his discovery. Brasseur de Bourbourg had been a parish priest in Guatemala. There he had learnt Quiché, the local Mayan language, published an orally preserved pre-conquest drama, and translated the text of a religious epic (written in Quiché but in Spanish letters) from a previously unknown manuscript. But his great discovery was made in a Madrid library. It was an extensive account of the Maya and their civilization written by a Franciscan friar (who later became a bishop), Diego de Landa. Unfortunately the manuscript Brasseur found was not the original of 1562. It was a copy, and a summarized copy at that, made about a hundred years later. Nevertheless it gave two important pieces of information about Maya writing.[6] One concerned the calendar and was an unmixed blessing. It rapidly led to an appreciation of Maya astronomical knowledge and dating techniques. The other, the purported alphabet, has been like the proverbial guide who tells the truth only half the time. Misunderstanding was inbuilt. When Landa said a letter (*a*, *b*, *c*, etc.), he will have meant a single sound, but he will have called it by its Spanish name (for example 'bay' for *b*, 'élé' for *l*). Landa's informant on the other hand can only have thought in terms either of syllables or of whole words: furthermore the Mayan script (like our own) often has more than one sign for the same sound. The result was that the equivalents he provided were sometimes a single sign, sometimes two, and on one occasion four.

Partly because of this and partly because the science of comparative philology (see p. 104) was still new and had not yet set to work to reconstruct the pre-history of the Mayan languages, the would-be decipherers, including Brasseur himself, who now moved in were unsuccessful. The most dedicated of them was Cyrus Thomas, an American from Tennessee. In a brief note in *Science* in May 1892 Thomas, an anthropologist and a scientist, announced preliminary success. Landa's alphabet, he wrote, 'was to a large extent correct', the 'great majority of the characters' were 'truly phonetic', and 'the writing was of a higher grade than had been previously supposed'. He had established its direction too: both the glyphs and the signs within the glyphs were to be read from left to right and from top to bottom. His second article, two months later, attempted to substantiate these claims, and gave rise to a sharp response from a German Americanist, Edward Seler, attacking not only Thomas's specific claims but also his whole phonetic approach on the ground that Linda's alphabet dated to well after the Spanish conquest when the scribes might well have begun to use some signs phonetically. Thomas did not give up immediately, but after ten years admitted defeat. 'The crucial test,' he had once written, 'was that the characters should give like results in new combinations.' The test was not satisfactorily passed and in 1903 he acknowledged 'that the inference of phoneticism was doubtful'. Seler had won the argument.

The Maya calendar

The attention of reputable Mayanists now focussed on the calendar. Here the information provided by Landa was an unqualified help. In fact when added to what was already known of Aztec practice it left little decipherment to do. The numerals operated, as do our own and as did the Babylonian, on a place system. On the lowest register a dot meant one, a stroke five, and a shell zero. On each ascending register this was multiplied by twenty. A single dot might therefore stand for 1, or 20, or 400, or 8000, just as our 1 stands for one or ten or hundred or thousand depending on where it comes in the sequence.

The calendar was more complicated. There was a ritual cycle of 260 days, a cycle of 360 days (18 months of 20 days each), and a civil year of 365 days. Great importance was also attached to the apparent (or synodic) Venus year of 584 days, while for the prediction of eclipses the moon was of prime consequence and the Maya knew the average length of the lunar cycle to within half a minute. Various periods resulted from the combination of these cycles. Of these the most interesting one for the historian is the so-called 'long count'. This consisted of 1,872,000 days ($=7200 \times 260$ or 5200×360), and it served the Maya as the Christian era serves us or the Year of the Hegira serves the Mohammedan world. Maya monuments regularly record the number of days since the start of the era. This works out as the equivalent of our 13 August 3114 BC and means that Maya dates can be known with total accuracy.

For more everyday purposes the Maya used a span of 37,960 days (=104 civil years=65 Venus years=146×260 days) or the half of that, their so-called round count, a period of 52 years.

These calculations, which can be extremely complicated, were carried out (together with much solid work in the way of the publication and indexing of the inscriptions) by a series of scholars from Ernst Förstemann at the end of the nineteenth century to Eric Thompson who died in 1975. But attempts at phonetic decipherment were largely abandoned. Conventional wisdom had it that at most there might be apparent phoneticism of rebus type – that is to say a kind of visual punning as if the English word 'be' were to be represented by the drawing of a honey-bee – but no more.

Reading the texts

The first serious attempt to dent this view was made by an American linguist, Benjamin Whorf, in 1933. He pointed out among other things that Landa had given separate glyphs for *ca* and *cu*, *ka* and *ku*, and that this must be genuine information because it indicated a syllabary. He suggested too that the sign for *u* might be another nugget of truth. In the codices it is often found on the left hand side of glyphs, and in Mayan languages it is a frequent grammatical prefix. These were perceptive, indeed seminal, observations. Unfortunately Whorf was tempted into building on them some over-speculative decipherments. Their demolition discredited his whole approach.

The next scholar to propose a phonetic decipherment was a Russian, Yuri Knorosov. Working at the Leningrad Institute of Ethnology and using an edition of the Maya codices which was rescued from the flames of the National Library in Berlin in 1945 (perhaps by Knorosov himself who was a soldier in the Red Army at the time though he himself later played down the story), he managed to break new ground. He did not simply propose phonetic readings that were plausible in themselves, but was able to point to other words which used the same signs in different combinations. Interlocking phonetic values, as we have seen in all the other decipherments in this book, are what is needed to establish proof.

Thus already in 1876 de Rosny had suggested *cu-tzu* as the phonetic reading for two signs prefixed to a glyph depicting a turkey in the Madrid Codex, because the first sign resembled Landa's *cu* and *cutz* is a Mayan word for 'turkey' (ill. 123a). But now Knorosov substantiated this. In the Dresden Codex a glyph generally recognized as standing for a dog deity was accompanied by two signs of which the first was de Rosny's *tzu* and the second was one of Landa's signs for *l*. From an early dictionary which was compiled in the seventeenth century or perhaps even earlier (though only published in the twentieth), *tzul* is given as meaning 'dog' (ill. 123b). Nor was this all. In another part of the Codex where the numeral

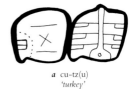

a cu-tz(u)
'turkey'

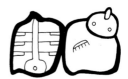

b tzu-l(u)
'dog'

c [bu]-lu-c(u)
'eleven'

123 The first steps in the phonetic decipherment of the glyphs, made by de Rosny (a) and by Knorosov (b) and (c)

11 was to be expected there were instead three signs. The first was illegible, the second was Landa's *l*, the third was Landa's *cu*. It was evidently the word for 'eleven' (*buluc* in Mayan) written out in full (ill. 123c).

Korosov offered other interlocking words, but these were the most convincing. However he had published in Russian, it was during the Cold War, and he followed up his first article with some less secure speculations. So he failed to win conviction, at any rate in the west.

What shook the orthodox view was a discovery not about language at all, but about history. It was made by another Russian, but this time one bred and educated in America, Tatiana Proskouriakoff. In front of the pyramids on top of the acropolis at Piedras Negras are groups of inscribed stones, or stelae. They

124 Stela 14 at Piedras Negras shows the accession of Ruler 5 in AD 758. Texts on its sides record the particulars of his early life

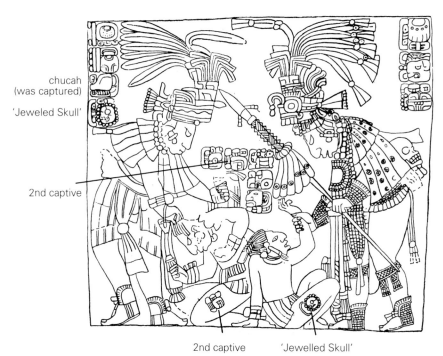

chucah
(was captured)

'Jeweled Skull'

2nd captive

u bac
(his captive)

'Bird Jaguar'

Yaxchilán
Emblem Glyph

2nd captive   'Jewelled Skull'

were erected in groups at five-year intervals and bore a series of Maya dates. Conventional wisdom had it that they recorded temple dedications, regular sacrificial occasions and the like. Proskouriakoff noticed that the first stela in each group showed the same scene (a figure seated in a raised niche) and that this was associated with a particular hieroglyph and a specific date. This was always preceded by another event which took place between 12 and 31 years earlier. The total time-span covered by each group never exceeded 64 years. The simple explanation was that the stones recorded human lifetimes, and since the monuments had such a prominent position, royal lifetimes. In that case, the first stone in each group described the ruler's birth and accession (this being 12 to 31 years later than his birth); the rest, subsequent events in his career.

The stones were therefore historical monuments. Their texts recorded dynastic names, titles and achievements. This doubled the interest of Mayan decipherment. It also confirmed Knorosov in a small particular. One of his words had been *chu-ca-h(a)* 'captured' (the *chu* interlocking with *cu-ch(u)* 'burden'). It had accompanied a captured god in the Dresden Codex: the same glyph was now to be read at Yaxchilán next to a captive prisoner of war on a limestone relief.

The process of confirmation was at first slow. There were good reasons for this. The language, classical Mayan, was known only from its descendants. Publication of the numerous, and elaborate, stone inscriptions, often from remote sites, was inherently difficult. So was the indexing and cross-referencing needed to establish a reliable sign-list. All these, in their different ways, have been major

chu-ca-h(a)
'captured'

125 A limestone relief showing the capture of Jeweled Skull by Bird Jaguar of Yaxchilán

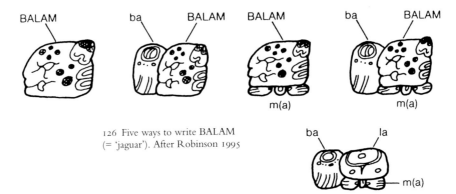

126 Five ways to write BALAM
(= 'jaguar'). After Robinson 1995

feats of organization. There was also considerable scepticism to
overcome. With Mayan as with Akkadian and Linear B (see pp. 114
and 177) a main stumbling-block has been the apparent laxity of
spelling conventions. Quite different-looking glyphs can represent
126   the same word. One's natural reaction is to think 'How impossible!'
But of course the same kind of thing can happen in our own script.
Consider

    53   LIII   liii   FIFTY-THREE   fifty-three

These are five ways of writing the same number, and visually
speaking they scarcely have a sign in common. Likewise with dates.
There are many ways to write, say, the Fourth of July, but
whichever way we use familiarity makes it instantly recognizable. It
must have done the same for the Maya. But a decipherer is not so
automatically familiar with the language or the script. He has to
proceed glyph by glyph and word by word with frequent doubt and
occasional error.

However for specialists the decipherment is now a fact of life,
and for the public it has already passed the acceptance point. The
credibility given to Akkadian by the 'unseen translation' of the
Tiglath Pileser cylinder (p. 14), to Luvian by the Karatepe bilingual
(p. 142), and to Linear B by the tripod tablet (pp. 176–7) has been
given to Mayan by a cup which carried a glyph that could be
transliterated *ca-ca-u(a)* and which, when it was sent to a laboratory
on Michael Coe's initiative, was found to have contained chocolate. (Our word cocoa for a chocolate-derived drink is descended
from the Mayan word.)

Origins and conclusions

The first origins of Maya writing may go back as far as 250 BC and
of its apparent ancestor, Zapotec, to around 600 BC and it was still
flourishing when the Spaniards came. Had the Spaniards kept the
tradition of Maya literacy alive there would have been no need for
a decipherment. But they did not. The missionaries taught Spanish
and the Spanish alphabet, and far from preserving Maya books
destroyed them. The result was that the glyphs died out and were
replaced by the Spanish alphabet even for writing in Mayan.

This is easy enough to understand, however sad for historians and anthropologists. What is more surprising is the previous failure of the Maya script to spread within America itself. Like Egyptian, but unlike nearly all other old-world scripts (see table on p. 180), it never travelled. Not even the Aztecs, who ultimately dominated the area and had a very similar tradition of painting and of book production (though their paper was made from a different substance), took it over. This is a problem if you believe that phonetic writing is a kind of evolutionary stage and comes more or less automatically once a society has achieved a certain level. For how could the Aztecs, who were as civilized as the Maya, have kept the pictures but dropped the script? Or can it be that phoneticism is not necessarily the most sophisticated stage, and that for their purposes the Aztecs found that pictures served better than words? After all we ourselves are far more graphicate than our grandparents and perhaps less literate: at any rate there are many contexts, from packaging to computer-screens, where we seem to prefer icons to the written word.[7] Another possible explanation is that Maya writing, even though phonetic, might not have appeared transferable for use in another language either to the Aztecs or to the Maya themselves.[8]

But whatever the truth on this matter there can no longer be any doubt that the Maya glyphs are genuine writing. And it was clearly invented or evolved, not borrowed. Whatever contact there may or may not have been between America and Asia after the first crossing of the Bering Strait, its date, its general appearance, and the system by which it operates proclaim its originality. It is the only script whose independent invention can be so firmly stated. Even Chinese appeared late and at a time when Mesopotamian influence cannot be excluded.

The originality of the Maya script gives it a unique interest, quite apart from the light it sheds on human history in what can no longer, thanks to its decipherment, be thought of as a New World.

127 Glyph on a cup found to have contained chocolate. After Robinson 1995

Notes on the Text

INTRODUCTION (pp. 9–10)

1 In the 18th century the Japanese public were forbidden contact with Europe and America, but some medical students caught sight of a textbook of anatomy at Nagasaki (where Dutch ships were permitted an annual visit) and were greatly impressed by the illustrations which showed bodily organs looking like the real thing and not as their Chinese professor described them. At considerable personal risk they got hold of a copy, smuggled it ashore, and by 1775 had succeeded in translating it. Though one of them knew a little spoken Dutch and they had managed to get hold of a small Dutch dictionary, they none of them knew the values of the European letters or how they operated. The feat must therefore count as a genuine decipherment, and one partially outside the Western tradition. An autobiographical account of it was written by Gempaku Sugita in 1815 (when he was 83) and is summarized in English by Eikoh Ma (1959).

CHAPTER I (pp. 11–42)

1 It is remarkable that in his account of his travels in the Greek islands, written in 1422, Buondelmonte gives the position, height, and pedestal inscription of the Constantinople obelisk, but makes no mention at all of its clearly carved hieroglyphs. He calls the monument an *agulia* and shows no awareness of its Egyptian origin – see note 3.

2 Cyriac describes the inscription (ed. Mehuns, p. 51) as 'a most ancient epigram in Phoenician characters, a thing unknown to men of our age presumably because of the long time that has elapsed and of the falling into disuse of the greatest and most ancient arts and our ignorance of them'. It is generally considered (e.g. Weiss 155) that the reference is to a specifically hieroglyphic inscription, and hieroglyphs are certainly referred to as having been seen by Cyriac in Marsupino's verses to him printed in Mehuns' edition. I am not sure why he calls them Phoenician, nor how he saw them on the Great Pyramid, as he seems to claim.

3 The precise term used to describe an obelisk is a small matter in itself, but it is symptomatic of the state of historical awareness. *Obelus* or *obeliscus* (variously spelt) is used in the *Notitia de regionibus urbis Romae* (a description of Rome, basically third-century A D, but with subsequent additions – see Nordh's edition, Lund 1949) together with the mention of 'Egyptian signs' (*notae Aegyptiacae*), and in a Carolingian itinerary (printed by Valentini and Zucchetti *Codice Topographice della Città di Roma* II 163–207). After this it seems to have fallen out of use. The only medieval instance of the word I have found is the phrase *obeliscus Neronis* in the *ordo Romanus* of the Benedictine canon (Valentini and Zucchetti III 212), which is presumably taken over verbatim from an earlier version.

The medieval terms for an obelisk are *aguglia* or *guglia*, Latinized as *agulia* or *Iulia* – the latter being either a phonetic transliteration or taken as agreeing with *columna* in reference to Caesar's tombstone. This is perhaps more probable, as I do not think *Iulia* occurs except where it relates specifically to the Vatican obelisk. Alternatively the word may be translated *acus*, 'needle'. Or a specific term may be avoided, and *lapis* or *saxum* used as for example by Petrarch (*Familiarium rerum lib.* vi 2).

The technical term of classical Latin, *obelus* or *obeliscus*, was revived by Poggio and Biondo in the mid-fifteenth century, and used by subsequent writers, who thereby identify themselves as humanists, and who are at the same time aware of what Pliny and others said of the Egyptian origin of obelisks.

Strozzi's immediate source for his captions on the map (ill. 1b) was perhaps Tortellius *Commentariorum Grammaticorum de Orthographia dictionum* (Rome 1471), who took much of his topographical information from Biondo (see Weiss, p. 71). For prototype of the maps see Scaglia (*J. Warb. Inst.* 27, 136–63).

4 The detail illustrated shows in about a third of the whole mosaic. The temple is marked out as Egyptian by the twin obelisks and the sacred lake. Animals, apart from those in the detail illustrated, include a lioness, tiger, lynx, giraffe, deer, and various unreal, or at least unidentified creatures such as a kêpien, a sphingia, an ass-centaur, a crocodileopard, and a crocottas (perhaps a cross between a wolf and a dog or a hyena and lioness).

Gullini (1956) takes it that the mosaic was laid down at the same time as the building in the early first century. Peters (1963) dates it half a century later on grounds of landscape style.

5 Cicero *de leg.* ii 2. The authority for Cicero's poem on the Nile is the writer in *Script. Hist. Aug.* 20, 3, 2.

6 Meroë was some nine hundred miles south of Aswan, near the modern Khartoum. It was the southernmost city of which the Romans had any knowledge. The Iseum in the Campus Martius was next to the so-called *ovile* or *Saepta* where voting had taken place in Republican times.

7 The plaque was discovered by A. Rowe in his excavation of the Serapeum. Its translation, after Rowe (1946), reads:
Hieroglyphic Text: The King of the South and North, heir of the Brother-Gods, chosen of Amun, powerful in the life of Rê, the son of Rê, Ptolemy, living for ever, beloved of Ptah, made this Temple and Sacred Enclosure of Serapis.
Greek Text: King Ptolemy, son of Ptolemy and Arsinoe, the Brother-Gods, [dedicates] to Serapis the Temple and the Sacred Enclosure.

8 Ill. 3d is reproduced from the publication of the papyrus by Bauer and Strzygowski (1905). The sack of the Serapeum is described by various authors, notably Rufinus *Hist. Eccl.* II 23 ff., and Eunapius *Vit. Soph.* vi 11.

9 The fullest references are still to be found in Zoëga (1797) who cites (458–9) several dozen passages in some twenty-five ancient authors in support of these different usages of the hieroglyphic script.

10 The references are Cicero *de nat. deorum* iii 56; *Corpus Hermeticum Asclepius* i 8; Lactantius *Div. Inst.* i 6, 2 and iv 6, 4.
The ultimate source for the ideas is Plato's *Timaeus*, though Lactantius thought that Plato was following Hermes Trismegistus, since he accepted the authenticity of the Hermetic tracts (see his *de ira dei* 11). Ficino, the Renaissance exponent of Neoplatonism, in the preface to his edition of Lactantius (1471), says the same: 'The founder of theology is said to be Mercurius Trismegistus. The next most important part in ancient theology was played by his follower Orpheus. . . .' The tradition, Ficino continues, then passed through the Orphic mysteries to Aglaophemus, Pythagoras, Philolaus, and eventually to Plato.
The Hermes Trismegistus mosaic, together with mosaics of the ten Sibyls (also on the authority of Lactantius via Ficino), on the pavement of Siena Cathedral, were laid during the rectorship of Alberto Aringhieri, a Knight of St John of Jerusalem and Rhodes, which terminated in 1498.

11 *pensiculate* in Aulus Gellius (i 3, 12 and xiii 20, 11). Pointed out by Pozzi (1959, p. 87).

12 Poliphilus' interpretation of the first three hieroglyphs is *patientia ornamentum custodia protectio vitae* ('endurance is the ornament, guard, and protection of life'), which Pozzi and Ciapponi in their edition explain simply by the five symbols taken in the order ox-head, branches, dog, helmet, lamp.
Poliphilus' rendering is rather bald, and its relevance to his situation none too clear. It is tempting to try to improve on it. This would certainly not be legitimate purely on the grounds that Poliphilus is still at an early stage of his journey, but it may be made so by the fact that Pierius suggests a richer meaning for some of the symbols. He says that the helmet, though it stands for defence, can also signify that the sources of life are temporarily hidden since it is an attribute of Pluto's. The dog is fidelity rather than just guardianship. The festooned ox-head means labour rewarded. These symbolisms, together with the order of the inscription, would suggest to me an interpretation on the lines of 'be faithful, wary, and persevering, and you will be rewarded as you go through life'. This would be more interesting sense and very much more appropriate to the siting of the inscription on the bridge that leads Poliphilus, now escaped from the City of the Past, into the country of Nature.
There is no difficulty over the other two signs on the other side of the bridge. The circle means 'always'. The dolphin ('speed' and 'life-saving') and anchor ('security') together mean 'make haste slowly'. This was adopted by Aldus as the emblem for his press – see Pozzi and Ciapponi, 1964, ii 62.

13 The subject of Pierius' Book xxxiii is the symbolism of the human sense organs, its immediate context a lecture on Pindar (*Nemeans* viii 43) *à propos* of pleasure showing itself in the eyes, and its form a dialogue between leading scholars of the time. They are Pierius' uncle Urbanus (1440–1524), the first to publish a Greek grammar in Latin, and who had himself travelled in Egypt; Raynerius, a Senator of Venice, a Procurator of St Mark's, and a member of the 'Aldine Academy'; Thomaeus (1456–1531), the Aristotelian philosopher; and Leonicenus (1428–1524), Professor of Medicine at Ferrara. According to Cosenza (1967), Thomaeus' pupils included Copernicus and Latimer, Leonicenus' pupils included Latimer, Linacre, and Ariosto.
The participants in the dialogue, which Pierius represents as having actually taken place, are an eloquent testimony to the importance attached at the time to the subject of hieroglyphics.

14 See Jequier (1921, p. 177), Sbordone (1940) on Horapollo i 55, 56, and Pierius xvii.

15 In 1582 the Matthaean obelisk was moved by Kyriacos Matthaeus to his garden on Monte Celio: in 1586 the Vatican obelisk was moved by Sixtus V to the area in front of St Peter's: in 1587 the Esquiline, in 1588 the Lateran, in 1589 the Flaminian obelisks were re-erected by Sixtus V in front of S. Maria Maggiore, the Lateran Palace, and in the Piazza del Popolo respectively: in 1589 or thereabouts the Florence obelisk was erected by Cardinal Medici in his gardens on the Pincio before being taken to Florence a few years later.

16 Caussin defines a hieroglyph as 'an image or figure arbitrarily agreed on by men to express a particular meaning, which was employed by the philosophers of Egypt instead of letters.'

17 For an English translation of Kircher's interpretation of the scarab (ill. 18), I do my best:

CENTRE: *the parts of the picture*: winged ball; serpent; rear of beetle and ball of dung; shoulder of beetle(?); head of beetle; circle of headdress; ornament on headdress; device (according to the Kircher the Coptic word for 'love'.

LEFT SIDE: *proper sense*: by the soul of the universe and life of the world • the ruler of the earth • the orbits of the Heavens • the Sun • the Moon • and the Elements • are joined in Love and conserved in their being.

RIGHT SIDE: *mystic sense*: Hemphta, the supramundane Spirit, the Archetypal Sun • Osiris • the Genii of the Heavens • Horus • Isis • the Sublunar Demons wrapped in the mighty chain of Love are taken and drawn along.

18 Kircher's Egyptian interpretations were so wild that they gave little handle for scholarly disproof. His seventeenth-century critics tended to concentrate their attack on his derivation of Greek from Coptic and his reconstruction and translation of an alleged Hebrew inscription found on what he imagined to be the site of the burning bush on Mount Horeb and reading, 'God shall make a Virgin conceive and she shall bear a son.' Readers with a taste for polemic will find lively demolitions of Kircher's methods and results in these two matters in Hottinger (1662), preface, Wagenseil (1681), 428–44, and Leuthof (1691), 442–3. The learned Archbishop Ussher had already seen through him, and told Evelyn that 'Kircher was a mountebank' (*Diary* 21st August, 1655).

Incidentally, in expounding on the Bembine Table Kircher quite ignored Pignorio's book, though he knew of its existence.

19 In the *Phaedrus* (229 D) and in the *Republic* (378 D) Plato dismisses the method of allegorical interpretation. Juvenal's main attack on Egyptian religion is at the beginning of his fifteenth satire. Pignorio's reference to Agustin is to his *de numism. dial.* 4.

20 Stillingfleete also tries to discredit Manetho on various grounds, the most interesting from our point of view being that his alleged translation of the hieroglyphics into Greek was an impossibility since hieroglyphic characters are not, and do not express, a language.

21 Comparisons between Mexican picture-writing and Egyptian hieroglyphic are as early as Mercati (1589, p. 96), though in Mercati's case it is Diodorus' supposed Ethiopian picture-writing, not directly Egyptian, which he thinks comparable.

22 *de aug. scient.* vi 1, published in 1623. Many of the positions taken up on this matter in the next two centuries (and even beyond – see Evans' ideas recounted in chapter 8) as orthodox are succinctly stated by Bacon in this chapter. These are the internationalism of gesture, particularly in making commercial transactions, and its status as a sort of 'transitory Hieroglyph'; the existence of Chinese writing as a Real Character, independent of linguistic barriers; the priority of Egyptian Hieroglyphic, a sort of pre-writing, to any alphabet except perhaps the Hebrew; even the undesirability of spelling reform since it would obscure etymologies and render old books hard to read. On Real Characters Bacon has this to say: 'Real Characters have nothing of the Emblem about them (as do Gestures and Hieroglyphs). Their outward appearance is as uncommunicative as that of the letters of the alphabet. Their creation is arbitrary and their acceptance is by usage, as if by tacit agreement. One thing that is clear is that a very great number of characters is needed for such writing: For there must be as many characters as there are root words.'

But though Bacon lists a Real Character among his *Desiderata*, he is not enthusiastic about its likely usefulness, words and letters of the alphabet being in his view very much the most convenient means of writing. A Real Character was little more than a theoretical alternative, just as it would be theoretically possible to have money made out of material other than gold and silver.

Nevertheless, the theoretical alternative was freely explored. David (1965, p. 40) lists six attempts made in the ten years before the appearance of Wilkins' book, by Lodowyck (London 1657), Beck (London 1657), Edmundson (London 1658), Dalgarno (London 1661), Becher (Frankfurt 1661), Kircher (Rome 1663).

CHAPTER 2 (pp. 43–59)

1 This was the first recognition of non-hieroglyphic Egyptian script, not of Egyptian mummies. These had long been familiar, chiefly for their reputed medical properties. Mummy substance was thought particularly beneficial in cases of broken bones and contusions, but also for many other things. There was a massive export trade in it from Egypt to Europe throughout the Middle Ages and beyond. 'Mummy is become merchandise, Mizraim cures wounds, and Pharaoh is sold for balsams', as Sir Thomas Browne put it. The trade continued into the eighteenth century. For facts and figures see Dannenfeldt (1959), 7–22.

1a The stela (*Corpus Inscr. Semiticarum* 2.1.141) is now at Carpentras where Rigord donated it. Its date is c. 500 BC when Egypt was under Persian rule. The writing is Aramaic (so Rigord's guess was not far out) but the embalmed woman, called Taba, was evidently Egyptian.

2 It was accompanied by a second article (printed in the July 1704 issue) on the origin of language and of writing. Rigord argues Hebrew for the one, and Samaritan (or Old Hebrew) for the other.

3 The first of these suggestions is partly anticipated by Menestrier, a Jesuit of Lyons and expert in heraldry, in the second of two papers on an Egyptian mummy-case which was publicly exhibited in France in 1692. Menestrier is suspicious of Kircher's interpretations, because they leave no room for the plain historical meanings in the inscriptions, which are vouched for by Greek and Roman writers. Menestrier applies the term hieroglyphic to the large-scale figures only and thinks the small ones (i.e. the real hieroglyphs) to be an example of the cursive or alphabetic script. I am not sure that this confusion entitles him to the credit, awarded him by Miss David (p. 50), of having been the first to make the suggestion that the hieroglyphs had a phonetic element.

4 By accepting the evidence of poets about the divine ancestry of their heroes Newton dated various gods to two generations before the Trojan War, and thus, by assuming that the gods were really just great men who introduced particular arts, he was able to date the invention of those arts, for example agriculture. Again, the difference between the true rate of the precession of the equinox and the rate as computed by the Greek astronomer Hipparchus enabled him, he thought, to bring down the date of the Argonaut expedition from 1247 to 937 BC. The basis of his argument was that since our traditional names of the constellations all refer to the Argonauts or earlier heroes, our star-map must have been made at the time of the Argonautic expedition and for its use – presumably by Chiron.

5 Warburton includes 'arbitrary marks' because not all the signs on the monuments are pictorial and because

of the celebrated description of the look of an Egyptian book in Apuleius (*Met.* xi 22), 'written with unknown characters, partly painted with figures of beasts . . . partly with lines whose tops and tails turned round in fashion of a wheel, joined together above like unto the tendrils of a vine, whereby they were wholly strange and impossible to be read of the profane people' (tr. Adlington, adapted).

The inclusion of animal forms in this description showed Warburton that it did not refer to alphabetic writing. On the other hand the inclusion of what were obviously arbitrary marks showed that it was on the way to it. Apuleius must therefore, he thought, be referring to the sort of 'running hand of hiero-glyphics' such as accompanied the large-scale figures on the Bembine Table. These are, of course, what we should call hieroglyphics. Warburton, who still thought of the word as primarily referring to the large-scale figures, classified the small writing as a subdivision of hieroglyphics, and suggested the name 'hierographical' for it.

6 This passage was added in the second edition of *The Divine Legation*.

7 Thus Warburton – like Rigord, though without mentioning him – takes διὰ τῶν πρώτων στοιχείων in Clement as meaning 'alphabetically'. His interpretation of the passage is, however, as one would expect, both original and ingenious (IV iv 2). Clement, he says, describes three kinds of Egyptian writing – *epistolic*, *sacerdotal*, and *hieroglyphical*. The first two proceed in 'the plain and ordinary way of writing by the first elements of words, or letters of an alphabet' (that is, curiologically): the last, to which Clement gives the name 'symbolic', can be either plainly representational (curiologic), or tropical or allegorical. The difficulty arises, according to Warburton, from Clement's having run together the two classes of hieroglyphic, the plain and the symbolic.

What shows Warburton that he has done so is Porphyry *de vita Pythag.* xi–xii, where Porphyry distinguishes between *hieroglyphic*, 'speaking openly by imitation' (κοινολογούμενα κατὰ μίμησιν) and *symbolic*, 'allegorizing enigmatically' (ἀλληγορούμενα κατά τινας αἰνιγμούς). The supposed latter class is what Warburton sometimes calls 'hierographical'.

8 For the extent of Warburton's influence on French thought see David (1965, pp. 100 ff.), and, outside France, Iversen (1961, p. 110).

9 Zoëga's vocabulary for the concepts of evolution and development includes the following: adverbs *sensim*, *lente*, *paullatim*, *gradatim*; verbs *transire*, *progredi*, *adolescere*; phrases *lento passu et per multos gradus*; analogies *quod vero evenire videmus in linguis gentium, ut natae augeantur, atque ubi ad maximam adoleverint vigorem et elegantiam, luxuriari incipiant, post marcescant, atque ad aliquam velut infantiam redeant* (541 – the stages of hieroglyphic script) and *plerumque ab exiguis initiis natae, post sensim adolevere, ac diu singulorum hominum privato commodo inservientes, paullatimque ad plures diffusae, denique nemine advertente in publicum usum transiere* . . . (550 – the diffusion of the alphabet compared to the diffusion of most very ancient human inventions).

10 Zoëga's firmest single piece of evidence was a remark

of Aristides (ii 360), an author of *c.* A D 180, that Egyptian was unwritable in Greek (*dysgrammaton*). Indeed, his date for Christian Coptic was approximately right – our earliest MSS. are late third century. It is just possible that Christian Coptic was an independent, or partly independent evolution, and not derived from the script of the magical papyri. See Kahle 244 *n.* 1, and 253.

CHAPTER 3 (pp. 60–84)

1 The French Expedition to Egypt may have been imaginative in concept and glorious in execution, but it was dogged throughout by a certain element of farce, which even extended to the publication of its results, the great *Description d'Égypte*. The historical preface, impeccably composed by the great Fourier to the highest standards of Academic French, had to be submitted to Napoleon (in a printed edition of three copies) for his approval. The alterations he made fall into two main types. The one attempted to represent the invasion of Egypt (a Turkish province) as an act of friendship to Turkey: the other referred to his own part. As an instance of the latter, Fourier, confronted with the delicate and difficult task of saying something positive about the final results of the expedition after the surrender of the whole French army, wrote that the French occupation had afforded the Egyptians the experience unusual to them of good government, and that in their hearts there still reigned the name of Bonaparte. Napoleon amended this to 'the immortal name of Bonaparte'. In the 1821 edition, in which all references to Napoleon were deleted, the phrase was changed to 'the name of France'. See Champollion-Figeac (1844, p. 130).

2 Sacy's Chinese is somewhat confused. The following comment was kindly supplied to me by Mr Ray Dawson. 'The modern word for barber is *ti-tou-de*, the *ren* having dropped off. *ti-tou-de-ren* would match Sacy's spelling except that his "*ten*" for "*tou*" seems to be a mistake. *ti* = shave, *tou* = head, and *ren* = man. *de* is a very common particle with either possessive or determinative function: so
ti-tou-de-ren = shave-head-kind of-man (det.)
ti-ren-de-tou = shave-man-'s-head (poss.)'

3 The theory of writing as the fixative agent of language, which remained in vogue until well into the nineteenth century, is at least as early as Sir William Jones, who made much use of it in his Presidential Addresses to the Asiatic Society of Calcutta. It lent itself well to the purpose of explaining how there had emerged so many different languages in the world in the very few millennia since Adam, a problem of which Jones shows himself particularly conscious.

4 'On sait que les Chinois éprouvent cet embarras, et qu'ils sont obligés quelquefois d'employer un certain signe pour avertir que les caractères qui entrent dans l'expression d'un nom propre, sont réduits à cette seule valeur. Je conjecture que dans l'inscription hiéroglyphique de Rosette, on a employé au même usage le trait qui entoure une série d'hiéro-glyphes', *Magasin Encyclopédique*, 1811, iv 184 *n.* 2. It is likely that the reflection only occurred to Sacy in the latter part of the year. Otherwise he would have

surely mentioned it in his recommendation of Rémusat's book to the *Corps Législatif*, where his whole purpose was to stress the utility of Chinese studies.

Mr Dawson informs me that in *tsie* the first character gives the initial sound and the second the final sound (not vowel + consonant, as stated by Bayer), and that in fact the device is only used in lexicons. It is not used for foreign words. For these it is enough to use words for their phonetic value and not for their meaning. Thus 'cocoa' is written by duplicating the character for *ko* (which means 'may', 'can'), and *ko* + *han* in Rémusat's example is an attempt to get as close as possible to the Mongolian *khan*, which was originally a two-syllable word.

5 In the Advertisement to his Egyptian Dictionary, of which he was correcting the proofs when he died, he denies all utility to Champollion's 'system of phonetic values' except as a possible mnemonic to serve 'in assisting the memory'.

6 Renouf's harsh, but just, conclusion is 'Champollion learnt nothing whatever from Young, nor did anyone else.'

A magnanimous attempt to present Young's claims in a favourable light is made by Henri Sottas in the preface of his centenary edition of the *Lettre à M. Dacier*. He gives Young a score of 100 correct out of the 212 hieroglyphic groups whose meaning he attempted to identify in his *Encyclopaedia Britannica Supplement* article of 1819. But this is too generous. Sottas includes over a dozen numeral signs counted separately, some quite obviously identifiable pictures, and whole cartouches (e.g. that of Ptolemy) whose meaning nobody then doubted. The problem was how the meaning was arrived at. Nevertheless, enough of Young's conjectures remain (e.g. 'God', 'feminine', 'year', 'month', 'day') to show that he had some precise and correct ideas on the subject; this much Champollion always acknowledged. But it was not enough for Young, who wanted to be recognized as the guide who had first demonstrated the correct way. Unfortunately he never achieved demonstration. A good instance of the random nature of his work is his transliteration of the name of Ptolemy. To the seven hieroglyphs which make up the name Young gave the values *ole, ma, os, p, t, i*, and nothing at all. Of these some are right, some half-right, some wrong. But as he offers neither coherent argument nor interlocking evidence to support them, it is impossible to place any confidence in them.

Sottas puts forward some interesting arguments to show that the Rosetta Stone was in itself not enough to allow a decipherment. The demotic letters for the name of Ptolemy were either not descended or not recognizably descended from the hieroglyphs used in the Ptolemy cartouche (whereas had the cartouche of Alexander survived on the stone, there would have been several mutually recognizable signs). Moreover there is only one word in the whole of the remainder of the inscription which contains two hieroglyphs from the Ptolemy cartouche: indeed there are only three instances where hieroglyphs of the cartouche recur at all in known Coptic words that could have been recognized from the Greek translation. It was thus virtually impossible for conjectural values to be

cross-checked within the Rosetta Stone itself, and during 1814, the only year in which Young pursued his Egyptian researches seriously, the Rosetta Stone was more or less his only resource.

But it is hard to sympathize with him. He had a second chance with Bankes' discovery of Cleopatra's cartouche on the Philae obelisk, which was known to him long before it was known to Champollion. Yet he let it slip. Moreover, as Sottas points out (47 *n*. 1; 66 *n*. 2), it was not only Champollion whose discoveries Young tried to annex for himself. He claimed that his results on the demotic text of the Rosetta Stone were independent of Åkerblad, and he even tried to claim that it was his suggestion which led Bankes to identify the Philae obelisk cartouche as Cleopatra's. Åkerblad, as we have seen, was little better, claiming independence for results of his which were the same as those previously published by Sacy. In contrast, Champollion always freely acknowledged the value of the work of his predecessors (e.g. *Lettre* 2, mentioning Sacy, Åkerblad, and Young himself).

7 Champollion's views on Coptic were very much of his time. (*a*) *Monosyllabic nature*. 'Monosyllabic languages' form a separate group in Adelung's classification (*Mithridates oder allgemeine Sprachkunde*, 4 vols., 1806–17). They include Tibetan, Siamese, and Chinese, and are thought by him to be essentially the earliest languages, perhaps descended directly from Adam who may have gone to live in Tibet after leaving Eden. The theory of the monosyllabic nature of Chinese was demolished in an article by Rémusat of 1813, which would have appeared too late for Champollion to take into account. The significance of monosyllabicness in proving the priority of a language is sharply questioned by Townsend (1815), citing English 'blame' from 'blaspheme', etc. (*b*) *Philosophical structure*. Champollion's remarks on Coptic are in the same key as Adelung's on English: 'Its simplicity depends in some measure on a philosophical accuracy which is carried systematically through the whole language, so that the adjective, participles, and the article are indeclinable, being in their nature destitute of gender, case, and number. . . .' (*c*) *Chinese analogy*. Cf. Adelung under (*a*) above, and Sacy's linguistic theory summarized on page 65. In his refusal to conclude that China was an Egyptian colony, Champollion was more cautious than some. The thesis had been argued by de Guignes (*Mem. de l'Acad. des Inscr.* xxix 1 sqq.), approved, at least as far as a common origin was concerned, by no less a person than the Abbé Barthélemy (*ibid.* xxx) on the grounds of the Chinese appearance of the boat and the boatman's hat in the Praeneste Mosaic (ill. 2), and was at least half-held by Young who in his contribution to the *Encyclopaedia Britannica Supplement* quotes reports that the Chinese physiognomy of the ninth century resembled that of the Arabs, and only later became of its present type owing to intermixture with the Mongols.

8 All three of these necessary prior assumptions were common ground at this time, the first since Sacy's suggestion in 1811, the other two since Zoëga (464; 435/6). See pages 57 and 58.

9 The signs for *kh* and *sch* are not to be found in the *Lettre à M. Dacier*. Both of them happen to belong to the small class of letters taken over by the Coptic alphabet from the demotic. St Martin in his communication to the Académie (read 20 December 1822) quotes the Coptic letter-forms in support of the identification of the hieroglyphic values, an argument that he would seem likely to have got from Champollion. Champollion himself in the *Précis* (179) quotes 'other Pharaonic names' as his collateral evidence for *sch* and a private name *Petkhem* for the *kh*. If he was aware of this at the time it would mean that he had already begun to apply his phonetic alphabet on a wider front. But since he may have suspected the value from his table of Demotic/Hieratic/Hieroglyphic equivalences, the point must remain uncertain.

Champollion's reading of the hieroglyphs outside the cartouche as 'irina' is wrong. In fact they mean 'Great King'. Champollion got the meaning of the last two signs ('great') correct later on (274; *Tabl. gén.* 299, 443–4), but did not revise his previous interpretation in the light of it – one of the comparatively few traces of the haste with which the book must have been written.

10 Mr Dawson tells me that about nine-tenths of Chinese characters are of the signific + phonic variety described by Rémusat, and not just 'a good half'. Moreover, it is greatly exaggerating the case to talk of 'many thousands of compound characters' with symbolic significance.

Rémusat's description of hîng-chîng (now romanized as xing-sheng) is as follows (1822, p. 8): 'The characters called hîng-chîng, or "representing sound" are half representational, half syllabic. One part, the image, determines the general meaning and fixes the genus. The other, which is an arrangement of strokes that has lost its representational significance, indicates the sound and characterizes the species.' He gives as examples:

魚 FISH
鯉 PLACE (pronounced *li*) } together 鯉里 = *li* ('carp')

木 TREE
柏 WHITE (pronounced *pě*) } together 木白 = *pě* ('cypress')

11 Intellectual fashion of the time praised 'facts' and decried 'system'. It was therefore inevitable that Champollion should stress the part played by the former in his discoveries (e.g. *Précis* 41), and talk of theories as if their construction was a natural foible against which one must struggle (251–2). But his honesty in admitting this temptation, as well as the whole tenor of his work, suggests that the desire to make coherent sense of the problem as a whole marched step by step in his mind alongside the desire to solve individual difficulties independently on their own merits.

12 The Dendera zodiac had been detached from its temple at Dendera, brought to Paris, and exhibited to an enthusiastic public as a monument of the most tremendous antiquity and importance. It was in fact a worthless product of the astrology of Roman times, as was made clear by Champollion's identification of

the cartouches on the walls below it as those of Roman emperors.

13 In the text of Champollion's *Précis* Letronne's translation of διὰ τῶν πρώτων στοιχείων is given as 'by the letters of the alphabet', comparison being made to phrases like *prima elementa*. Letronne then changed his mind in favour of 'the original letters of the alphabet' (as opposed to the compound letters like *x*). According to these second (and rather less plausible) thoughts, which were published by Champollion in an appendix, there are two categories of Egyptian writing, the 'vulgar' (called 'demotic' or 'public' by Herodotus and Diodorus, 'enchorial' on the Rosetta Stone, 'epistolographic' by Clement) and the 'sacred'. The 'sacred' is further subdivided by Clement into hieratic (=priestly writing) and hieroglyphic. Hieroglyphic may be either 'cyriologic' (i.e. by the letters of the alphabet) or 'symbolic', and this in its turn may be either straightforwardly representational (also called 'cyriologic') or 'tropical' or 'enigmatic'.

The main objection to this is the two contrary meanings attached to 'cyriologic' (either 'alphabetic' or 'representational'), depending on whether it is describing phonetic or ideographic writing. Champollion, however, thought it certain and important enough to bring into the title of his book, the full form of which is: *Précis du système hiéroglyphique des anciens égyptiens, ou Recherches sur les élémens premiers de cette écriture sacrée, sur leurs diverses combinaisons, et sur les rapports de ce système avec lec autres méthodes graphiques égyptiennes.*

CHAPTER 4 (pp. 85–110)

1 For instance Shiraz is given as the site of ancient Persepolis in Ferrari's standard *Epitome Geographica* of 1605.

2 Herbert was a member of a diplomatic mission to Persia which set out in a fleet of seven 'great and well-manned ships' in March 1626. His first account of the journey was published in 1634. A somewhat enlarged second edition was printed in 1638 with the same plate of Persepolis. The third and final edition of 1677 is virtually a different book, far fuller in content and rewritten to conform to the literary style of the new age. It has a different plate of Persepolis.

3 Hyde's reproduction of the inscription is taken from the Royal Society's *Philosophical Transactions* xvii no. 201 of June 1693, where it is said that they were drawn by Samuel Flower, an English merchant at Aleppo and Agent of the East India Company. Apparently Flower took them in November 1667 on a visit to Persepolis made in response to the Royal Society's published desiderata (see page 88). Soon afterwards, however, he died and most of his papers were lost.

4 Hyde's views on this did not influence Leibnitz, who, in a letter of 1707 (VI i 204) used the existence of the Persepolis script, so clearly independent of Hebrew writing, as an argument against the divine origin of the alphabet.

5 Kaempfer frequently complains of his engraver (*morosus et infelicis ingenii sculptor*), particularly for bunching up the cuneiform characters and thus making them hard to distinguish. The engraver

presented a perennial problem for authors of the time. Hyde makes a good pun about the one responsible for the plate of the Sassanid inscriptions – *qui eas caelaverit Sculptor eâdem operâ celasse dicatur.*

6 Chardin adds his tribute to that of Figueroa's 'perspicuae et distinctae' and Herbert's 'simmetry and order', saying of the script that it is 'fort beau, il n'a rien de confus, ni rien de barbare'. These reports evidently impressed Leibnitz, who refers more than once to the 'singularis simplicitas' of the Persepolis script.

7 Sacy, with his customary clarity, lists the reasons for supposing that the inscriptions are in different scripts: (i) each has a different total repertoire of characters; (ii) they differ in degrees of simplicity; (iii) perpendicular or horizontal strokes predominate in one class, oblique in another; (iv) the most frequent character of one class may be absent in another; (v) one class allows perpendicular strokes to be cut by horizontal ones, another not (1793, pp. 7–8).

8 Leibnitz's letter is printed in his collected works (VI ii 193) and also in Chamberlayne's *Oratio Dominica.*

9 The language of the Achaemenid inscriptions and the language of the Avesta are known together as Old Iranian. The language of the Arsacid and of the Sassanian periods, and of the so-called Book-Pahlavi in which are written the traditional and religious texts of the Zoroastrians of Persia and India are known together as Middle Iranian. New Iranian embraces the stages and dialects of the language from the time of the national poet Firdausi (*c.* A D 1000) till today. See Kent (1950).

10 Both Arsacid and Sassanian Pahlavi are written with numerous Aramaic xenograms. The custom is similar to and perhaps carried over from the use of Akkadograms and Sumerograms in cuneiform and may have originated when Persian government offices, staffed by Aramaic-speaking officials, were converted from writing on clay to parchment in the time of Darius. The Arsacid and Sassanian forms of the writing system are not the inventions of the particular dynasties but the end-results of two different housestyles that grew up in the chancelleries of Achaemenid Persia, one centred in Pars and the other in the north. See Herzfeld (1924), 72–3.

11 The account was in fact written by T. C. Tychsen, the Professor of Theology at Göttingen, who later became interested in oriental languages. Gesenius and Ewald were his pupils.

12 Despite the clarity of the proof of the left-to-right direction of the script, it was not always accepted. There had even been a 'decipherment' of it (by Wahl) which read it backwards! There has also been a more serious attempted decipherment by O. G. Tychsen (a Norwegian-born orientalist who became Professor at Rostock) in 1798. Tychsen had argued, very sensibly though as it turned out wrongly, from the fact that the script went from left to right and that it contained word-dividers, that it must be subsequent to Greek writing. He also thought that the palace could not have been that of the Achaemenids which was known to have been burned down by Alexander. He therefore read in the inscriptions the name of Arsaces, the founder of the Arsacid or Parthian dynasty. Parthian power rested on its archers, and

that, he thought, was why they had invented an alphabet composed of arrows! After Grotefend's publication Tychsen withdrew his proposed solution.

In assessing the merits of Grotefend's decipherment one should not forget its superiority to these previous attempts, though he may have owed a real debt to F. C. Münter, a Danish scholar, who in 1800 had championed the case for Persepolis being of Achaemenid date.

13 In principle, of course, Grotefend's critical approach to the texts offered by Niebuhr and Le Brun was perfectly justifiable, and indeed some of their mistakes (or *sphalmata* as he calls them) are correctly pointed out by him.

The mistakes in his own plate (which was drawn by T. C. Tychsen) include *forum* and *retis* for *fortis* and *regis* in the Latin, and Daiheausch for Darheausch in the transliteration.

14 Lipsius' views are expounded in his letter to Schott (no. 44 of the *centuria tertia ad Belgas*). What ostensibly occasioned them was the extraordinary thesis of Goropius Becanus that the sacred language of Egypt was Dutch. Lipsius was not unaware of the inflectional similarities between German, Latin, and Persian, but he does not attach any greater weight to them than to similarities of vocabulary.

Salmasius, in his *de Hellenistica commentarius*, published in 1643, came close to propounding the theory of a common origin for Greek, Persian, German, and Slavonic. He amassed a quite impressive list of common vocabulary words, and even observed some consistent sound changes. But he preferred to account for the similarities by supposing that in early times the languages had been close neighbours with much mutual borrowing, rather than that they had originally been identical.

15 Leibnitz VI i 121 and 299 ff. There is a good instance of what I have called the arithmetical approach to language in an article by Thomas Young in *Philosophical Transactions* of 1819. He thinks that there are six words in Basque and Coptic which are apparently the same, and calculates that if the identity is a real one then the chances that 'at some remote period an Egyptian colony established itself in Spain' must be reckoned as 1700 to 1 in favour. In the light of our modern organic view of language such a calculation looks ridiculous: then it was still legitimate hypothesis.

15a The change originated with William Wotton, a friend of Isaac Newton and Richard Bentley. In 1715 Wotton put forward 'as his own notion' that 'the essential Difference of one Language from another is to be taken from their respective *Grammars*, rather than from their *Vocabularies*.' His essay was published in Latin in Chamberlayne's *Oratio Dominica* (the same volume which contained Leibnitz's suggestion that decipherment could proceed from proper names) and in English translation in 1731. The idea that a shared numeral system was likely to show family relationship and not be due to borrowing was first argued by James Parsons in 1767. See Pope (1989).

16 Jones calls the proposition that the ancient Egyptians, the Goths, Greeks, Romans, Persians, and Indians 'originally spoke the same language and professed the same religious faith' something that was 'capable of

incontestable proof'. He thought that the language had reached Europe from Egypt. The argument is put forward in his ninth anniversary discourse.

17 Rask's essay was completed in 1814, published in 1818, and translated into German in 1822. Its ideas were developed and systematized by Grimm, after whom Grimm's Law is named. Bopp's first publication on the verb system of Sanskrit was in 1816.

18 Rask (1826), Burnouf and Lassen (1826), Burnouf (1833). Burnouf, himself the son of a Professor of Latin, became Professor of Sanskrit at the Collège de France in 1833, and was elected to the Académie on the vacancy caused by Champollion's death. Beer published in the *Hallische Allgemeine Zeitung* and Jacquet in the *Journal Asiatique*.

Chapter 5 (pp. 111–122)

1 The principle on which the Persian cuneiform signary was made up is ingeniously discussed by Hallock (1970). He concludes that the inventor must have worked on a basic text, giving as he worked along it the simpler sign shapes to the sound values he needed first. Since the signs for *ku* (made of two wedges) and for *ru* (three wedges) are among the simplest shapes, but also among the least frequent in general occurrence, Hallock argues that the basic text must have contained very early on the name of Cyrus. Whether the script was devised in his reign or in that of Darius is still a disputed question. Hallock's argument would support the former.

2 For the main tree (Akkadian, Babylonian, Assyrian) see von Soden and Röllig (1967). For the derivation from it of Hurrian and Hittite see Speiser (1941), 13–14 and Sturtevant and Hahn (1951), 2–3. For the derivation of Elamite see Reiner (1969), 68–71.

3 Though this was the age of Layard and the most active era of Mesopotamian excavation, bricks, seals, and other objects inscribed in cuneiform had been arriving in Europe since the eighteenth century. A good description of the finding of 'written bricks, perhaps the most curious article of the Babylonian antiques', and the perplexity to which they gave rise is to be found in Rich (1813).

4 The most recent discussions of the Proto-Elamite tablets have been by W. C. Brice – see Bibliography.

5 Before 1949 the earliest material evidence that we had for the existence of our alphabet was the first five Hebrew letters on a graffito from Lachish of the eighth century BC. It was also known that the Greek alphabet must have been borrowed at about this time. But there had been put forward various theoretical arguments based on South Arabian letter forms, and in particular the retention in the Ethiopian alphabet of the letter-name 'harm', which suggested that the stems of the Phoenician and South Arabic/Ethiopic alphabets must have diverged in the fourteenth or thirteenth century BC. There is also a growing corpus of proto-Canaanite and proto-Sinaitic inscriptions of the second millennium. The Ugaritic abecedaria thus fit comfortably into the pattern of our present knowledge about the antiquity of the alphabet. Forty years ago they would not have fitted it at all.

See under F. M. Cross, W. F. Albright, and E. A. Speiser (1951) in the Bibliography.

6 Windfuhr's own view of the course of events is (1) the knowledge in Ugarit of the linear alphabet; (2) the creation of the cuneiform alphabet; (3) the introduction, still in Ugarit, of our own alphabetic order. His reason is that if the ABC order had already existed the allocation of sign shapes to sound values would have taken cognizance of it. This seems highly dubious. The same argument would place the invention of the typewriter before that of the ABC because its keyboard runs 'qwertyuiop'.

Chapter 6 (pp. 123–135)

1 The legend on the first coin reads *e-u-wa te-o-se pa-si* Εὐϝά(ν)θεος βασι[λῆϝος] 'of King Euanthes'; on the second coin *e-u-wa-ko-ro pa-si-le-wo-se* Εὐαγόρω βασιλῆϝος 'of King Euagoras'. Under the goat on the reverse are the first two letters of the Greek form of the king's name.

Both coins are from Salamis. The date of Euanthes was *c.* 450 BC, of Euagoras 411–374 BC.

See Masson nos. 324*a*, 325*b*.

2 Smith's restoration of the form of the word for 'king' on its second appearance in the text is wrong. It should be βασιλεύϝο(ν)τος, the genitive present participle. However, what he restored was a correct nominative case, which he knew of from elsewhere. So as far as deciphering the word went he was not seriously misled.

3 Answers (in Attic Greek): ἡ π(τ)όλις, ἄνθρωπος, τὸς (= ὁ) κῆπος, τὸν κῆπον, κήπῳ, τῷ Ἀπόλλωνι.

4 It took time for the success of Schmidt and of Deecke and Siegismund to penetrate into England. As late as 1876/7 Fox Talbot, then in the last year of his life, felt it necessary to read a paper introducing their work to the Society of Biblical Archaeology.

Chapter 7 (pp. 136–145)

1 Burton said of the drawings he published that 'the fancy of the copyist had been allowed to run wild'. Though he corrected them himself he realized that better copies were possible, and advised the Palestine Exploration Society to procure them; also that the stones should be taken to Constantinople. This was done, to the anger and dismay of the local inhabitants, at the end of November 1872, and plaster casts taken of the stones by the Rev. W. Wright, a missionary at Damascus, who travelled to Hama for the purpose with the Turkish Governor of Syria. The story is told in the Society's *Quarterly Statement* of 1873.

2 Recently a rather more sophisticated use of such a distribution curve has been made by Dr Mackay, of Birkbeck College, to predict the total number of syllabic or alphabetic signs in a script for which we have only incomplete evidence. See *SMIL* (1965).

3 In so far as he had a positive expectation in the matter, Sayce expected that the language of the inscriptions would turn out to be a relation of Urartian, which he thought was an ancestor of modern Georgian. See Sayce (1880*a*).

4 In 1931 Gelb was prepared to read the cuneiform *n tar-qu-u-tim-me šar mât âli me-ra* and the Luvian Hieroglyphic *tarku-tu+me* KING LAND *e-me+ri*. The most recent interpretation, and one that is likely to be

right as it carries on from the work of others (particularly Güterbock) and can be supported from newly discovered material is by Hawkins and Morpurgo-Davies 1998. In the cuneiform the name of the king (of the land of Mira/i) is written ᵐtar-kaš-ša-na-wa, *and in the hieroglyphic* TARKASNA – *wà/i.* The name itself is no longer to be derived grandly from a storm-god but earthily from a mule or donkey!

5 The first of the three signs interpreted in the caption to ill. 90 gives the classification GOD, the second gives the specific meaning STORMGOD or *Tarhuns,* and the third is a phonetic indicator confirming this by giving the final sound of the name to be read. The writing can be made fuller and clearer by the inclusion of more of the final sounds of the name, e.g. DEITY STORMGOD, *-huins.*

6 The failure to distinguish the two ideograms for KING and TOWN was originated by Sayce, and caused much confusion. For instance, Jensen in 1894 tried to interpret the Carchemish group as meaning King of Carchemish, as did Cowley in 1917, even though Sayce had clearly stated the distinction with apologies for his previous error in 1903. The confusion was only finally dispelled by Meriggi (1929), 199.

7 I use Laroche's numeration for the signs.

8 Homer *Iliad* 24, 602 ff. Herodotus ii 106–7. This rapid forgetfulness is paralleled by the way Ctesias, who lived in Persia in the fifth century B C, had no knowledge at all of what the great Behistun inscription meant, and did not even know that it had been put there by Darius a bare hundred years before.

CHAPTER 8 (pp. 146–158)

1 The letter was sent on 25 April and published on 23 June 1894. It argued that the script was independent of both Egyptian and Hittite Hieroglyphic, and that it could be divided into three stages, picture, hieroglyph, and linear, the last of which was 'certainly a syllabary'. Two of these points had been made and the other implied even earlier, in an announcement made by Evans to the Hellenic Society on 27 November 1893 before he had even been to Crete (see *JHS* xiv, pp. xi and 266).

2 Theoretically Evans' distinction between 'pictograph' and 'hieroglyph' should have depended on recurrence, the 'pictograph' being drawn differently to suit each context, the 'hieroglyph' never changing its form. In practice it did not. For instance, the man in ill. 84b is unique, but is nevertheless listed as a 'hieroglpyh'.

On the subjectiveness of Evans' dating of the early seals see Warren (1970), p. 30.

3 Evans' extraordinary description of the appearance of the letter forms as 'European' was not a momentary oversight. He repeated it nine years later in *Scripta Minoa I* (p. 39). His reason for calling cuneiform more primitive may puzzle the reader, since it is much less picture-like in appearance than the Aegean script. To judge from the later passage in *S.M. I,* Evans' reason was that he thought cuneiform 'cumbrous and obscure'.

I suppose that nowadays anybody who wrote in the way Evans did at this time about Mycenaean writing, or talked of 'the great Thraco-Phrygian race', or expressed incredulity at evidence which seemed to suggest that there was an aspect of Red Indian culture which was superior to that of Bronze Age Europe, would be labelled a racist. It is therefore important to point out that in the late nineteenth century the word race did not evoke images of political oppression. Had it done so, Evans would have been the last to use it. Its aura was a very different one, that of scientific and sociological up-to-dateness. Disraeli was being modern, not reactionary, when he said that race was all, and Sayce was a brilliant young cleric when he informed the Society of Biblical Archaeology in its first year of existence that 'the Aryan founded inductive science' and 'civilization and culture were on the side of the Turanians (viz. Sumerians)', while the great thing taught to us by the decipherment of cuneiform was the enduring character of the Semite 'by nature highly receptive and well-fitted to be the future trader of the world'.

Sayce retained his view of the all-importance of race throughout his life, and in his *Reminiscences* (1923) tried to explain his own character and career by his racial constitution. On the other hand it is my impression (no more) that Evans made very much less use of the concept of race in his later years when he was writing the *Palace of Minos.*

4 For the axe, see Evans (1935), p. 733; for the throne and sceptre sign in proper names, *ibid.,* p. 700.

The latter is a very clear instance of the confusion in Evans' mind. As an analogy for 'the inclusion of the symbol of dominion in personal names' he cites Melchizedeck, Vercingetorix, Vladimir, and others. But though the word implying royalty or power is present in these names and can be heard when they are spoken, it cannot be seen when they are written: there is no visible sceptre or crown among the Hebrew, Roman, or Slavonic letters of which they are composed.

There is an equal confusion in a remark that Evans makes on p. 682. After estimating the number of phonograms in ordinary use in Linear A and B as 85 and 62 respectively, he comments that the latter shows 'a certain advance towards the alphabetic standard of 24 letters'. Now, it may be legitimate to call an alphabet more advanced than a syllabary. But it would be obvious nonsense to call a smaller alphabet of 22 letters more advanced than a larger one of 28. But Evans' remark about his two syllabaries is precisely like this.

The only way it makes sense is on the assumption of a gradual and continuous evolution, as if the transition from syllabary to alphabet were accomplished by the casting-off of a character every ten or twenty years. If this is what was at the back of Evans' mind it would also help to explain the point of the comparisons he made between Cretan signs and Greek or Phoenician letter-forms.

5 But, of course, Evans did not expect and might well have found it difficult to welcome a Greek solution. He did himself see that a sign-group accompanying a horse-ideogram could be transliterated according to the Cypriot likenesses of its signs *po-lo,* which was very like the Greek *pôlos,* 'foal'. But he dismissed it, suggesting a Carian disyllabic word for horse, *ala* (1935, p. 799 *n.* 3). His belief that the language could

not be Greek was doubly entrenched. It was the general opinion of the time that the Greeks only arrived in the area with the fall of the Mycenaean palaces. In the second place Evans was led by his theory of writing to suppose that Linear B was essentially just a reformed version of Linear A and likely to have been used for writing the same, Minoan, language.

CHAPTER 9 (pp. 159–180)

1 By this time the Pylos tablets had been discovered, but their publication had been delayed by the war. With a characteristic caution Kober classified them as 'Mainland Script' as distinct from 'Knossos Linear B'.

2 For anybody who may wish to check my figures I had better explain that in assessing correctness of placing I have ignored the consonant and vowel values tentatively suggested by Ventris at the time but have given to each series the value later allotted to the majority of its members, thus:

Work-Note 1: vowels, *o, i, e, a*
consonants, *t, w, w, s, nil, r, k, -, -, y*

Work-Note 15: vowels: *i, o, e, -, a*
consonants, *nil, -, w, p, d, t, s, n, y, m, k, r, r, nil, q*

Work-Note 17: vowels, *i, o, e, a, -*
consonants, *nil, -, w, p, y, d, t, s, n, m, k, r, r, nil, q*

3 The argument (Work-Note 14, pp. 135 ff.) is ingenious and detailed. Briefly summarized it runs as follows. Nouns must end either in a vowel or in a consonant. Affixes must be of the form VC(V), C, or CV. This gives six possible combinations. On Cypriot spelling rules their treatment would be as follows (the words are imaginary):

| word | as written with or without suffix | | | |
	none	-ar	-r	-ra
kup	*ku-pe*	*ku-PA-re*	*ku-pe-re* or *ku-PU-re*	*ku-PA-ra* or *ku-PU-ra*
tesi	*te-si*	*te-si-JA-re*	*te-si-re*	*te-si-ra*

It can be readily seen that the use of affixes ought to lead to a frequent change of sign (shown in small capitals). The apparent fact that it does not can only be explained either by assuming that nearly all words in the Linear B language ended in vowels or that the spelling rules were not the same as in the Cypriot syllabary.

4 The tripod tablet was unearthed in the 1952 season's excavation, cleaned that winter, and first seen by Blegen in the spring of 1953. His letter to Ventris of 16 May appears in Chadwick (1958, p. 81).

5 An attempt to explain the existence of the Cypriot syllabary was made by Ernst Grumach, one of the main champions of the case for rejection, just before his death. According to him it was an artificial creation of around 700 BC motivated by a sort of national-ist revival and made by allotting syllabic values of the Hittite Hieroglyphic type to indigenous Bronze Age characters whose shapes had somehow been preserved or remembered (Grumach 1970, pp. 332–3). But there is no evidence whatever for this having happened, and no parallel for such a revival of a disused script can be cited from either the ancient or the modern world.

The apriorism behind the case for rejection can be clearly seen in a remark of Grumach's on the next page of the same article. 'There are in Linear B about 150 signs which are manifestly employed as ideographic object-signs: and there even seems to be an increase in the number of such signs after the transition from Linear A to Linear B. This is just the opposite of what is to be expected in the genesis of syllabic writing, which allows objects and notions to be described without the help of ideographic signs, and therefore normally leads to a decrease in size of the ideographic element, and to its eventual disappearance.'

But why should this be expected in a syllabic script? It does not happen in an alphabetic script. We employ a signary three or four times that employed by a Greek of classical times – and nearly all the growth has been in the 'ideographic element'. It is easier to write £5=$8 than 'five pounds are the same as eight dollars'. The rule, if there is one, is that newly borrowed scripts are lean, but if they enjoy an unbroken tradition for any length of time there is a tendency for them to grow fat. Broadly speaking, this would seem to hold for the cuneiform scripts and for Egyptian hieroglyphic as well as for our own alphabet.

6 See Kitchen in *BASOR* 181, 23 f., and T. G. H. James in the *Minutes of the London Mycenaean Seminar* of 18 November 1970.

POSTSCRIPT (pp. 192–194)

1 A detailed history of this period of Carian studies is given by Adiego (1993, pp. 101–125).

2 The Greek text can be reconstructed partly from our knowledge of similar decrees, and partly by inference from what survives of the Carian. Thus the *nik* at the end of line 2 and the lùsikrat$_2$as in line 5 of the Carian text allow one to restore the names Νικοκλεα and Λυσικρατουσ. The decree is published and discussed by Frei and Marek, 1997.

3 Kowalsky (1975, pp. 86–89) considers the problem, as does Boisson (1994, pp. 223–229), and in greater detail than either, Adiego (1993, pp. 292–300), but, as Adiego himself admits, no comprehensive explanation has yet been put forward

POSTSCRIPT (pp. 195–203)

1 Anglerius (1516 *Decad 3, lib. 10*). Peter Martyr Anghiera was a learned Italian from Milan who had become a trusted member of the Spanish court. His story of the discovery of the New World was published as a whole in 1536, but parts had appeared earlier under pressure from the great Spanish scholar, Antonio Nebrissensis. Antonio had a special interest

in writing – it was he who first showed how Latin must have been pronounced by the ancient Romans – and it cannot be ruled out that he may have influenced Anghiera's ideas on the subject.

2 Acosta (1589, *lib. I cap. 4) Nam cum apud Indos nullae literae in usu sint, nulla certa monumenta maiorum.* Acosta also refused to allow 'letters' to the Chinese, only 'characters', 85,000–120,000 of them. However the Japanese, he felt, 'have some kinde of letters', employed for writing names (1590, VI, iv). Evidently therefore what he means by 'letters' is phoneticism, a word not yet invented – see p. 58.

3 Bacon's dialogue 'An advertisement touching a holy war' was written in 1622 and published in 1692. The Royal Society's list is in *Philosophical Transactions* 1667.

4 For the likelihood that the Dresden Codex was one of the books that had been seen by Anghiera and of how it may have come to Dresden, see Coe 1992/1994, p. 79.

5 Rafinesque engaged in too many fields of science and scholarship for the good of his own reputation as an *homme sérieux*. See Coe 1992/1994, pp. 81/89ff. and Stuart 1989.

6 Landa was first and foremost a priest, not an ethnographer, and did not hesitate to destroy evidence where he thought destruction would serve a more important good. 'We found a great number of books of their lettters' he wrote about an incident that took place in 1562. 'But since they contained nothing in which there was not superstition and falsities of the devil, we burned them all – which they felt to an extreme extent and which caused them great pain.'

7 David Kelley (1975, p. 167) plays with this idea, pointing out (like me – see pages 183 and 213 n. 5 – but quite independently) that in Egyptian too it was the ideographic element that grew as the civilization got older.

A full discussion of the relationships between the Maya script and its neighbours is given by Marcus (1992).

8 It seems to be a universal human foible to suppose that written languages are a thing apart. Even as late as the 15th century in Italy 'knowing grammar' meant knowing Latin. Italian was not supposed to have any. In South Africa it was once assumed that you could not *write* Afrikaans, only speak it. And in the 1st century AD an educated man who was familiar with Greek and Latin, both manifestly phonetic scripts, could say of Egyptian that it was unwritable (see note 10 page 207).

Glossary of Technical Terms

I hope I have avoided using pretentious technical terms. But it is better for language to be consistent than for it to be arbitrary. Thus I have had to use some specialist words, and some customary words in an uncustomarily technical sense. This list is intended as a guide to my own usage in this book: it is not a comprehensive glossary of the specialized words that can be used in the study of writing, such as is given for instance by Gelb (1952, pp. 248–53).

acrophonic means 'how the beginning sounds'. The *acrophonic principle* is not infrequently invoked to explain the origin of a phonetic writing system by supposing that the picture of an object was read as the initial sound of its name. Applied to English the principle would explain the letter 'a' as originating in its stalked form *a*, the picture of an apple; 's' as the picture of a snake, and so on. What saves us from this is the knowledge that the English alphabet was inherited from Latin. The main justification that used to be put forward for the acrophonic principle was the names of the Hebrew letters (*aleph*=ox, *beth*=house, etc.). But it is likely that these are subsequently bestowed nicknames – see Gelb (1952, pp. 140–1).

allogram see *xenogram*.

alphabet the set of phonetic signs in an alphabetic script. Gelb would limit the use of the word alphabetic to the Greek script and scripts derived from it, their characteristic being that they make no formal distinction between the signs for vowels and the signs for consonants. In the Semitic scripts on the other hand the primary signs denote consonants. Vowels were originally not specified at all: later this was done by a system of diacritic marks or pointings. Gelb would call this system a consonantal syllabary, which is logical. But it is clumsy, and there is also something unnatural in denying the alphabet to those who used the letters *aleph* and *beth*!

Where it is necessary to distinguish the two types, the Semitic alphabet may, *pace* Gelb, be called consonantal.

bilingual is used of inscriptions or other texts where the same content is expressed in two languages.

They may or may not be also *biscript*.

biscript describes texts in two different writing systems, such as one finds today on the more tourist-frequented roads in Greece and the Arab countries. *Biscripts* may of course be, indeed usually are, also *bilingual*, as at Palmyra.

I owe the word to Professor Bennett of the University of Wisconsin, who coined it and triscript at my request. In the past there have been other candidates proposed, triliteral (Rawlinson), trigrammatical (Cull *TSBA* vi 550), digraphic (Pierides *TSBA* iv, 38), and I think I have seen biscriptural, but none of them has survived its sponsor.

boustrophedon means 'the way an ox turns' and is used of writing where alternate lines proceed in opposite directions, like an ox ploughing.

character is an older term for *sign*.

consonantal scripts are those in which the phonetic signs represent consonants only, as in the Semitic scripts. Gelb, however, prefers to think of these scripts as being syllabaries in which each sign stands for a consonant *plus* an undefined vowel.

consonantal syllabary is an intelligible name for the phonetic signs of such a script. The difference between consonantal-syllabic signs and purely consonantal ones is of limited functional importance, but historically it makes the evolution of writing simpler to explain.

cursive a 'running' form of a script developed for greater ease or speed of writing. Even though the outward forms of the signs in cursive may be quite different from their equivalents in monumental writing (as with Pompeian graffiti or modern miniscule compared to capital letter forms – e.g. a, A; g, G), they may be said to belong to the same *script* if the systems as a whole are identical and there is a one-to-one correspondence between the signs of each form.

decipherment means the explanation (by transliteration or otherwise) of the individual signs of a script. It does not mean understanding the sense of particular texts written in it. For instance, the

Etruscan script is deciphered even though the language is unknown and the texts have not been interpreted.

determinative a sign which is written to help define the meaning, but which is not intended to be read out loud, for instance in Egyptian or Akkadian the conventional sign for GOD which accompanies the spelling of a divine name. There is no equivalent in our own script except perhaps the capitalization of the initial letters of proper names.

Gelb would prefer the expression 'semantic indicator' (to balance 'phonetic indicator'), but *determinative* is an entrenched as well as a neater term.

diacritic marks are attached in some scripts, which originally possessed simple *consonantal syllabaries*, to the consonantal signs to show what vowel is to be read with it. They differ from vowel *pointing* in being attached to the signs instead of standing independently.

grammatology a word of Gelb's to denote the science of writing.

grid a way of conveniently displaying a syllabary so that the signs that share the same vowel value are ranged below each other and the signs that share the same consonant value are ranged beside each other.

heterogram see *xenogram*.

hieroglyphic is an evocative word and has evoked many false ideas. Its proper application is to the monumental script of ancient Egypt. To the Greeks who coined it, the word meant 'sacred carving': to later antiquity and the Renaissance it implied anything from mystery to metaphor. Egyptian hieroglyphic can now be seen to have been a writing system like any other, with a signary composed of phonetic, logographic, and determinative signs, and differing only in its degree of elaboration and its aesthetic appeal. But the belief that the hieroglyphs were all originally pictures, together with the aura of mystery which the script collected about it during its long life and which it has not altogether shed even now, led to the romantic application of the term to describe other scripts possessing the triple qualification of appearing mysterious, early, and pictorial. In some cases, notably Hittite Hieroglyphic, the name has stuck.

homophone a sign which has the same phonetic value as another, for instance the English *q* which is homophonous with *k*. Whether or not a sign is a homophone of another depends, of course, not on their shapes or essential natures but on the language of the script for which they are being used. *z*, despite Kent's remark in *King Lear*, is not an 'unnecessary letter' in English, though it was in Latin where it was at one time homophonous with *s*. The opposite of *homophone* is *polyphone*.

ideogram ought to mean *pictogram* but is generally used to mean *logogram*. This is confusing, and the word obviously should be avoided. However, *praeceptis sum minor ipse meis*, and I have hopelessly failed to avoid it. The reason, in part at least, is that this has been a historical book, and I have been reluctant to make a nineteenth-century researcher describe a script as logographic when in real life he would never have used the word or thought very much about the distinctions implicit in it. What he would have said was ideographic, and what he would have meant was non-phonetic.

letter is even more confusing when used in technical discussion. For one thing, it is generally used for the sign of an alphabet but not for the sign of a syllabary. For another, a phrase like 'the English letter a' has no single meaning: it may be taken graphically or phonetically – and in either case may mean a variety of things (viz. the shapes A, a, *a*, or the sounds in m*a*n, g*a*me, p*a*lm).

ligature two or more signs joined as one. ff, fi, ffi in the lower-case type of this book provide examples of phonographic ligature, the signs for per cent (%) and for fractional quantities ($\frac{1}{2}$, $\frac{1}{4}$, $\frac{3}{4}$) are logographic ligatures, and the sign &, though nowadays treated as a simple logogram, was once a xenographic ligature (the Latin *et* read as 'and').

linear was meaningfully used by Champollion in the phrase 'linear hieroglyphic' to describe a form of cursive in which the hieroglyphs were sketched by outline only. But the word passed from respectability when it was seduced by Evans to cohabit with the term script in the phrase *linear script*. Here it is supposed to mean non-pictorial, but the application of the term is highly subjective, and in so far as it claims to tell us something about the inner structure of a script from the outward appearance of its signs it is an impostor. Unfortunately, the labels Linear A and Linear B have become too firmly attached to two scripts of the Aegean family to be easily discarded. Elsewhere, though, there is never any need to use the term, and it should not be used.

logogram a sign for a complete word, differing from a *determinative* in that it furnishes additional information instead of classifying information already given. Chinese characters are logograms, and Chinese can be called a logographic script. But most, perhaps all, other scripts contain a class of logograms. English examples include £, $, =, + as well as all the numeral signs. Abbreviations, though composed of *phonograms*, are logographic in function. At the other end of the spectrum are symbols like the telephone and the crossed knife and fork in a hotel directory. These are too purpose-made to form a part of the general currency of the script, and should not be called logograms. They can be referred to by those who like long words as *semasiograms*, by others as special signs. See also *ideogram*.

metrical signs, denoting the unit of measurement, like £, $, °, ′, ″, form a sub-class of logographic signs.

monumental describes the more prestigious or public form of a script as distinct from its cursive form.

numeral signs form a sub-class of logographic signs.

phoneme is not a word for a written sign but for a unit of speech which is recognized as significant in a particular language. For instance Chinese speakers hear and use aspirated and unaspirated *p* as separate sounds, English speakers do not. The sounds therefore form two phonemes in Chinese, only one in English. An individual language generally has about forty phonemes, and an ideal writing system would see to it that each one was represented by a distinct and unique sign.

phonetic indicator is Gelb's phrase to denote a phonetic sign placed after a logogram which has two ways of being read in order to show which one is meant. An English example would be the letters *nd* placed after the numeral sign '2' to compel the reading 'second'.

phonetic, or *phonographic*, *signs* are those that express the sounds of speech as opposed to *logographic* or *ideographic* signs and *determinatives*.

phonogram a *phonetic sign*

pictographic has been used as the opposite of *linear*. It is an unnecessary term. If we know the function of a sign we can call it logographic or phonetic as the case may be. If we do not, it cannot be helpful and may be misleading to call it *pictographic* or *linear*.

polyphone is a phonetic sign that may stand for two or more different sounds, like the English *c* (= *k*, an unvoiced guttural, or *s*, an unvoiced sibilant). The opposite of *homophone*.

rebus sign is a sort of punning logogram in which the picture of something easy to draw represents something which is difficult to draw but the name for which sounds the same. The Sumerian example most often quoted is an arrow (*ti*) to stand for life (also *ti*). An English example of a *rebus* message would be the picture of a bee followed by the picture of a well sent to an invalid to wish him a quick recovery ('be well!').

script a writing system in its totality, that is to say a signary and the conventions which govern its use. Strictly speaking no two languages can have the same script, since the phonetic values of the signs are bound to differ, and even the signaries may not be exactly the same. But of course scripts of the same family may have a very large degree of overlap.

Scripts may contain (and most do) several different classes of sign – punctuation, determinative, logographic, and phonetic. The last of these is the one that comes first to mind, and for pur-poses of temporary convenience it is legitimate to refer to a script as *alphabetic*, *consonantal*, or *syllabic* in order to indicate the nature of its phonetic signs, just as it is legitimate to refer to a man as Arabic-speaking, provided one remembers that there is more to the whole script and more to the whole man.

semasiogram a possible term for a special sign not sufficiently standard in use to rate as a *logogram*.

sign the unit of a *script*.

signary the set of *signs* of all classes in a *script*, or the set of signs in one of these classes, as in *phonetic signary*.

syllabary the set of phonetic signs in a script where the representation of speech is carried out by means of separate signs for each syllable. The unit of a syllabary is sometimes called by the ugly and rather unnecessary word *syllabogram*. Syllabograms may be of the type V, CV, VC, CVC, or even CVCV (C standing for consonant, V for vowel). Where a syllabary is restricted to the first two types it is called an *open syllabary*.

syllabogram see *syllabary*.

transcription re-writing a text from another script according to the conventions of one's own, so as to represent in an approximate manner the pronunciation of the original.

transliteration re-writing a text from another script by means of the signary of one's own (if necessary artificially augmented) in such a way that there is a one-to-one correspondence between the signs or sign-groups used. It is possible to reconstruct the original spelling from a transliteration, but not from a transcription.

trilingual, or *triscript*, as for *bilingual* and *biscript*, but with three languages or scripts instead of two.

vowel-pointing see *diacritic marks*.

writing is well defined by Gelb as 'a system of inter-communication by means of conventional visible marks'.

xenogram a word written in another language but to be read as if it were one's own. For instance in English we write lb, which stands for the Latin word *libra*, but read it as the English word 'pound'. Aramaic words, to be read as Persian, are frequent on Parthian and Sassanian inscriptions, and Sumerian words on Akkadian tablets.

The term originally employed for this device, allogram, was already in use for other purposes and has since been dropped. The current term is heterogram, but this is a miserable substitute, clumsy, obscure to most people, and etymologically inaccurate. *xenogram*, an infinitely preferable word in all respects, was suggested to me by Professor Crossland of the University of Sheffield.

Bibliography

Preliminary Notes

These remarks are presented simply as a first guide to readers who wish to pursue for themselves the subjects treated in the various chapters. The books and articles are summarily referred to by author and year; fuller citation will be found under the name of the author in the Bibliography below.

Chapter One: An admirably documented account of the activities of Renaissance scholars in general is to be found in Weiss (1969). More specifically concerned with the rediscovery of Egypt are two articles by Dannenfeld (1953, 1954).

Different aspects of Graeco-Roman attitudes to Egypt are dealt with by Witt (1971), Griffiths (1970), and in Sbordone's (Italian) edition of Horapollo (1940). There is a French translation of Horapollo by van de Walle and Vergote (1943), and an English one by Boas (1950).

On the cult of hieroglyphic wisdom and the reaction to it see Iversen (1961 and 1968) and David (1965, in French). Kircher is treated by Godwin (1979) and Janssen (1943) attempts to say what good things can be said about his Egyptology.

Festugière is the most recent scholar to have made a speciality of the Hermetic writings: they are available in English translation (though with much needless re-arrangement of the text) by Scott (1924), who in his introduction discusses the Siena pavement mosaic as does Cust (1901).

There are Coptic grammars of the Saidic dialect by Steindorff (1951), Till (1961) and Lambdin (1983); and of the Bohairic dialect by Mallon (1956); a Coptic Dictionary by Crum (1939); lives of Peiresc by Gassendi (1641) and Cahen-Salvador (1951). The bearing of Coptic on the decipherment of the hieroglyphs is discussed (in German) by Cramer (1953).

Chapter Two: Evaluations of Warburton and his influence will be found in Iversen (1961) and David (1965). The liveliest exponent of his theories is, needless to say, Warburton himself.

There is no English book on Zoëga, nor have his books, which are in Latin, been translated. His memory, however, is still alive in Denmark, and entries on him will be found in the standard international biographies.

Chapter Three: It would be worth having a full-scale study of Sacy's life and influence. None exists, though Dehérain (1938) provides a sketch for one. There are several biographies of Thomas Young, the

most recent being by Wood (1954) and Kline (1993): his Egyptian researches are most knowledgeably evaluated by Renouf (1897) and Sottas (1922).

Fourier's public career is the subject of a book by Champollion's elder brother (Champollion-Figeac 1844). The standard book on Champollion is that of Miss Hartleben (1906, reprinted 1983). The most detailed account of his decipherment is in Sottas (1922). Its most vigorous defender was Sir Peter le Page Renouf, and the trouncings meted out by him to its opponents on various occasions can be found in his collected works (1902). The ancient Egyptian language, as now known, is described by Loprieno (1995).

Chapter Four: Booth (1902) gives the fullest account in English of the discovery and initial decipherments of cuneiform. The basic publication of the site of Persepolis is by Schmidt (1953): a splendidly illustrated introduction to the glories of the Achaemenid empire is given by Ghirshman (1964).

Ghirshman (1962), Frye (1962), and Colledge (1967) give the general historical background of the period of the Palmyrene and Sassanid inscriptions. Aramaic writing is discussed by Driver (1948, 1956). The standard modern grammar in English on Archaemenid Persian is by Kent (1950).

Henry Rawlinson's remarkable life is well told by his brother George Rawlinson (1898) and Edward Hincks is given his due credit by Cathcart (1994).

Chapter Five: Of the many books which may be recommended as giving a general historical perspective on the cuneiform-using world the ones most likely to interest the reader of this book are perhaps those of Oppenheim (1964) and Dalley (1998). The importance of the Ugaritic discoveries is well summarized in a general article by Ullendorff (1964). References to the more specialized modern literature dealing with this and other cuneiform scripts have been given in the chapter notes and need not be repeated here.

For a modern treatment of Sumerian from a linguistic point of view see Thomsen (1984).

Chapter Six: On all matters relating to the Cypriot syllabary Masson's book (1961 rev. ed 1983) is exhaustive, but on the general archaeology and history of the island no book can be – so diverse has been its past and so rich are the monuments which testify to it. Spiteris (1971) gives a finely illustrated survey and Karageorghis (1964) describes a single site for the general reader.

Chapter Seven: Gurney (1952 rev. ed. 1990) gives the best and most readily available account of the Hittites in English, but he does not go into detail on the script or its decipherment. For this see the introduction to Hawkins (1999).

Chapter Eight: Sir Arthur Evans' work has not yet been made the subject of a dispassionate critical survey. There exists, however, an excellent picture of his life, given by his half-sister Joan Evans (1943) and there are memories of him from Harden (1983).

Chapter Nine: The first fruits of the decipherment of Linear B were assembled by Palmer (1963). Shelmerdine and Palaima (1984) show how the palace accounts can illuminate everyday Mycenaean life. The best general book on the course of the decipherment is by Chadwick (1958), now in a second edition with a substantial postscript. Meredith *et al.* (1984) give a very human account of Michael Ventris's life. For information on other Aegean scripts see Pope (1978) and Chadwick (1987).

Conclusion: The history of writing was a favourite subject in the eighteenth century when there was very little evidence available for it. It then fell into disfavour, until stimulated no doubt by the discovery that our alphabet already existed in the second millennium BC (see pages 121–122), there was a revival of interest – witness Driver (1948), Gelb (1952), Jensen (1958), and Diringer (1962, 1968). Modern techniques of reproduction have now made possible even more comprehensive treatments of the subject, for example DeFrancis (1989), Daniels and Bright (1996) and, with particularly magnificent illustrations, Robinson (1995).

Abbreviations

Standard works and periodicals referred to on more than one occasion have been abbreviated as follows:

ABSA *Annual of the British School at Athens.* London.

AJA *American Journal of Archaeology.* Princeton.

BASOR *Bulletin of the American Schools for Oriental Research*, Jerusalem and Baghdad.

BRL *Bulletin of the John Rylands Library.* Manchester.

CE *Chronique d'Égypte.* Brussels.

HO *Handbuch der Orientalistik.* Leiden.

JA *Journal Asiatique.* Paris.

JHS *Journal of Hellenic Studies.* London.

JNES *Journal of Near Eastern Studies.* Chicago.

JRAS *Journal of the Royal Asiatic Society.* London.

PSBA *Proceedings of the Society of Biblical Archaeology.* London.

RHA *Revue Hittite et Asianique.* Paris.

TSBA *Transactions of the Society of Biblical Archaeology.* London.

ACOSTA, J. 1589–1590 *De natura novi orbis.* Salamanca.

—1590. *Historia natural y moral de las Indias.* Salamanca.

ADELUNG, J. C. and VATER, J. S. 1806–17. *Mithridates, oder allgemeine Sprachenkunde.* 4 vols. Berlin.

ADIEGO LAJARA, I.-J. 1993. 'Les identifications onomastiques dans le déchiffrement du carien' in GIANNOTTA 1994, 27–63.

—1993. *Studia Carica: investigaciones sobre la escritura y lengua Carias.* Barcelona.

AGUSTÍN, H. L. 1587. *Dialogos de medullas, inscriciones, y otros antiquedades.* Tarragona.

AHRENS, H. L. 1876. 'Kypriote Inschriften', *Philologus*, 35, 1–102.

ÅKERBLAD, J. D. 1802. *Lettre sur l'inscription égyptienne de Rosette, addressée au Citoyen Silvestre de Sascy.* Paris.

ANGLERIUS (=PIETRO MARTIRE D'ANGHIERA), 1516. *De orbe novo decades.* Alcala.

—1521. *De Insulis nuper repertis et Incolarum moribus.* . . . Seville.

ANQUETIL DUPERRON, A. H. 1771. *Zend-Avesta.* . . . Paris.

BACON, F. 1623. *De Dignitate et Augmentis Scientiarum.* London.

BARNETT, R. D. 1953. 'Karatepe, the key to Hittite Hieroglyphs', *Anatolian Studies*, 3.

BARTHÉLEMY, J. J. 1754. *Reflexions sur l'Alphabet et sur la langue dont on se servoit autrefois à Palmyre.* Paris.

—1760. *Explication de la Mosaique de Palestrine.* Paris. (See also CAYLOS, below.)

BAUER, A. and STRZYGOWSKI, J. 1905. *Eine Alexandrische Weltchronik.* Vienna.

BAUER, H. 1930. *Entzifferung der Keilinschriften von Ras Schamra.* Halle.

BAUER, G. S. 1730. *Museum Sinicum.* Petrograd.

BECANUS, GOROPIUS 1580. *Opera . . . hactenus in lucem non edita, nempe Hermathena, Hieroglyphica, etc.* Antwerp.

BELON, P. 1553. *Les observations de plusieurs singularités et choses mémorables, trouvées en Grèce, Asie, Indée, Égypte, Arabie, etc.* Paris.

BENNETT, E. L. 1951. *The Pylos Tablets, a preliminary transcription.* Princeton.

BESOLDUS, C. 1632. *De natura populorum . . . et de linguarum ortu atque immutatione.* 2nd ed. Tübingen.

BIONDO, F. 1446. *Romae Instauratae, lib. iii* (first printed ed. Rome, 1470 or 1471).

BIRCH, S. 1872. 'Cypriote Inscriptions', *TSBA*, 2.

BLÜMEL, W., 1990. 'Zwei neuen Inschriften aus Mylasa . . .' *Epigr. Anatol.* 16, 29–43.

BOAS, G. 1950. *The Hieroglyphics of Horapollo.* New York.

BOISSON, C. 1994. 'Conséquences phonétiques de certaines hyphèses de déchiffrement du carien' in GIANNOTTA 1994, 207–232.

BOOTH, A. J. 1902. *The Discovery and Decipherment of the Trilingual Cuneiform Inscriptions.* . . . London.

BOPP, F. 1816. *Über das Conjugationssystem der Sanskritsprache in Vergleichung mit jenem der griechischen, lateinischen, persischen, und germanischen.* Frankfurt.

BOSSERT, H. T. 1932. 'Santas und Kupapa', *Mitt. der Altorient. Ges.*, 6, 3, 1–88.

—1948. 'Karatepe', *Oriens*, 1, 2, 147–207.

BRANDIS, J. 1873. 'Versuch zu Entzifferung der

Kyprischen Schrift', *Monatsbericht Preuss. Akad.* 649–52.

BRASSEUR DE BOURBOURG, C. E. 1864. *Relations des choses de Yucatán de Diego de Landa.* Paris.

BRICE, W. C. 1962. 'The Writing System of the Proto-Elamite account tablets of Susa', *BRL*, 45, 15–49.

—1963. 'A comparison of the account tablets of Susa with those of Hagia Triada', *Kadmos*, 2, 27–38.

—1967. 'The Structure of Linear A . . .', *Europa* (*Fest, für Ernst Grumach*), 32–44.

BRIGHT, W. 1996. *The World's Writing Systems.* Oxford. See DANIELS, P. T., below.

BROWN, P. 1971. *The world of late antiquity.* London.

BRUIN, C. DE 1714. *Reizen over Moskovie, door Persie, en Indie.* Amsterdam. (French ed. 1718, English tr. 1737, 1754).

BUONDELMONTE 1422. *Liber Insularum Archipelagi* (ed. de Sinner, Leipzig and Berlin, 1824).

BURCKHARDT, J. L. 1822. *Travels in Syria and the Holy Land* (ed. W. M. Leake). London.

BURNOUF, E. 1826. *Essai sur le pali* (with Lassen). Paris.

—1833. *Commentaire sur le Yaçna.* Paris.

—1836. *Mémoire sur deux Inscriptions Cuneiformes trouvés près d'Hamadan.* Paris.

BURTON, R. 1872. *Unexplored Syria* (with Tyrwhitt Drake). London.

CAHEN-SALVADOR, G. 1951. *Un grand humaniste, Peiresc 1580–1637.* Paris.

CASAUBON, I. 1614. *de rebus sacris et ecclesiasticis exerc, xvi . . . .* London.

CASSON, S. (ed.). 1927. *Essays in Aegean Archaeology.* Oxford.

CATHCART, K. J. 1994. *The Edward Hincks Memorial Lectures.* Dublin.

CAUSSIN, N. 1618. *De symbolica Aegyptiorum sapientia.* Paris.

CAYLUS, Comte de 1752–67. *Recueil d'antiquités égyptiennes, étrusques, grecques, et romaines.* 7 vols. Paris.

CHADWICK, J. 1953. See VENTRIS, below.

—1958. *The Decipherment of Linear B* (2nd ed. 1967). Cambridge.

—1987. *Linear B and related scripts.* London.

CHAMBERLAYNE, J. (ed.) 1715. *Oratio Dominica in diversas omnium fere gentium linguas versa.* Amsterdam.

CHAMPOLLION, J.-F. 1814. *L'Egypte sous les Pharaons.* Paris.

—1822a. 'Lettre . . . relative au Zodiaque de Dendêra', *Rev. Enc.* 44 (August).

—1822b. *Lettre à M. Dacier.* Paris.

—1824. *Précis du système hiéroglyphique des anciens Égyptiens.* Paris.

—1836. *Grammaire égyptienne* (ed. J.-J. Champollion-Figeac). Paris. (For life see HARTLEBEN, below.)

CHAMPOLLION-FIGEAC, A. 1887. *Les deux Champollions: Leur vie et leurs œuvres.* Grenoble.

CHAMPOLLION-FIGEAC, J.-J. 1819. *Annales des Lagides.* Paris.

—1844. *Fourier et Napoléon: L'Égypte et les cent jours.* Paris.

CHARDIN, J. 1711. *Voyages . . . en Perse. . . .* 3 vols. Amsterdam.

COE, M. D. 1992/4. *Breaking the Maya Code.* London and New York.

COLLEDGE, M. A. E. 1967. *The Parthians.* London.

COLONNA, F. 1499. *Hypnerotomachia Poliphili.* Venice. (Facsimile ed. with commentary by G. Pozzi and L. A. Ciapponi, 1964.)

COSENZA, M. E. 1962–7. *Dictionary of Italian Humanists.* 6 vols. Boston.

COWLEY, A. E. 1917. 'Notes on Hittite hieroglyphic inscriptions', *JRAS.* 561–85.

—1920. *The Hittites.* London.

—1927. 'A note on Minoan writing', in CASSON, 1927, above.

CRUM, W. E. 1939. *A Coptic Dictionary.* Oxford.

CULL, R. 1878. Obituary of Fox Talbot. *TSBA*, 6.

CUST, R. H. H. 1901. *The Pavement Mosaics of Siena 1369–1562.* London.

CYRIAC D'ANCONA *c.* 1435. *Kyriaci Anconitani Itinerarium* (ed. Mehuns, Florence 1742).

DALLEY, S. 1998. *The Legacy of Mesopotamia.* Oxford.

DANIELS, P. T. and BRIGHT, W. 1996. *The World's Writing Systems.* Oxford.

DANNENFELD, K. H. 1953. 'The Renaissance and pre-classical civilisations', *J. of Hist. of Ideas,* 435–49.

—1954. 'Egypt and Egyptian Antiquities in the Renaissance', *Studies in the Renaissance* 6, 7–27.

DAVID, M. V. 1965. *Le débat su les écritures et l'hiéroglyphe aux xviie et xviiie siècles.* Paris.

DAWKINS, J. and WOOD, R. 1753. *The ruins of Palmyra.* London.

DEECKE, W. and SIEGISMUND, J. 1875. *Doe wichtigsten Kyprischen Inschriften.* Leipzig.

DEFRANCIS, J. 1989. *Visible Speech.* Honolulu.

DEHÉRAIN, H. 1938. *Silvestre de Sacy, ses contemporains et ses disciples.* Paris.

DELRIO, A. 1822. *Description of the Ruins of an Ancient City.* London.

DHORME, E. 1930. 'Un nouvel alphabet sémitique', *Rev. Biblique,* 39, 571–7.

—1931. 'Première traduction des Textes phéniciens de Ras Shamra', *id.* 40, 32–56.

DIRINGER, D. 1962. *Writing.* London.

—1968. *The Alphabet* (3rd ed.) 2 vols. London.

DRIVER, G. R. 1948. *Semitic Writing.* London.

—1956. *Aramaic Documents of the 5th c. B.C.* Oxford.

EIKOH MA. 1959. 'Japan's Encounter with Western Medical Science'. *Bulletin of the History of Medicine.* Baltimore.

EMERY, C. 1948. 'John Wilkins' Universal Language', *Isis* 38, 174 ff.

EVANS, A. J. 1894a. Letters from Candia, in *The Athenaeum* of June 23rd.

—1894b. 'Primitive Pictographs and a Prae-Phoenician Script from Crete and the Peloponnese', *JHS*, 14, 270–372.

—1897. 'Further discoveries of Cretan and Aegean script with Libyan and proto-Egyptian comparisons', *JHS*, 17, 327–95.

—1900a. Letter from Knossos, in *The Athenaeum* of May 19th.

—1900–3. 'Knossos Excavation Reports' in *ABSA*, vols. 6–9.

—1903b. *Syllabus of a course of Three Lectures on Pre-Phoenician Writing in Crete and its bearing on the history of the Alphabet.* Royal Institution, London.

—1908. 'The European Diffusion of Pictography and its bearing on the Origin of Script', in MARETT,

1908, below.
—1909. *Scripta Minoa*, vol. i. Oxford.
—1921. *Palace of Minos*, vol. i. London.
—1935. *Palace of Minos*, vol. iv. London.
—1952. *Scripta Minoa*, vol. ii (ed. Myres). Oxford.
EVANS, JOAN. 1943. *Time and chance: the story of Arthur Evans and his forebears*. London.
FALKENSTEIN, A. 1936. *Archaische Texte aus Uruk*. Berlin and Leipzig.
FERRARI, P. A. 1605. *Epitome Geographicum*. Pavia.
FESTUGIÈRE, A. J. 1945–54. *Corpus Hermeticum* (with A. D. Nock); Paris.
—1950–4. *La Révélation d'Hermes Trismégiste*. 4 vols. Paris.
FICINO, M. 1492. *Plotini opera omnia . . .* Florence.
FIGUEROA, GARCIAE SILVA 1620. *de rebus Persarum epistula*. Antwerp.
FÖRSTEMANN, E. 1906. 'Commentary on the Maya Manuscript in the Royal Public Library of Dresden.' *Papers of the Peabody Museum IV2*. Cambridge, Mass.
FORRER, E. 1931–2. *Die hethitische Bilderschrifte*. Chicago.
FOURMONT, E. 1737. *Meditationes Sinicae*. Paris.
—1742. *Linguae Sinarum Mandarinicae, Hieroglyphicae, grammatica duplex*. Leipzig.
FRANK, C. 1923. *Die sogenannten hettitischen Hieroglyphen-inschriften*. Leipzig.
FRASER, P. M. 1960. 'The Cult of Sarapis in the Hellenistic World', *Opusc. Atheniensia* 3, 1–54.
FREI, P. and MAREK, C. 1997. 'Die karisch-griechische Bilingue von Kaunos' *Kadmos* 36, 11–89.
FRIEDRICH, J. 1932. *Kleinasiatische Sprachdenkmäler*. Berlin.
—1954. *Entzifferung verschollener Schriften und Sprachen*. Berlin.
—1969. Articles 'Churritisch' (1–30) und 'Urartaisch' (31–53), in *HO*, I, ii, 1–2 (ii).
FRUTAZ, A. P. 1962. *Le Piante di Roma* 2 vols. Rome.
FRYE, R. N. 1962. *The Heritage of Persia*. London.
GASSENDI, P. 1641. . . . *Peireskii vita . . .* Paris.
GELB, I. J. 1931, 1935, 1942. *Hittite Hieroglyphs* I, II, and III. Chicago.
—1952. *A Study of Writing*. London.
GHIRSHMAN, R. 1962. *Iran: Parthians and Sassanians*. London.
—1964. *Persia: from the origins to Alexander the Great*. London.
GIANNOTTA, M. E. 1994. *La Decifrazione del Cario... Atti del 1° Simposio Internationale*. Rome.
GODWIN, J. 1979. *Athanasius Kircher: a Renaissance man and the quest for new knowledge*. London.
GORDON, C. 1968. *Forgotten Scripts: the story of their decipherment*. London.
GRIFFITHS, J. G. 1970. *Plutarch's De Iside et Osiride*. Univ. of Wales.
GROTEFEND, G. F. 1802. 'Praevia de cuneatis, quas vocant, inscriptionibus Persepolitanis legendis et explicandis relatio', *Gött. gel. Anz.* 3, 1481–7.
—1815. see HEEREN, below.
GRUMACH, E. 1970. 'The Structure of Minoan Linear Scripts', *BRL*, 52, 326–45.
GURNEY, O. 1952 2nd edition (rev.) 1990. *The Hittites*. London.

HALBHERR, F. 1903. 'Resti dell'età micenae scoperti ad Haghia Triada', *Mon. Ant.*, 13. 33 ff.
HALÉVY, J. 1903. 'Introduction au déchiffrement des inscriptions pseudo-hittites . . .', *Rev. Sém.*, 1, 55–62, 126–137.
HALLOCK, R. T. 1970. 'On the Old Persian signs', *JNES* 29, 52–5.
HARDEN, D. B. 1983. *Sir Arthur Evans 1851–1941: a 'memoir'*. Oxford.
HARTLEBEN, H. 1906. *Champollion: sein Leben und sein Werk*. 2 vols. Berlin.
—1909. *Lettres et journaux de Champollion le jeune*. 2 vols. Paris
HAWKINS, J. D. 1999. *Corpus of Hieroglyphic Luwian Inscriptions*, Vol. 1. Berlin.
HEEREN, A. H. L. 1815. *Ideen über die Politik, den Verkehr, und den Handel der vornehmster Völker der Alten Welt*. 3rd ed. Göttingen.
HEKSCHER, W. S. 1947. 'Bernini's Elephant and Obelisk', *Art Bull.* 29, 155–82.
HERBERT, T. 1634. *A Discription of the Persian Monarchy and other parts of the greater Asia and Africa*. London. (3rd ed. rewritten and enlarged 1677.)
HERZFELD, E. 1924. *Paikuli*. 2 vols. Berlin.
HINCKS, E. 1847. 'Some Passages of the Life of King Darius, the son of Hystaspes, by Himself', *Dublin Univ. Mag.* Jan., 14–27.
—1857. see Tiglath. Pileser, below.
HOOD, M. S. F. 1967. *The Home of the Heroes*. London.
—1971. *The Minoans*. London.
HOTTINGER, J. H. 1662. *Cippi Hebraici*. Heidelberg.
HROZNY, B. 1915. 'Die Lösung des hethitischen Problems', *Mitt. der Altorient. Ges.*, 56, Dec., 17–50.
—1917. *Die Sprache der Hethiter*. Leipzig.
—1933. *Les Inscriptions hittites hiéroglyphiques*. Prague
HUMBOLDT, A. VON. 1816. *Vues des Cordilliéres et Monumens des Peuples Indigènes de l'Amérique*. Paris.
HYDE, T. 1770. *Historia Religionis veterum Persarum*. . . . Oxford.
IVERSEN, E. 1961. *The myth of Egypt and its hieroglyphs in European tradition*. Copenhagen and London.
—1968. *Obelisks in Exile: I The Obelisks of Rome*. Copenhagen and London.
JABLONSKI, P. E. 1750. *Pantheon Aegyptiacum*. Frankfurt.
JANSSEN, J. 1943. 'Athanase Kircher, Égyptologue', *CE* 18, 240 ff.
JEFFERY, L. H. 1961. *The Local Scripts of Archaic Greece*. Oxford.
JENSEN, H. 1958. *Die Schrift . . .* 2nd ed. Berlin. (Eng. tr. 1970).
JENSEN, P. 1894. '. . . der Chatischen oder cilicischen Inschriften', *Zeit. d. morg. Ges.*, 48, 235 ff., 429 ff.
JEQUIER, G. 1921. *Les Frises d'objets des sarcophages du Moyen Empire*. Cairo.
JONES, A. H. M. 1971. *The Cities of the Eastern Roman Provinces*. 2nd ed. Oxford.
KAEMPFER, E. 1712. *Amoenitatum exoticarum politico-physico-medicarum*. Lemgow.
KAHLE, P. E. (jr) 1954. *Bala'izah: Coptic texts from Deir el-Bala'izah in Upper Egypt*. London.
KAMMENHUBER, A. 1969. 'Hetitisch, Palaisch, Luwisch, und Hieroglyphenluwisch', *HO*, I, ii, 1–2 (ii), 119–357.

KARAGEORGHIS, V. 1969. *Salamis in Cyprus: Homeric, Hellenistic, Roman.* London.

KELLEY, D. H. 1976. *Deciphering the Maya Script.* Austin.

KENT, R. 1950. *Old Persian.* New Haven.

KIRCHER, A. 1636. *Prodromus Coptus sive Aegyptiacus.* Rome.

—1643. *Lingua Aegyptiaca restituta.* Rome.

—1650. *Obeliscus Pamphilius.* Rome.

—1652–4. *Oedipus Aegyptiacus.* Rome.

—1663. *Polygraphia nova et universalis.* Rome.

—1666. *Obelisci Aegyptiaci nuper inter Isaei Romani rudera effossi interpretatio hieroglyphica.* Rome.

—1667. *China monumentis . . . illustrata.* Rome.

KITCHEN, K. A. 1965. 'Theban topographical lists old and new', *Orientalia* 34, 1 ff.

—1966. 'Aegean place-names in a list of Amenophis III', *BASOR*, 18r, 23 ff.

KLAPROTH, J. 1832. *Examen critique des travaux de feu M. Champollion sur les Hiéroglyphes.* Paris.

KLINE, D. L. 1993. *Thomas Young, forgotten genius.* Cincinnati.

KNOROSOV, Y. V. 1952. 'Drevniaia pis'mennost' Trsentral' Noi Ameriki' *Sovetskaya Etnografia 3(2)*, 100–8.

—1958. 'The problem of the study of the Maya hieroglyphic writing'. *American Antiquity* 23, 248–291.

KOBER, A. E. 1945. 'Evidence of inflection in the "chariot" tablets from Knossos', *AJA*, 49, 64–75.

—1946. 'Inflection in Linear Class B: I. Declension', *AJA*, 50, 268–76.

—1948. 'The Minoan Scripts: fact and theory', *AJA*, 52, 82–103.

—1949. '"Total" in Minoan Linear Class B', *Archiv Orientalni*, 17, 286–98.

KOWALSKI, T. W. 1975. 'Lettres cariennes: essai de déchiffrement', *Kadmos* 14, 73–93.

LACROZE, M. V. 1715. 'de variis linguis', in Chamberlayne 1715.

—1775. *Lexicon Aegyptiaco-Latinum.* Oxford.

LAMBDIN, T. O. 1983. *Introduction to Sahidic Coptic.* Macon 1983.

LANG, R. H. 1871. 'On the Discovery of some Cypriote Inscriptions', *TSBA*, I, 123–8.

—1905. 'Reminiscences', *Blackwoods Magazine* (May 1905), 622–39.

LANTSCHOOT, A. VAN 1948. *Un précurseur d'Athanase Kircher.* Louvain.

LAROCHE, E. 1960. *Les Hiéroglyphes hittites: I L'écriture.* Paris.

—1971. 'Liste des documents hiéroglyphiques', *RHA*, 27, 110–31.

LARSEN, M. T. and TROLLE, M. 1996. *Conquest of Assyria: excavations in an antique land 1840–1860.* London.

LASSEN, C. 1826. See BURNOUF, above.

—1836. *Die Altpersischen Keil-Inschriften von Persepolis. Entzifferung des Alphabets und Erklärung des Inhalts.* Bonn.

LEIBNITZ, G. W. VON 1768. *Opera omnia* (ed. Dutens). Geneva.

LEVITA, E. 1525. *Grammatica Hebraea Eliae Levitae Germani per S. Munsterus versa.* Basle.

LEWIS, G. C. 1862. *An Historical Survey of the Astronomy of the Ancients.* London.

LIPSIUS, I. 1602. *Epistolarum selectarum centuria tertia ad Belgas.* Antwerp.

LOPRIENO, A. 1995. *Ancient Egypt: a linguistic introduction.* Cambridge.

LUDOLFUS, I. 1691. *ad suam historiam Aethiopicam commentarius.* Frankfurt.

LUYNES, H. DE. 1852. *Numismatique et Inscriptions cypriotes.* Paris.

MALLON, A. 1956. *Grammaire Copte.* 4th ed. Beirut.

MALPEINES, L. DE 1744. *Essai sur les hiéroglyphes des Egyptiens.* (tr. from W. Warburton) Paris.

MARCUS, J. 1992. *Mesoamerican Writing Systems: Propaganda, Myth, and History in four ancient civilisations.* Princeton.

MAREK, C. 1997. See FREI above.

MARETT, R. R. 1908. *Anthropology and the Classics.* Oxford.

MASSON, O. 1961. *Les inscriptions, chypriotes syllabiques.* Paris 2nd ed. (rev.) 1983.

MENESTRIER, C. F. 1692. *Lettre . . . à l'occasion d'une Momie apportée d'Egypte. . . .* Paris.

MERCATI, M. 1589. *Degli obelisci di Roma.* Rome.

MEREDITH, A. G. *et al.*, 1984. *Michael Ventris remembered.* Stowe School.

MERIGGI, P. 1929. 'Die hethitische Hieroglyphenschrift', *Zeit. f. Ass.*, 29, 165–212.

—1933. 'Zur Lesung der H.H.', *Or. Lit. Zeit.*, 36. 73–84.

—1934. *Die längsten Bauinschriften. . . .* Leipzig.

—1937. 'Listes des hiéroglyphs hittites', *RHA*, 27 and 29, 69–114, 157–200.

—1966–7. *Manuale di Eteo Geroglyphico.* 2 vols. Rome.

MESSERSCHMIDT, L. 1900–6. *Corpus Inscriptionum Hettiticarum.* Berlin.

MONTFAUCON, B. 1719–24. *L'Antiquité Expliquée.* 5 vols.+sup, Paris.

MORPURGO, A. 1963. *Mycenaeae Graecitatis Lexicon.* Rome.

MUNSTER, S. 1525. see LEVITA, above.

NEWTON, SIR ISAAC 1728. *The Chronology of the Ancient Kingdoms amended.* London.

NIEBUHR, C. 1774. *Reisebeschreibung nach Arabien und andem umliegenden Ländern.* Copenhagen. (Eng. tr. 1792.)

NORDH, A. (ed.) 1949. *Libellius de regionibus urbis Romae.* Lund.

OPPENHEIM, A. L. 1964. *Ancient Mesopotamia: portrait of a dead civilization.* Chicago.

PALAIMA, T. G. 1984. See SHELMERDINE, C. W.

PALMER, L. R. 1963. *The Interpretation of Mycenaean Greek Texts.* Oxford.

PEISER, F. E. 1892. *Die Hettitischen Inschriften.* Berlin.

PERROT, G. 1862. *Exploration archéologique de la Galatie et de la Bithynie.* Paris.

PETERS, W. J. T. 1963. *Landscape in Romano-Campanian Mural Painting.* Assen.

PIERIUS VALERIANUS, J. 1556. *Hieroglyphica.* Basle.

PIGNORIO, L. 1605. *Vetustissimae tabulae aeneae Sacris Aegyptiorum Simulachris coelatae accurata Explicatio.* Venice.

POGGIO BRACCIOLINI 1431–48. *Historiae de varietate fortunae* (ed. Georgius, Paris 1723).

POPE, M. W. M. 1964. *Aegean Writing and Linear A.* Lund.

—1965. 'The origin of Near Eastern writing', *Antiquity*, 40, 17–23.

—1971 (with Jacques Raison) *Index du Linéaire A*, Rome.

—1978 (with Jacques Raison) 'Linear A: changing perspectives' *Études Minoennes* I. Louvain

—1989 'Ventris's Decipherment – First Causes' in *Problems in Decipherment* (ed. Duhoux, Palaima, Bennett) Louvain-la-Neuve.

POZZI, G. and CIAPPONI, L. A. 1964. See COLONNA, above.

PROSKOURIAKOFF, T. 1960. 'Historical implications of a pattern of dates at Piedras Negras, Guatemala'. *American Antiquity* 25, 454–475.

—1963/4. 'Historical data in the Inscriptions of Yaxchilán'. *Estudios de Cultura Maya* 3, 149–167 and 4, 177–202.

QUATREMÈRE, É. 1808. *Recherches . . . sur la langue et la littérature de l'Égypte*. Paris.

—1811. *Mémoires géographiques et historiques sur l'Égypte*. Paris.

RASK, R. C. 1818. *Undersögelse om des gamle Nordiske eller Islandske Sprogs Oprindelse*. Copenhagen. (German tr. under title *Über die trakische Sprachklasse* included in Vater, 1822).

—1826. *Über das Alter . . . der Zend-Sprache. . . .* Berlin.

RAWLINSON, G. 1898. *A Memoir of Major-General Sir Henry Creswicke Rawlinson*. London.

RAWLINSON, H. C. 1846. *The Persian cuneiform inscription at Behistun deciphered and translated . . .* (=*JRAS*, 10). London.

—1850. *A Commentary on the Cuneiform Inscriptions of Babylonia and Assyria*. London.

—1857. see TIGLATH PILESER, below.

RAY, J. D. 1981. 'An approach to the Carian script' *Kadmos* 20, 150–162.

—1987 'The Egyptian approach to Carian' *Kadmos* 26, 98–103.

—1994 'New Egyptian names in Carian' in GIANNOTTA 1994, 195–206.

REINER, E. 1969. 'The Elamite Language', *HO*, I, ii, 1–2, (ii), 54–118.

RÉMUSAT, J. P. A. 1811. *Essai sur la Langue et la Littérature chinoises*. Paris.

—1813. 'Utrum Lingua Sinica sit vere monosyllabica?', *Fundgraben des Orients* 3, 279–88.

—1822. *Élémens de la grammaire chinoise*. Paris.

RENOUF, P. LE P. 1897. Young and Champollion', *PSBA* 19, 188–209.

—1902–7. *Collected Works*. Paris.

RICH, J. C. 1813. 'Memoir on the ruins and antiquities of Babylon', *Fundgraben des Orients*, 3, 129–62, 197–200.

RIGORD, J. P. 1704a. 'Sur une Ceinture de Toile trouvée en Égypte autour d'une Mumie', *Mém. de Trévoux art.* 89.

—1704b. 'De l'origine des langues et de l'écriture', *Mém. de Trévoux art.* 104.

RIPA, C. 1593. *Iconologia*. Rome.

ROBINSON, A. 1995. *The Story of Writing*. London and New York.

ROLLIG, W. 1967. See W. VON SÖDEN, below.

ROWE, A. 1946. 'Discovery of the Famous Temple and Enclosure of Serapis at Alexandria', *Suppl. aux Ann. du Service des Ant. de l'Égypte, Cahier 2*.

SACY, A. I. SILVESTRE DE. 1787. 'Sur les Inscriptions de Nakshi Roustam' (printed in Sacy 1792).

—1792. *Mémoires sur diverses antiquités de la Perse*. Paris.

—1800. 'Lettre à M. Millin sur les inscriptions des monumens Persépolitains', *Magasin Encyclopédique*. an. 8, v, 438 ff.

—1802. *Lettre au Citoyen Chaptal . . . au sujet de l'inscription Égyptienne du monument trouvé à Rosette*. Paris.

—1808. Review of Quatremère 1808 in *Mag. Enc.* 1808, iv, 241–82.

—1811a. Recommendation of Rémusat's *Essai* delivered to the Corps Législatif, and printed in *Discours sur divers sujets*, Paris. 1823.

—1811b. Review of Quatremère 1811 in *Mag. Enc.* 1811, iv. 177 ff.

—1825. Review of Champollion's *Lettre à M. Dacier, Précis*, and of Young's *Account*, in *Bull. Univ. des Sciences et de l'Industrie*, Sect. 7.

SALMASIUS, C. 1656. *Epistularum lib. primus* (ed. Clement).

SAYCE, A. H. 1872. 'The origin of Semitic Civilisation', *TSBA*, 1, 294–309.

—1874. 'The Languages of the Cuneiform Inscriptions of Elam and Media', *TSBA*, 3, 465–85.

—1876. 'The Hamathite Inscriptions', *TSBA*, 5, 22–32.

—1880a. 'The monuments of the Hittites', *TSBA*, 7, 248–93.

—1880b. 'The Bilingual Hittite and Cuneiform Inscription of Tarkondimos', *TSBA*, 7, 294–308.

—1887. 'The Karian Language and Inscriptions', *TSBA*, 9. 1. 112–154.

—1903. 'The Decipherment of the Hittite inscriptions', *PSBA*, 25, 141 ff.; 347 ff.

—1923. *Reminiscences*. London.

SBORDONE, F. 1940. *Hori Apollinis Hieroglyphica: saggio introduttivo, edizione critica del testo, e commento*. Naples.

SCAMUZZI, E. 1939–47. *La 'Mensa Isiaca' del Regio Museo di Antichità di Torino*, Rome.

SCHMIDT, E. F. 1953. *Persepolis*. Chicago.

SCHMIDT, M. 1874. *Die Inschrift von Idalion und das Kyprische Syllabar*. Jena.

SCHÜRR, D. 1992. 'Zur Bestimmung der Lautwerte des Karischen Alphabets 1941–1991'. *Kadmos* 31, 127–156.

SCOTT, W. 1924–36. *Hermetica*. 3 vols. Oxford.

SEBEOK, T. A. 1966. *Portraits of Linguists*. Bloomington.

SELER, E. 1892. 'Does there really exist a key to the Maya Hieroglyphic Writing?' *Science* 20, 121–122.

ŠEVOROVŠKIN, V. 1994. 'Carian – Three Decades later' in GIANOTTA 1994, 131–166.

SHELMERDINE, C., W. and PALAIMA, T. G. 1984. *Pylos comes alive: industry and administration in a Mycenaean palace*. New York

SIEGISMUND, J. 1875. See DEECKE, above.

SMITH, G. 1871. 'On the Reading of the Cypriote Inscriptions', *TSBA*, 1, 129–44.

SÖDEN, W. VON. 1967. *Das Akkadische Syllabar* (with W. Rollig), 2nd ed. Rome.

SOTTAS, H. 1922. Centenary edition of Champollion's *Lettre à M. Dacier*. Paris.

SPEISER, E. A. 1941. *Introduction to Hurrian*. New Haven.

—1951. 'A Note on Alphabetic Origins', *BASOR*, 121, 17–21.

SPITERIS, T. 1970, *The Art of Cyprus*. Amsterdam and London.

STEINDORFF, G. 1896–1901. *Grabfunde des Mittleren Reichs*. 2 vols. Berlin.

—1951. *Lehrbuch der Koptischen Grammatik*. Chicago.

STILLINGFLEETE, E. 1662. *Origines Sacrae, or a Rational Account of the Grounds of Christian Faith*. . . . London.

STRZYGOWSKI, J. 1905. See BAUER, A., above.

STURTEVANT, E. H. and HAHN, E. A. *A Comparative Grammar of the Hittite Language* (revised ed.). New Haven.

SUNDWALL, J. 1948. 'An attempt at assigning phonetic values to certain signs of Minoan Linear Class B', *AJA*, 52, 311–20.

SWINTON, J. 1754. 'Letters to the Royal Society on the Palmyra Alphabet', *Phil. Trans.* 48, 690 ff.

TALBOT, H. F. 1857. see TIGLATH PILESER, below.

—1876. 'On the Cypriote Inscriptions', *TSBA*, 5, 447 ff.

THOMAS, C. 1892a. 'A Key to the Mystery of the Maya Codices', *Science* 19, 294.

—1892b. 'Key to the Maya Hieroglyphs', *Science* 20, 44–46.

—1892c. 'Is the Maya Hieroglyphic Writing Phonetic?' *Science* 20, 197–201.

—1903. 'Central American Hieroglyphic Writing', *Annual Report of the Smithsonian Institution*, 705–721.

THOMPSON, J. E. S. 1962. *A catalog of Maya Hieroglyphs*. Norman.

—1972. *A commentary on The Dresden Codex: a Maya Hieroglyphic Book*. Philadelphia.

THOMPSON, R. C. 1912. 'A new decipherment of the Hittite Hieroglyphs', *Archeologia*, 64, 1–144.

THOMSEN, M.-L. 1984. *The Sumerian Language: an introduction to its history and grammatical structure*. Copenhagen.

TIGLATH PILESER 1957. *Inscription of Tiglath Pileser I King of Assyria BC 1150 as translated by Sir Henry Rawslinson, Fox Talbot Esq., Dr Hincks, and Dr Oppert*. London.

TILL, W. C. 1961. *Koptische Grammatik*. 2nd ed. Leipzig.

TORTELLIUS, J. 1471. *de Orthographia*. Rome.

TOWNSEND, J. 1815. *Character of Moses*. Bath.

TRIGAULT, N. 1615. *de Christiana expeditione apud Sinas suscepta a Societate Jesu*. Augsburg.

TROLLE, M. 1996. See LARSEN, M. T.

TYCHSEN, O. G. 1798. *de cuneatis inscriptionibus Persepolitanis lucubratio*. Rostock.

ULLENDORFF, E. 1964. 'Ugaritic Studies within their Semitic and Eastern Mediterranean Setting', *BRL*, 46, 236–49.

VALENTINI, R. and SUCCHETTI, G. 1940–53. *Codice topographici della città di Roma*. 4 vols. Rome.

VALLE, P. DELLA 1650. *Viaggi di Pietro della Valle . . . La Persia, Parte Secunda*. Rome.

VALPERGA DE CALUSO. 1783. *Didymi Taurinensis Litteraturae Copticae Rudimentum*. Parma.

VAN DE WALLE, B. 1943. "Traduction des Hiéroglyphes d'Horapollon', *CE* 35, 39–89, 199–239.

VANSLEB, J. M. 1677. *Nouvelle relation d'un voyage fait en Égypte*. Paris.

VATER, J. S. (ed.) 1822. *Vergleichungstafeln der Europäischen Stamm-Sprachen und Süd-West Asiatischer*. Halle.

VENTRIS, M. G. F. 1940. 'Introducing the Minoan Language', *AJA*, 44, 494–520.

VENTRIS, M. G. F. and CHADWICK, J. 1953. 'Evidence for Greek dialect in the Mycenean archives', JHS, 73, 84–103.

VIROLLEAUD, C. 1929. 'Les inscriptions cunéiformes de Ras Shamra', *Syria*, 10, 304–10.

—1931. 'Le déchiffrement des tablettes alphabétiques de Ras Shamra', *Syria*, 12, 15–23.

—1940. 'Les villes et les corporations du royaume d'Ugarit', *Syria*, 21, 123–51.

—1957. Textes en cunéiformes alphabétiques …= vol. 2 of Le Palais Royal d'Ugarit, ed. C. F. A. Schaeffer. Paris.

VOGUÉ, M. DE 1868. 'Inscriptions cypriotes inédites', *JA* (6th series), 11, 491–502.

WAGNESEIL, J. C. 1681. *Tela ignea Satanae*. Altdorf.

WARBURTON, W. 1738–44. *The Divine Legation of Moses demonstrated on the principles of a Religious Deist, from the Omission of the Doctrine of a Future State of Reward and Punishment in the Jewish Dispensation* (Bk. IV on Egypt appeared in 1740: for French tr. see MALPEINES, 1744, above).

WARREN, P. 1970. 'The primary dating evidence for early Minoan seals', *Kadmos*, 9, 29–37.

WEISS, R. 1969. *The renaissance discovery of classical antiquity*. Oxford.

WEISSBACH, F. H. 1890. *Die Achämeniden-Inschriften Zweiter Art*. Leipzig.

WILKINS, D. 1715. Contributions to Chamberlayne's *Oratorio Dominica*.

—1716. *Novum Testamentum Aegyptiacum*. Oxford.

WILKINS, J. 1668. *An Essay towards a Real Character and a Philosophical Language*, London.

WINDFUHR, G. L. 1970. 'The Cuneiform Signs of Ugarit', *JNES*, 29, 48–51.

WITT, R. E. 1971. *Isis in the Graeco-Roman World*. London.

WOOD, A. 1954. *Thomas Young: natural philosopher 1773–1829*. Cambridge.

WOOD, R. 1753. See DAWKINS, above.

YOUNG, T. 1823. *An account of some recent discoveries in hieroglyphical literature, and Egyptian antiquities, including the author's original alphabet as extended by M. Champollion*. London.

—1855. *Miscellaneous works of the late Thomas Young M.D., F.R.S.*, 3 vols. London.

ZOËGA, G. 1787. *Nummi Aegyptiaci*. Rome.

—1797. *De origine et usu obeliscorum*. Rome.

—1810. *Catalogue codicum Copt. mss. qui in museo Borgiano adservantur*. Rome.

ZUCCHETTI, G. 1940–53. See VALENTINI, above.

Photographic Acknowledgments

The photographs used for the undermentioned illustrations are reproduced by courtesy of:

Archives Photographiques, Paris, 33
Archivo Fotografico Generale, 31
Ashmolean Museum, Oxford, and Mrs L. Ventris, 110–114
Bodleian Library, Oxford, 9, 12, 13d, 20, 22, 23a, 26a, 27, 28, 46–51, 53, 54, 59b, 60, 62a,b, 63, 64a,b, 65, 84
Trustees of the British Museum, 68, 69, 86
Maurice Chuzeville, 42a, 43a,b
Peter Clayton, 3b, 15, 19, 32, 34
Dr Halet Cumbal, 89
Dr Silvio Curto, Soprintendenza per le Antichità

Egizie, Turin, 17a
Deutsches Archäologisches Institut, Athens, 91a
Ray Gardner, 3c, 13c, 77, 78b
Professor Ignace J. Gelb, 87
Giraudon, 25
Hirmer Fotoarchiv, 44c(ii), 91b,c
K. A. Kitchen, 118a
Kongelige Bibliotek, Copenhagen, 29, 61
The Mansell Collection, 2, 4
National Portrait Gallery, London, 24, 99
Oriental Institute, University of Chicago, 45, 56, 57, 58a, 59a, 72
Mrs L. Ventris, 109
Roger Wood, 66
Map by Nicholas Rous

Index

For Renaissance and modern authors see also in the Bibliography

Italic numerals refer to the illustrations

ACHAEMENID, Achaemenids, 100, 102, 104, 106, 108, 110, 112, 210
Achôris, 82; *frontispiece, 42a, b*
Acosta, J. d', 39, 195, 214
Acts vii 22, *see* Moses
Adam and the origin of language, 28, 51, 208
Adelung, J. C., 208
Adiego Lajara, I. J., 193–4
Aegean writing, 123–35, 146–79, 180, 182
Agustìn, A., 34
Ahrens, H. L., 131–4
Åkerblad, J. D., 64, 71, 208
Akkadian cuneiform, 111, 113, 117, 122, 141, 182; *70, 76, 115*
Aldus, 24, 205
Alexander the Great, 14, 73, 210
Alexander VII, Pope, 30–1
Alexandria, 15
Amenophis III, 178–9; *44c, 118*
American Indians, Evans on, 148, 154; Warburton on, 51; *see also* Aztec, Maya, Mexican
Ammianus Marcellinus, 12, 19, 20, 21
Amun, 80, 81; *40a*
Andros, 11
Anghiera (= Anglerius), P. M. d', 195, 213
animals and Egyptian writing, 18, 52, 58, 75
Anquetil Duperron, A. H., 99, 101, 102, 106
Antinous, 77; *38c*
Antonio Nebrissensis, 213–4
Anubis, 45; *40c*
Apuleius, 15, 20, 207
Aramaic, 15, 44, 99, 180, 181, 183
Ardashir, 98, 99; *64c*
Aristides, 207

Aristotle, 25
Armenian script, 181, 183
Arsacid, *see* Parthian
Assyrian cuneiform, 111, 113, 114
Augustus, 11, 73
Avesta, 103, 105, 106, 210
Aztec, 203

BABYLONIAN CUNEIFORM, 111–17
Bacon, Francis, 39, 53, 195, 206
Bankes, W., 72, 189, 207; *34* (obelisk)
Barberini obelisk, 77; *37*
Barnett, R.D., 138
Baron, Cardinal, 34
Barthélemy, J. J., 49, 53, 95–7, 120, 187, 189, 191, 208; *22c, 23c, 63*
Basque, 111, 210
Bauer, H., 118–20; *73*
Bayer, G. S., 65
Becanus, Goropius, 7, 210
Behistun, 106, 111, 188, 212; *66*
Bembine Table, 24; *17–19*; Kircher on, 32, 205–6; Pignorio, 33; Warburton, 207
Bennett, E. L., 169; *117*
Bentley, Richard, 210
Bernini, 30; *15*
Besoldus, C., 103
Biondo, F., 12
Birch, S., 130
Blegen, C., 170, 176
Blümel, W., 193
Bopp, F., 63, 104, 211
Bossert, H. T., 143
Brandis, J., 130
Brasseur de Bourbourg, 197
Brice, W. C., 211
Bruin, C. de (= Le Brun), 89, 102, 186; *52, 55*
Buondelmonte, 11, 204
Burckhardt, J. L., 136
Burnouf, E., 105, 106, 188, 211
Burton, R., 137, 211; *85*

CALIGULA, 11
Cambyses, 14, 100

Carchemish, 144; *90*

Carian, 192–4

cartouches, Barthélemy on, 53; in Champollion's decipherment, 72–9, 81–2; Kircher, 31; Sacy, 66, 189, 190, 191; Zoëga, 57

Casaubon, I., 34–5

Cassiodorus, 21

Caussin, N., 28; *14*

Caylus, Comte de, 49, 53; *22c, 23c, 25, 26c*; biscript vase, 74, 100, 102, 105, 42a

Chadwick, J., 9, 163, 175–6; *116*

Chairemon, 17, 18

Chamberlayne, J., 38, 210

Champollion, J.-F., 68–84, 209; *33, 35–44*; *l'Égypte sous les Pharaons*, 69–70; *lettre à M. Dacier*, 71–4, 76; *Précis*, 75–84, 209; *also mentioned*, 9, 19, 20, 38–9, 42, 46, 53, 54, 60, 63, 102, 120, 173, 178, 189, 190, 191, 208

Champollion-Figeac, J.-J., 68

Chardin, J., 88–9, 97, 198; *50, 53*

China and Egypt, 196

Chinese, 10, 30, 39, 40, 182, 190, 203, 206; Adelung, on, 208; Champollion, 70, 71, 77; Evans, 148; Hyde, 88; Kaempfer, 89; Rémusat, 75–6, 208; Sacy, 63, 65–6, 207; Warburton, 48–9; Young, 67; Zoëga, 56, 58–9

chocolate, 202; *197*

Cicero, 15, 2–2–, 31, 47

Clarke, Hyde, 137–8

Claudius, 18, 33, 73

Clement of Alexandria, on the types of Egyptian writing, 17, 43, 44, 50–1, 83, 207, 209 (Letronne and Champollion); 'the Diospolis inscription', 21, 25, 36 (Stillingfleete), 44 (Rigord); other, 20, 28, 34, 47

Coe, Michael, 202

Colonna, F., 23; *5–8*

Condillac, E. B., 53

Constantinople obelisk, 204

Coptic, 36–9, 181–3, 197, *20*; Champollion, 68–70, 79–80; Horapollo's knowledge of, 19; Kircher, 28, 30; Montfaucon, 46; Quatremère, 64, Rigord, 43–4; Young, 67; Zoëga, 57–8

Cowley, A. E., 144, 157–8, 159, 174, 191, 212; *104*

Crete and Cretan writing in general, 146, 147, 148, 178–9, 212; *92; see also* Aegean

scripts; 'Cretan Hieroglyphic', 148–9, 152, 154, 156, 177, 182, 212; *92–5, 98, 102*

Crick, F. H., 9

Ctesias, 212

cuneiform, beauty, 210; different cuneiform scripts, 111, 210; name, 88; not known to Greek or Roman public, 16; speculations, 88, 210; spread, 123, 182; *see also* Akkadian, Assyrian, Babylonian, Elamite, Hurrian, Persian, Sumerian

Curtius, Quintus, 85

Cypriot syllabary, 15, 123–35, 136, 138, 144, 148, 177, 182, 186, 187, 213; *77–83*; in decipherment of Linear B, 157–8, 162, 170, 172, 174, 188, 189, 213

Cypro-Minoan writing, 135, 182

Cyriac of Ancona, 11, 23, 204

Cyrillic script, 181

Cyrus, 100, 211

DALI, *see* Idalion

Daniel v 8, 7

Darien, 195

Darius, 100, 101, 105, 106, 111, 210, 211, 212

Dawkins, J., 95, 96, 187

decipherment, Champollion, 71, 73, 75, 78–9; in Luvian Hieroglyphic, 143–5; Hyde Clarke, 137–8; Kober, 159–60; Leibnitz, 95; Montfaucon, 46; Sacy, 63, 99; Schmidt, 130–1; theoretical considerations, 186–91; Ventris, 163, 173; Young, 67; Zoëga, 55–6, 58–9

Deecke, W., 131–4, 211

del Rio, A., 197

demotic, 17, 46, 50, 62–3, 64, 67, 71, 197; *36; see also* Clement of Alexandria on types of Egyptian writing

Dendera, Egyptian temple at, 69–70; zodiac, 75, 77, 209

Dhorme, E., 118, 120; *74*

Diodorus Siculus, 17, 20, 22, 36, 84

Disraeli, 212

Drake, Tyrwhitt, 137

Dresden codex, 195, 199, 201, 214; *122*

EGYPT, Champollion's early views about, 69–70; French expedition to, 60, 207; the Roman image of, 14–21

Egyptian hieroglyphic, 11–84, 113, 123, 148, 150, 152, 180, 182, 188–9, 203

Elamite cuneiform, 111, 117
enchorial, *see* demotic
English language, Adelung on, 208
Enoch, 28
Epiphanius, Bishop of Salamis, 96, 97
Eteocypriot, 123, 135
Ethiopian and Ethiopians, 17, 18, 41, 53,
    211
Etruscan, 162, 166, 174, 183, 191;
    augury-lore, 24
Eusebius, 20
Evans, A. J., 135, 146–58, 161, 162, 166,
    194, 212, 213; *91–8, 99, 100–3, 105*

FICINO, M., 21, 192
Figueroa, Garcia Silva, 85, 117
Flaminian obelisk, 19, 81
Flower, S., 97, 198
Forrer, E., 141–2, 144, 145, 187
Förstemann, Ernst, 199
Fourier, J. B. J., 68, 69, 195
Fourmont, E., 65

GALEN, 35
Gelb, I., 141–3, 145, 187, 211; *87*
Gellius, 23, 205
Georgian script, 181; language, 212
Gothic script, 182
Greek, alphabet, 112–13, 178, 180, 181,
    183; biscripts, Greek and Egyptian, *see*
    Serapeum and Rosetta Stone; and
    Cypriot, 124; *79;* language not expected
    to be that of Linear B tablets, 162, 163,
    170, 172; Greek and Palmyrene, 95–6;
    62; and Sassanian, 97–9; *64;* so
    deciphered by Ventris, 174–9
Grimm, J., 211
Grotefend, G. F., 74, 94, 99–102, 105,
    106, 173, 188, 189; *65*
Grumach, E., 212
Guiscard, Robert, 11

HADRIAN, 15, 73, 77; *3c, 13c*
Hagia Triada, 154
Halbherr, F., 154
Hallock, R. T., 211
Ham and Hamitic languages, 104
Hama stones, 136–8, 191, 200; *85*
Hamadan, 106
Hamilton, Sir Wm., 68
Hawkins, J. D., 142, 143, 212
Hebrew, alphabet, 39, 44, 52, 78, 206,
    210, 211; *see also* Phoenician, Semitic;

language, 43, 51, 103, 118–19; place in
    history, 36, 46, 56
Heeren, A. H. L., 100
Herbert, T., 85–6, 88, 210; *46*
Hermapion, 19, 20, 21, 50, 81
Hermes Trismegistus, Siena mosaic, 22; *4*
Hermetic corpus, Casaubon's dating of,
    34–6; *Asclepius* quoted, 22, 36; first
    publication, 20
Herodotus, 14, 17, 20, 46, 50, 145, 192
hieratic, 71; *see also* Clement of Alexandria
    on types of Egyptian writing
hieroglyphs as a medium of
    communication, Bacon, 206; Caussin,
    28, 205; Champollion, 70, 75–6; Evans,
    148–51, 154–5, 190, 191, 212; Grumach,
    213; Kircher, 30–2; Plotinus, 21; Sacy,
    64–5; Sayce, 138; Stillingfleete, 36, 206;
    Warburton, 48–52; Wilkins, 39–42;
    Zoëga, 58–9; *see also* 'Cretan
    hieroglyphic', Egyptian, Luvian, *and*
    Mexican Hieroglyphs
Hillary, Sir Edmund, 9
Hincks, E., 102, 105, 108, 110, 114–16,
    117, 189
Hippocrates, 24
Hittite cuneiform script, 111, 113 ;
    language, 113, 138, 141, 144–5, 187
Hittite Hieroglyphic, *see* Luvian
    Hieroglyphic
Hogarth, D. G., *90*
Homer, 22, 46, 145, 151, 192
Horapollo, 11, 18, 19, 20, 21, 27, 28, 31;
    Aldus ed. 24; Champollion, 83; Pierius
    on, 24, 25; Pignorio, 34; Warburton, 48;
    Zoëga, 58
Horus, 19; *10*
Hrozny, F., 141
Humboldt, A. von 195–7; *122*
Hurrian cuneiform, 111, 141
Hyde, T., 88–9, 97, 186, 209; *48, 49*
hypnerotomachia Poliphili, see Colonna, F.
Hystaspes, 101, 105, 106

IAMBLICHUS, 20
Iberian script, 183
Idalion, 124, 125; bronze tablet, 124, 128,
    130–4
Indian scripts, 180
Indo-European linguistics, birth of, 102–4,
    210–1; *see also* Salmasius
Indus Valley script, 123, 180
'inherent vowels', 105, 108–9, 189

Isis, 11, 15
Iversen, E., 31

JAPANESE, decipherment of Dutch, 204;
    writing system, 214
Jeffery, L. H., 181, 183
Jones, Sir Wm., 103–4, 117, 207, 210
Josephus, 20, 21
Julius Caesar, 13
Juvenal, 15, 34

KAEMPFER, E., 88–9, 209; *51, 54*
Karakaiouli, 53
Karatepe inscription, 136, 142–3, 187,
    202; *89*
Kaunos bilingual, 194; *121*
Kelley, David, 214
Kent, R. P, 210; *67*
'king of kings', *see schahinschah*
Kings I ii 29–31, *see* Solomon
Kircher, A., 28–33, 37–8, 41, 46, 205–6;
    16, 17b, 18, 37
Kitchen, K. A., *118*
Klaproth, J., 84, 178
Knorosov, Yuri, 199–201; *123*
Knossos, 123, 146, 151, 154, 166, 173,
    178–9, 188; *114, 118*
Kober, Alice, 157, 159–61, 162, 163, 164,
    166, 169, 173, 174, 188, 189, 213; *106–8*
Kowalsky, T. W., 192
Ktistopoulos, C. D., 169

LACROZE, M. V., 38
Lactantius, 20, 22, 47–8
Landa, Diego de, 197–200, 214
Lang, R. H., 124–8; biscript from Idalion,
    126–9; *80, 81*
Laroche, E., 145
Lassen, C., 104–8, 188, 189, 211
Latin alphabet, 181
Layard, A. H., 211
Leibnitz, G. W. von, 95, 99, 103, 186,
    189, 210
Lemnos, 162
Letronne, J. A., 83, 209
Levita, E., 22
Lewis, G. C., 84
Lihyanic script, 183
'Linear' in Evans' speculations, 148–51,
    152, 154–5, 212; *94, 95, 97*; the Linear A
    script, 150, 154, 156, 159, 172–3, 177,
    182, 213; *96*; the Linear B script, 154,
    155, 157–79, 182, 186, 187, 188, 189,

213; *100, 103–8, 110–14, 116*
linguistic theories, *see* grammar,
    hieroglyphic, Indo-European, 'mixed
    languages', speech and writing
Linnaeus, 104
Lipsius, I., 103, 210
Lucan, 18
Luther, Martin, 27, 28
Luvian 141, 143, 144–5, 172, 187, 202
Luvian Hieroglyphic, 123, 135, 136–45,
    148, 172, 180, 182, 187; *84–6,
    88–90*
Luynes, Duc de, 124, 127, 134; *77, 78.*
Lycian, 172
Lycurgus, 22, 36

MAILLET, M. de, 43
Makridi-Bey, 141
Malcolm, Sir John, 106
Malpeines, Léonard de, 53
Manetho, 17, 19, 206
Marett, R. R., 154
Marlowe, Christopher, 85
Massaio, P. del, 13; *1*
Masson, O., *79, 82*
Matthaean obelisk, 205
Mausolus, Mausoleum, 192
Maya, 195–203
Medawar, P., 186
Median cuneiform, *see* Elamite cuneiform
Menestrier, C.-F., 206
Mercati, M., 206
Meriggi, P., 142, 212
Meroë, 15, 17, 204
Messerschmidt, L., 141
'Mexican hieroglyphs', 39, 190; Bacon on,
    206; Humboldt, 195–7; Mercati, 206;
    Sayce, 138; Warburton, 48–9; Zoëga, 59
Minervan obelisk, 30–1; *15, 16*
Minoa and Minoan, 151, 152, 156
Minuti, T., 37
'mixed languages', 103–4, 130, 210
Montfaucon, B. de, 45–6; *22b, 23b, 26b*
Morpurgo-Davies, Anna, 142
Moses, divine mission of, 46; and the
    wisdom of Egypt, 28, 36;
    and writing, 52; *4*
mummy-trade, 206
Munster, S., 22
Münter, F. C., 210
Mycenae and Mycenaean, 123, 146, 152,
    188; *91; see also* Linear B
Myres, J. L., 166, 175

NABATAEAN SCRIPTS, 183
Napoleon, expedition to Egypt, 60, 207; the Hundred Days, 70; and Sacy, 62
Naqš-i-Rustam, 97; *64*
Nebuchadnezzar, 114
Neoplatonists, 10, 34; *see also* Plotinus, Ficino
Nepherites, 82
Nero, 13, 18, 82
Neumann, G., 142
Newton, Sir Isaac, 47, 104, 206, 210
Niebuhr, Carsten, 54, 94, 100, 102, 186; *27, 28, 58b, 59b, 60, 61*
Nile, 14, 15
Noah and his children, 36, 104
numerals, diagnostic of language relationships, 210
numeral systems, in general, 182; Aegean, 182; Babylonian, 198; Mayan, 197, 198
Numidian script, 183

OBELISKS, 11–13, 15, 23, 26, 28, 50, 55, 58; their designation, 192; their re-erection in Rome, 27, 205; *see also* Barberini, Constantinople, Flaminian, Matthaean, Minervan, Pamphilian, Philae, Vatican
Obicini, T., 37–8
Oppert, J., 114–16, 117
Orpheus, 22, 48
Osiris, 18, 26, 77; *11, 38a*

PALESTRINA, *see* Praeneste
Palmyra, 62, 94–7
Pamphylian obelisk, 30, 79
Parsons, James, 210
Parthia and Parthians, 98, 99, 103, 187, 210
Peiresc, N. C. Fabri de, 37, 95
Perrot, G., 137; *84*
Persepolis, 85–90, 209; *45, 47–60*
Persian, 102–4, 105, 106, 188, 210
Persian cuneiform, 74, 85–94, 99–110, 111, 113, 187, 210; decipherment of, 67
Petit, S., 95
Phaistos disk, 156, 182
Philae obelisk, 72, 208; *34, 35c, d*
Philo, 20, 28
Phoenician script, 180, 204; Barthélemy's decipherment of, 97; Evans, 148, 181, 183; Hyde, 97; Lucan, 18; Rigord, 43; *see also* Cypriot biscript, 126; *80, 81, 83*; Hebrew and Semitic alphabet; Luvian

Hieroglyphic biscript, 136, 142–3, 187; *89*; language, 43, 118–19, 121–2 'pictographic' in Evans' speculations, 148–51, 154–5, 177; *see also* 'Cretan hieroglyphic' and hieroglyphic
Pierius Valerianus, 24–8, 205; *9, 12, 13d*
Pignorio, L., 33, 194
Plato on allegory, 33, 206; and Egypt, 20, 22; and *Hermetic corpus*, 204; Warburton on, 47, 48
Pliny the Elder, 11, 12, 20, 25, 54
Plotinus, 20, 21
Plutarch, 18, 20, 50, 85; on the Egyptian alphabet, 18, 58, 63; and the *Hermetic corpus*, 35; 'Sais inscription', 21, 25, 44
Poggio, 11, 12
Pope, Alexander, 46
Porphyry, 207
Praeneste mosaic, 15, 28, 208; *2*
Proskouriakoff, Tatiana, 200–201
Proto-Elamite, 117, 123, 177, 180; *70*
Psammetichus, 31, 43, 192–3; *44a, 119*
Ptah, 38, 80; *40b*
Ptolemy I, 14, 15
Ptolemy III, 15, 192; *3a*
Ptolemy V, 62
Punic, language, 34; script, 183
Puzur-Inšušinak, *70*
Pylos, 123; Linear B tablets, 164, 165, 170, 213; 'tripod tablet', 176, 213; *117*
Pythagoras and Egypt, 22, 36, 47

QUATREMÈRE, E., 64, 66

RAFINÉSQUE, C., 197
Rameses II, 50, 81; *44b*
Rask, R. C., 102, 104, 188, 211
Ras Shamra, *see* Ugarit
Rawlinson, H. C., 9, 100, 106–10, 113–17, 178, 188, 189; *67, 68*
Ray, John, 192–94
Rémusat, J. P. A., 66, 75–6, 190, 207, 208, 209
Renouf, P. le P., 66, 208
Rich, J. C., 211
Rigord, J.-P., 43–4, 49–50, 75, 206, 207; *22a, 23a, 26a*
Ripa, C., 27
Roget's *Thesaurus*, 40, 42
Rosetta Stone, 58, 59, 60, 62, 71, 72, 76, 79, 178, 186, 188–9, 208; *31, 35a, b, 36, 39c*
Rosny, 99; *123*

Royal Society of London, 39, 88, 195
Runic script, 183

SACY, A. I. Silvestre de, and Bopp, 63,
    104; and Champollion, 64, 68, 84; and
    Chinese, 66, 207; decipherment of
    Sassanid inscriptions, 94, 97–9, 100, 187;
    64a, b; on function of cartouches, 66,
    189, 190, 191; on hieroglyphical and
    grammatical languages, 64–5; on
    Rosetta Stone, 62–4
Safaitic script, 183
St Martin, A. J., 76, 102, 106, 209
Salmasius, C., on Coptic, 37; on origin of
    European languages, 210
Samaritan script, 183, 206
Sanskrit: Bopp, 104, 105, 211; Jones, 104;
    Rask, 102; Sacy, 63
Sassanid inscriptions, 88, 97–9, 100, 183,
    187, 210; *64*
Sayce, A. H., 117, 135, 138–41, 143, 189,
    191, 192, 211, 212
Sbordone, F., 19
Schaeffer, C., 117, 119, 170
schahinschah, 98–9, 100, 188
Schliemann, H., 146, 151
Schmidt, M., 130–4, 189, 211
Seler, E., 198
Semitic alphabet, 112, 121, 180, 183, 211
Serapeum, 15, 16, 205; *3d*
Serapis, 15 ; *3b, 3c*
Seth, *10*
Shapur, 98–9
Shem and the Semitic languages, 104
Siegismunde, J., 131–4, 199
Siena Cathedral mosaic, 22; *4*
Sinaitic script, 183
Smith, G., 127–9, 187, 211; *81*
Solomon and the wisdom of Egypt, 36
Solon, 22, 36
Sottas, H., 208
South Arabian script, 180, 183, 211
Stillingfleete, E., Bishop of Worcester,
    35–6, 40, 47, 48, 56
Strabo, 20, 36, 101
Strozzi, A., 13, 204; *1*
Suetonius, 13
Sulla, 15
Sumerian cuneiform, 112, 182; language,
    Sayce's view of, 138, 212
Sundwall, J., 172
Susa, *see* Elamite and Proto-Elamite
Swinton, J., 95, 187

Syriac, 96, 97, 183

TACITUS, 12, 18, 20, 21
Talbot, H. F., 114, 211
Tamachec script, 183
'Tarkondemos' seal, 139, 143, 144; *86*
Tensing, 9
Thales, 48
Thamudic script, 183
Thebes (Egyptian), 15; (Greek), 123
Theophilus, *3d*
Thomas, Cyrus, 198
Thomas, Eric, 199
Thoth, 50, 56; *see also* Hermes
    Trismegistus and *Hermetic corpus*
Tibet and Tibetan, 208
Tiglath Pileser I, 114, 202; *69*
Tortellius, J., 204
Townsend, J., 208 a
Trigault, N., 39
Tychsen, ⅔. G., 189, 210
Tychsen, T. C., 210
Tzetzes, J., 17

UGARIT and the Ugaritic alphabet,
    117–22, 164, 186, 187, *71–5;*
    in the decipherment of Linear B,
    173, 199; *115*
Urartian, 111, 113, 200
Ussher, James, on Kircher, 206

VALERIANUS, *see* Pierius Valerianus
Valle, Pietro della, 37, 86, 117; *46*
Vansleb, J. M., 37
Vatican obelisk, 11, 13, 204
Ventris, M., 9, 109, 155, 157, 158, 159,
    162–79, 188, 189, 191, 213; *110–14,*
    116, 117
Vergil, 67
Vico, E., 33; *19*
Virolleaud, C., 117–21, 164, 187, 191; *71,*
    72, 76, 115
Vogüé, Comte de, 124, 126; *79*

WARBURTON, W., Bishop of Gloucester,
    36, 43, 46–53, 56, 57, 194, 206, 207; *24*
Warren, P., 212
Watson, J. D., 9
Weissbach, F. H., 117
Whorf, Benjamin, 199
Wilkins, D., *20*
Wilkins, J., Bishop of Chester, 39–42; *21a, b*
Windfuhr, G. L., 121–2, 211; *75*

Winkler, H., 141
Wood, R., 95, 96, 187
Wotton, William, 210
writing, Evans, 154–5; history of, 181–3, 197, 202, 203, 212, 213, 214; Jones, 207; Kober, 160; relationship between writing and speech, 207, 214; according to Wilkins, 42; Rigord, 206; Sacy, 64–5; Sayce, 138; Warburton, 50–2

XENOGRAPHY, 99, 210
Xerxes, 74, 81, 100–1, 105, 106, 111

YOUNG, T., on Basque, 210; and Champollion, 77, 82, 84, 189, 190, 196; on China, 196; and Sacy, 65, 66–8

ZAPOTEC, 202
Zenobia, 94, 95
Zoëga, G., 38, 42, 55–9, 67, 80, 205, 207; *29, 30*
Zoroaster and Zoroastrianism, 98, 103, 210